PHARMOVATION®

Dr. Kimber Boothe, PharmD, MHA

ISBN#: 978-1-955342-25-4 (Paperback)
ISBN#: 978-1-955342-24-7 (Hardback)
ISBN#: 978-1-955342-26-1 (eBook)

Published by:

Holon Publishing & Collective Press
A Storytelling Company
www.Holon.co

CONTENTS

INTRODUCTION

"Innovation — the ability to see change as an opportunity — not a threat."
—Steve Jobs

Pause for a moment and imagine yourself at work. Close your eyes and imagine yourself in the room where you spend most of your working hours. Take a few deep breaths. Now, imagine what your week would look like if you had all the resources you needed.

If you weren't constantly frustrated by...

- Limited Resources
- Technician Shortages
- Drug Shortages
- Misaligned Reimbursement
- Having to Explain Your Value
- Being Asked to Do More with Less
- Being Overwhelmed
- Burnout
- Self-Sabotage

What would your week look like without daily discouragement? What if you had what you needed to succeed?

I've asked myself these questions for years, and have been on a quest to answer them for my team, departments I consult for, and other pharmacy leaders like you. My strengths have always been strategy and project management; creating bold strategic plans and executing them is what I do best.

But pharmacy practice is my true passion. I've supported the creation of well over 250 positions in different health systems throughout my career. I've been speaking on the topic of pharmacy practice advancement for over 6 years. **I'm on a journey to justify resources for**

pharmacy and inspire a bold practice advancement movement.

One milestone along this journey began in late 2017. I'm living in Connecticut with my family — my husband and three kiddos — scrolling through LinkedIn when I come across a post by Anna Garrett, a pharmacist leader I follow, but, at that time, hadn't yet met in person. I read groggily as I sip my tea. She's hosting a new conference in Asheville, North Carolina, the following spring called the Medipreneurs Summit.

One thing you should know about me is that I love conferences. I mean I REALLY love them. I get so jazzed learning about pharmacy practice and advancements in our field. In college, I ran for a leadership position and answered the question, "What would you do if you had unlimited funds?" with "I would require everyone to attend a conference of their choice for professional development every year. All expenses paid." To me, there's nothing like conference energy. Everyone is away from "regular life" for a few days, staying in a nice hotel, and getting to really geek out on things that excite them. You're with your people. You all love the same things. You're passionate about the field you're in. There's a certain inspiration from conferences that's hard to find anywhere else.

So when the inaugural Medipreneurs conference dates were announced for April 2018, I was excited to be part of the first group to attend.

The following season was one of immense transition. To date, in my career, I'd already justified the creation of over 75 new positions in pharmacy. I'd seen what pharmacy departments can do when properly equipped. I knew the tools that it took to get there. And I was looking for a way to share those tools with more pharmacy leaders.

Beyond my existential desire to affect change on a new level, I also accepted a new position in Cincinnati, moved my family to Ohio, and come April, we are definitely ready for a break from so much change and transition. We loaded up the car and drove five and a half hours to North Carolina, where my husband, Richard, found an outdoor zip-lining adventure for the kids and I drank lots of hot tea while planning and dreaming alongside other entrepreneurs in the medical field.

Saturday morning, I listened intently to Lisa Larter's keynote address titled, "Jump: Use your Gifts to Live your Dreams." She speaks about bringing your strengths to the forefront of your career and finding ways to integrate your passion and expertise. My mind begins to buzz. Something in my brain finally clicks.

I suddenly know my next steps as if they've been laid before me in stone. I write down — yes, I still have the notes! — a pharmacy-specific program. Later that afternoon in a break-out session the ideas keep flowing. Sitting at half-moon tables covered in crisp white tablecloths I brainstorm with other medical professionals. **A pharmacy-specific program training those in leadership to be bold and advocate for what we need to provide the services we want to provide. We can do more with more!**

That day, Pharmovation was born (and yes, I even wrote this name down to capture the need for innovation as we advance). Exactly one year later, at the second Medipreneurs conference, I launched the course. And two years later, this book came into being.

Pharmovation is a marriage of my strengths and passions, exactly what Lisa Larter prescribed in 2018. This book contains the information, skills, tactics, and strategies you need to innovate pharmacy practice at your organization.

•••

Before we jump in, let's get acquainted. This book assumes that you're a pharmacy professional or in some sort of leadership role adjacent to a pharmacy team. Perhaps you're both. You may serve at a stand-alone hospital, be part of a health system pharmacy or work in another area of pharmacy practice.

You're a professional dedicated to practicing at the top of your license, serving as many patients as possible in the most effective way you're able.

This book will help you determine what you need and strategically implement these needs so you won't have to only imagine what you could do with more. You'll finally be able to overcome the frustration of health system pharmacy chaos with career development & innovative strategic planning.

Pharmovation is the only method of its kind. It will not only show you exactly what to do to accelerate your career and advocate for resources, but ultimately, how to advance pharmacy practice to bring joy to your work and improve patient outcomes.

•••

Let's take a closer look at what we'll get into over the next few hundred pages. A mantra of mine that you'll see repeated throughout the book is:

***"Pharmacy can do more with more."*™**
—Kimber Boothe

I believe this in the very core of my being. Pharmacy can do more with more. We can improve patient safety, optimize medication use, and enhance patient care with more resources, more training, more advocacy, more everything. We CAN achieve the quadruple aim of quality, patient experience, cost, and provider engagement.

In designing the Pharmovation program, I've taken time to work with other leaders, investigated pharmacist perspectives and confirmed which key topics and competencies bring rapid success. Beyond that, I've created downloadable materials that will allow you to immediately apply what you are learning. You'll find the QR code at the end of each chapter that will take you to the Pharmovation Implementation Guide where you will find extra goodies and resources.

The chapters themselves are ordered in such a way to support your development. While you're free to skip around and read in whatever order you please, there is a method to the madness. In the first half of the book, we'll explore ways to innovate practice by taking an in-depth look at opportunity, enterprise, strategy, services, and technology. Later on, you'll be stretched to innovate *yourself* through leadership, development, and ultimately, the execution of all the knowledge you've acquired.

Briefly, each chapter will help you achieve a specific objective.

- **Mindset**: Learn the importance of mindset to your success and how to incorporate it in your pharmovation journey.
- **Opportunity**: Understand why staying aware of the bigger picture is vital. Realize that there is a huge need for pharmacists.
- **Enterprise**: Capitalize on the value of the integration and reach of the pharmacy enterprise.
- **Strategy**: Know how to justify resources for both small and large needs.
- **Services**: Be excited about the needs and opportunities for pharmacists and technicians to be accountable and innovative with their roles.
- **Technology**: Be empowered to justify new technology to meet

the needs of both you and your patients.

- **Leadership**: Practice increased leadership and accountability regardless of your level in the organization.
- **Development**: Take ownership of your career and encourage leadership growth by completing a 2-year development plan.
- **Execution**: Be confident and able to realize the tools in this book by integrating learning into practice.

Pharmovation Framework

Throughout the book, you'll also see these boxes with suggested action steps to accelerate your development.

TAKE ACTION NOW

- Access the Pharmovation Implementation Guide to support your journey and implementation at www.pharmovationguide.com or use the QR code on the next page.
- Join the Pharmovator Community and introduce yourself at www.kimberboothe.com/community!
- Set aside time to dedicate to this book each day or week. Put it in your calendar!

I encourage you to take your time digesting all that's within these pages. This is not a book that's meant to be speed-read or glanced through and forgotten about, doomed to gather dust on a distant shelf.

This book will, if you let it, change your pharmacy practice, bring joy back into your career, and help you develop into the healthcare professional you're meant to be.

You will see this QR code at the end of every chapter. It allows you to access the Pharmovation Implementation Guide. Alternatively, you can also visit www.pharmovationguide.com!

Now, let's do this!

Chapter 1
Pharmovation MINDSET

"Whether you think you can or you think you can't, you are right."
—Henry Ford

Jumping back in time to 2015, well before Pharmovation was a thought in my imagination, I'd started a business. I just wasn't sure exactly where it was going. It was two parts career coaching, one part speaking at pharmacy conferences. I enjoyed it but was looking for a bigger change. At the time I was working at Bayer, on the "Big Pharma" side of things and, while my time there had been positive, I realized this season was coming to a close. I felt ready to get back into a hospital with the skills I'd gained on the corporate ladder.

Through some career coaching, I'd identified that I wanted to stay in leadership and return to health systems. I knew I could have more of an impact there. So I went home. Back to my old stomping grounds. Back to a pharmacy enterprise.

Back to New Haven, Connecticut. I was hired as the Director of Clinical Services at Yale New Haven Health. During my interview we spoke a lot about advancing pharmacy practice and accelerating transformation. And practice advancement became my north star. I put forth a plan to prioritize medication reconciliation within the system. As you will find in the following chapters, research will agree that focusing on correct medication histories and safe transition of care decreases medication discrepancies while patients enjoy improved outcomes. I had an ambitious timeline and big plans — probably from my years in big pharma and fascination with the business side of things.

I knew there was room for improvement and was eager to work with my team. In our first meeting they said they were prepared to ask for funding to hire 2 new pharmacy technicians. The new positions would prioritize patients on 10 or more meds, and make sure medication lists were accurate. This would only provide 10% of total patients the additional team support for medical reconciliation.

It wasn't a bad plan. That wasn't the problem. It was timid. It was thinking small. Begging for the funding to serve merely 10% of their patients to the level they thought necessary? TEN PERCENT?! We can do better than that.

And we did.

For a year we worked on a business plan to get what we needed, not what we thought we could scrape by with. Within 18 months, we'd hired enough staff (more than 14 technicians and many other pharmacist and resident positions) to do 100% admission medication reconciliation. We had to justify it, plan for it, and fight to get it. It wasn't easy.

My team dared to think bigger. They opened their minds to what was possible instead of thinking small. This mindset is crucial to succeeding in innovating your pharmacy practice. We must think outside the box, ask for what we need (what we REALLY need), and work together to justify the expense. As leaders of the pharmacy community, we fight for the resources and positions our team (and patients) need to succeed. In order to succeed in innovating your pharmacy practice, you must have the right mindset.

In this chapter, you'll learn the importance of mindset to your success and how to incorporate it in your Pharmovation journey. We'll talk about the key aspects of innovation, intrapreneurship, change & transformation, and wrap up with mindset. These are foundational ways of thinking that will set you up for success throughout your career.

•••

Innovation

SECTION PREVIEW | SECTION PREVIEW |

In this section, we'll focus on...

- What is Innovation?
- Benefits of Innovation
- Barriers to Innovation
- How to Innovate

What is Innovation?

Developing your innovation skill and making it a habit is critical to success. A well-known innovator of our time is Steve Jobs, who said, "Innovation is the ability to see change as an opportunity — not a threat." But innovation is not restricted to CEOs. It's important at work and useful in daily life. As we grow and adapt to change individuals and managers need to break from traditional ways of thinking and create and nurture an environment of innovation.

To begin, let's define innovation for the purposes of this book. We've got to be on the same page to go on this journey together.

Innovation is...

- A new idea, method, or device.[1]
- The application of better solutions that meet new requirements, unarticulated needs, or existing market needs.[2]
- Executing an idea which addresses a specific challenge and achieves value for both the company and the customer (aka health organization and patient).[3]

The first definition of innovation above — a new idea, method, or device — is perhaps the most common. We tend to think of innovation as something new. And while this certainly is an example of innovation, the second and third definitions are often overlooked as innovative.

While we think of innovation as a single action or the introduction of something wholly "new," it's often part of a larger chain of events. For example, someone generally begins with an **idea**. This can be a concept, opinion, or belief. From there, they seek to solve a problem they perceive with a new invention. The **invention** is the creation of a product or introduction of a new process. At some point later on, someone (perhaps a different someone) improves on or makes a significant contribution to an existing product, process or service with commercialization. This improvement is **innovation**. For example, the bicycle was an invention, while the electric bicycle is an innovation on the original product. Or take the world wide web, a ground-breaking invention. Since the invention of the internet, many innovators have made their mark. Facebook, Google, and Skype, to name a few.

Let's look further at descriptions of different ways to describe innovations — outcome of the innovation, degree of innovativeness, and degree of change.

The Outcome of Innovation: Is typically a product, platform, service or process. Launching a new or improved product or service to the market, or even process innovation, which is finding better or more efficient ways of producing existing products for delivery of existing services.

Degree of Innovativeness or Novelty: Innovations may be expected or unexpected. Incremental innovation with new product updates or versions of technology are expected by the user. We expect to update our phones and have new features available to us every so often. This innovation sustains product use and does not significantly affect existing markets. Innovation can also be radical or revolutionary within a product, showcasing a much better version than previously available but still not affecting the existing market.

- An incremental innovation being where we do the same thing, only better.
- A radical innovation is wholly a new idea to the world but serves an existing market.

Degree of Change: Innovation can be sustaining or disruptive. Sustaining does not significantly affect existing markets compared to disruptive ones that creates a new market entirely by providing a different set of values, unexpectedly overtaking an existing market with unexpected change.

- A sustaining change meaning that the rules of the game remain the same.
- A disruptive change is a game changer completely, inventing or overtaking a market or industry.

Outcome of the Innovation	• **Product** • **Service** • **Platform** • **Process**
Degree of Innovativeness or Novelty	• **Incremental/Evolutionary:** innovation that is an expected improvement, a product in an existing market. • **Semiradical/Substantial** • **Radical/Revolutionary:** unexpected, but does not affect existing markets
Degree of Change	• **Sustaining:** does not significantly affect existing markets • **Disruptive:** creates a new market by providing a different set of values, which ultimately and unexpectedly overtakes an existing market

Innovation Descriptions

Through these descriptions we can think of innovation as existing on a graph. The x-axis is the degree of change moving from sustaining to disruptive and the y-axis is the degree of innovativeness moving from incremental to radical.

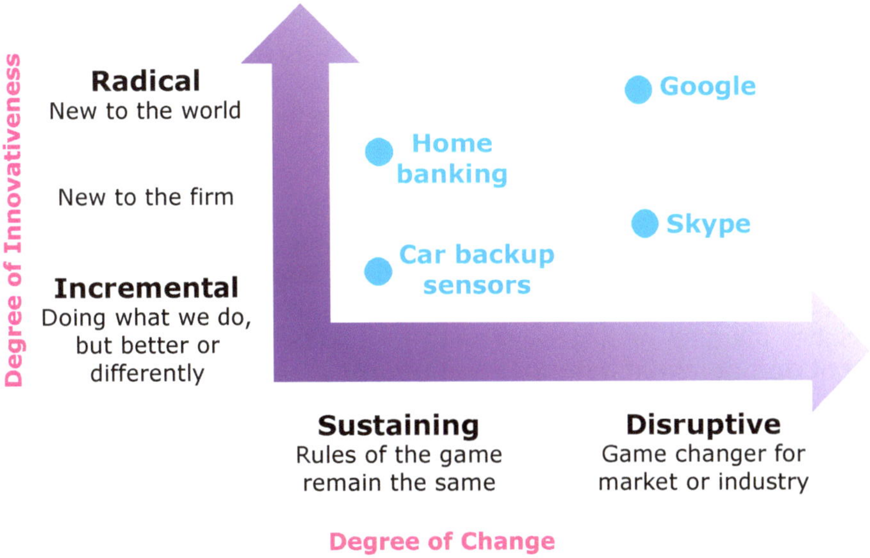

Innovation Examples

Examples of these would be...

Sustaining and Incremental: back up sensors in a car. Fundamentally, it is the same way we back up, and the car isn't new, but the backup sensor is an improved safety feature.

Sustaining and Radical: online banking. The nature of banking does not change. You still make deposits and withdrawals and track your expenses. But it's now online. It's a big change for the user but does not create a new market.

Disruptive and Incremental: Skype. Skype works almost exactly like a phone call. In fact, you can even use it to call landlines. But since it utilizes the connectivity of the internet, it's MUCH cheaper to call anywhere in the world. It completely changes the game for telecommunications companies.

Disruptive and Radical: Google. Google works like nothing else the consumer has seen until this point. It's similar to an encyclopedia, but you don't have to leaf through to find answers yourself. Plus, it searches the entire internet (including Wikipedia... Which is another great example of innovation) and gives you seemingly endless results. A complete game changer for both the user and existing markets.

Now that we have had innovation defined for us, we will learn about its benefits.

Benefits of Innovation

Now, what are the benefits of an innovation? Well, virtually all of the economic growth that has occurred since the 18th century is ultimately attributable to innovation.

Innovative companies are ones who are able to both innovate AND adopt new ideas quickly. They're **adaptable** with flexibility in their strategies, structure, and culture. They're **competitive** with better processes, services, and business models. Because of this, they have higher margins and stock returns (if publicly traded). **Companies that do not invest in innovation put their future at risk.**

> ***"Innovation is not just about disruption, it can also be about adopting new ideas faster."***
> —Kimber Boothe

In the book *Diffusion of Innovations*, author E. M. Rogers explains that ideas spread by the method of communication channels over time. He describes the diffusion through four steps[4]:

1. Innovation
2. Communication
3. Time
4. Social System

This means that innovation requires good communication, ample time, and a functioning social system in order to fully take root and affect change. You can see a common chart below where innovators create and early adopters and the early majority are taking advantage of this new innovation sooner compared to the late majority and laggards such that over time, you reach a hundred percent of diffusion. The goal, therefore, is to shorten the amount of time it takes for a new idea to be adopted. This requires more active communication as well as having early adopters of a new idea work as ambassadors (through the existing social system) to help others get on board.

In healthcare, we often see organizations putting their future at risk through what we call the Evidence-Practice Gap. The Evidence-Practice Gap looks at the time it takes to implement a new idea broadly. How long does it take a new idea (with sufficient evidence to validate its worthiness) to become common practice? Research suggests that it sometimes takes more than a decade to implement research results in clinical practice. Does this seem appropriate to you?

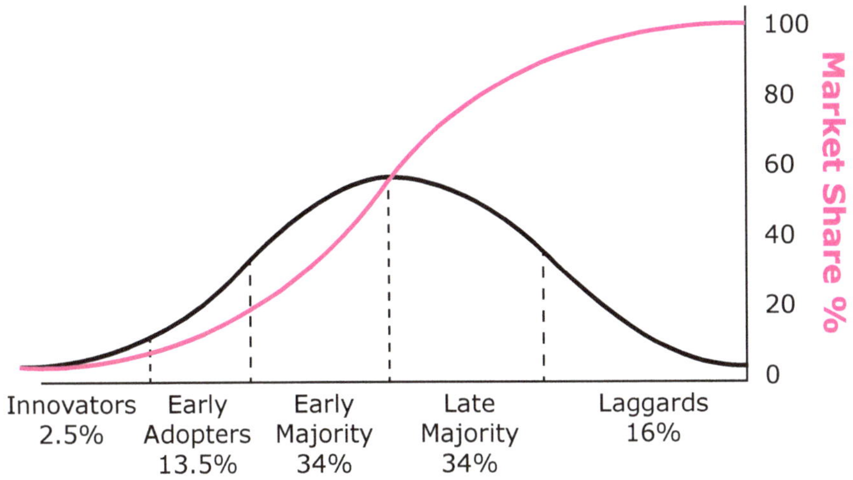

Adopter Categories[4]

Our goal should be, in most cases, to speed up the diffusion. So if you can move these curves to the left, you will speed up the time that something is adopted and implemented. If we have something that is of good evidence, for example, when we think about having pharmacists or medication history technicians in certain clinical areas, it should not take 10 years to put that into full use. The adoption of the electronic health record was sped up through the American Recovery and Reinvestment act, which tied an incentive to adoption.

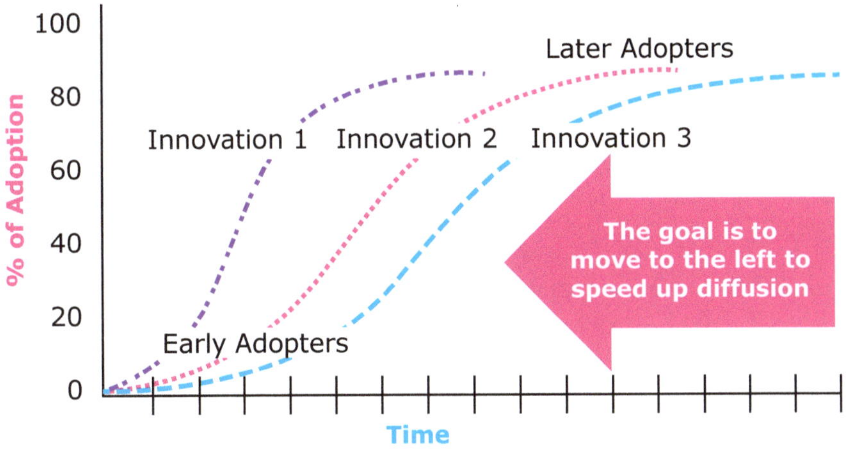

Innovation Adoption Differences[4]

This is something to watch for in your own organization. While many companies believe they are committed to innovation, they do not invest the time, people, or money needed to support any true innovation.

You can make a difference by advocating to support innovation and implement new evidence-based practices sooner rather than later.

Barriers to Innovation

Unfortunately, innovation isn't necessarily easy. You may encounter some of the following barriers to innovation and creative thinking in your organization[5]:

- **Negative Attitudes**: A tendency to focus on the negative aspects of problems and expend energy on worry, as opposed to seeking the inherent opportunities in a situation.
- **Fear of Failure**: A fear of looking foolish or being laughed at.
- **Executive Stress**: Not having time to think creatively. The over-stressed person finds it difficult to think objectively at all. Unwanted stress reduces the quality of all mental processes.
- **Following Rules**: Some rules are necessary, but others encourage mental laziness. A tendency to conform to accepted patterns of belief or thought — the rules and limitations of the status quo — can hamper creative breakthroughs.
- **Making Assumptions**: A failure to identify and examine the assumptions you are making to ensure they are not excluding new ideas. Many unconscious assumptions, in particular, restrict thinking.
- **Over-Reliance on Logic**: Investing all your intellectual capital into logical or analytical thinking — the step-by-step approach can exclude imagination, intuition, feeling, or humor.

Instead, organizations must adjust to a positive outlook by seeking opportunities in new situations and realizing that failure is a necessary stepping stone to success. Furthermore, it's been shown that long-term corporate success is linked to the ability to innovate.[5] Managing day-to-day operations is important, but it is new game-changing breakthroughs that will launch companies into new markets, enable rapid growth, and create high return on investment. Companies that challenge their own assumptions will be headed for a more successful future.

Now that we know the barriers of innovation, we will learn how to innovate.

How to Innovate

Innovation isn't something that just happens. It must be systematically fostered and supported within organizations. Companies aiming to encourage innovation should consider the following systematic steps, adapted from *Innovation and Entrepreneurship: Practice and Principles* by P.F. Drucker.[6]

Systematic Innovation Steps:

1. **Systematic Analysis of Opportunities**: Purposeful, systematic innovation begins with an analysis of the opportunities through the 7 sources framework.
2. **Analyze the Opportunity**: See if people will be interested in using the innovation — look, ask, listen. Innovation is both conceptual and perceptual. "Successful innovators look at figures, and they look at people. They work out analytically what the innovation has to be to satisfy an opportunity. And then they go out and look at the customers, the users, to see what their expectations, their values, and their needs are."
3. **Simple and Focused**: "An innovation, to be effective, has to be simple and focused. It should do only one thing, otherwise, it confuses. All effective innovations are breathtakingly simple. Indeed, the greatest praise an innovation can receive is for people to say: 'This is obvious. Why didn't I think of it?'"
4. **Start Small**: By appealing to a small, limited market, a product or service requires little money and few people to produce and sell it. As the market grows, the company has time to fine-tune its processes and stay ahead of the emerging competition.
5. **Aim for Market Leadership**: A successful innovation aims at leadership within a given market or industry. If an innovation does not aim at leadership in the beginning, it is unlikely to be innovative enough to successfully establish itself. Leadership here can mean dominating a small market niche.

Now, let's talk about those seven opportunities (or sources) that Drucker spoke of for innovation that you want to assess. Internal areas of opportunity are listed on the top section and external on the bottom.

The first source is the unexpected — the unexpected successes, the unexpected failures, and the unexpected outside events. You want to look to see where you have opportunities. Second, you want to look to see where there is incongruity between reality as it is and reality as it should be. If I give an example here of pharmacy and healthcare, when we look at nurses who are supposed to barcode scan medications when they're administering them. There's an incongruity between what is happening and what should happen because those rates are not always at a hundred percent. There is an innovation needed for the process. This is an important one that I think we have a lot of opportunity for.

Third, we want to look at how we can perfect a process that already exists, replace a link that is weak, or supply a link that is missing. We can find these process needs all over the place when we look at healthcare. Fourth is changes in industry structure or market that can catch everybody unaware. So we want to look at where there's opportunities for growth, maturing markets, converging markets, and other model markets. This is where it's important. And we'll talk about this in the strategy chapter for looking at what the changing forces impacting us are so we can be better prepared for them.

The fifth source is demographics, looking at changes in population size, age composition, educational level employment, status, or income are important. Even looking at the demographics of our own healthcare workforce is important. Then there are changes in perception, the sixth source, when the customer goes from seeing the glass half full to the glass half empty or vice versa. We want to understand those potential changes in perception.

And then finally, number seven is new knowledge. And this is not just having technical or scientific breakthroughs, but the innovative use of knowledge creates new products or services. These are the seven sources or opportunities that you can think about in an organized way to look for opportunities for innovation in your practice areas.

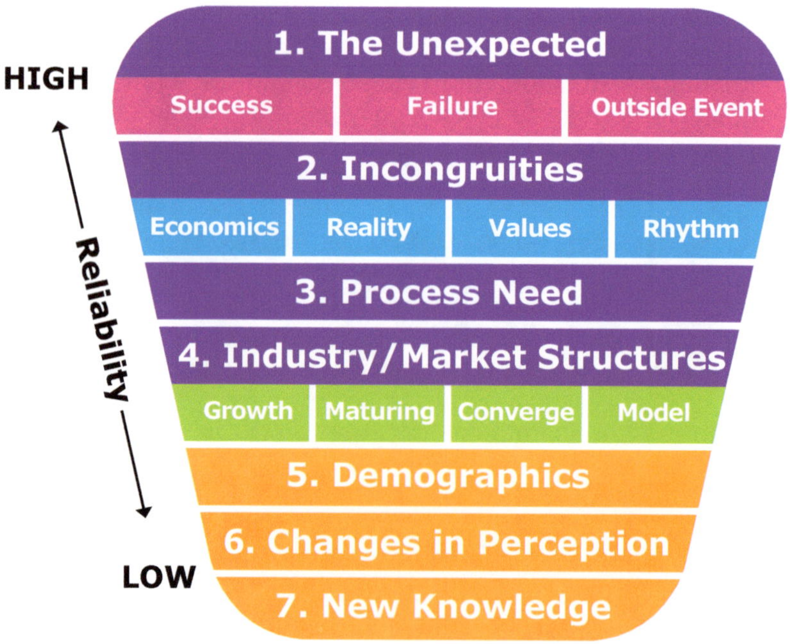

7 Sources for Innovation[6]

Now there are some innovation do's and dont's that I wanted to share with you as shown in this table. I want to make one highlight regarding customer feedback. Something that Steve Jobs had said years ago was he would never use a customer focus group to come up with innovations. Customers may not come up with these innovative ideas. You want to listen to their pain points and barriers to identify the innovative solution. He likes to say that a customer never would have come up with the iPod.

Innovation Do's	Innovation Dont's
Make innovation a process	Leaders just ask for ideas
Make innovation part of your culture	Accept the status quo
Build your persuasion skills	No buy-in from executives
Build change management skills	Same old thinking, same old results
Take customer input and build upon it as customers may not identify innovation	Avoid segmentalist organizations working in silos
Plan for integrative organization	Rely on customer feedback sessions
Accept big and small innovative ideas	Demand disruptive innovation
Consider a wide range of alternatives (resources, people, methods, business models)	Neglect alternatives
Know what you're trying to solve	Work on innovation only in a rush
Invest time, people, and money	Only have creative ideas and not implement innovation

Innovation Do's and Dont's

Another angle for tackling innovation comes to us from *The Innovation Secrets of Steve Jobs* by Carmine Gallo.[7]

7 Innovative Principles:

1. **Do what you love**: Think differently about your career.
2. **Put a dent in the universe**: Think differently about your vision.
3. **Kickstart your brain**: Think differently about how you think.
4. **Sell dreams, not products**: Think differently about your customers.
5. **Say no to 1,000 things**: Think differently about design.
6. **Create insanely great experiences**: Think differently about your brand experience.
7. **Master the message**: Think differently about your story.

While all these principles and ideas are well and good, innovation cannot be theoretical. It must become a habit. Following a process for innovative thinking and resulting behaviors will result in habitual innovation in a company or organization. Habit forming itself can become a habit, from the incorporation of key triggers, conditions, and words into your daily routine.

Here are few tips for making innovation a habit[8]:

1. Constantly connect the dots.
2. Commit to asking questions.
3. Actively try new things.
4. Find points of intersection with others.
5. Have a sense of purpose.
6. Cross-pollinate ideas.
7. Make innovation a regular part of your daily routine.

In summary, **innovation is executing an idea which addresses a specific challenge and achieves value for both the company and customer.** It does not have to be just disruptive innovation. Small incremental innovations are important for both products and services as well as our processes. Innovation has many benefits, but many barriers arise related to mindset, limiting belief, and lack of process. However, there are systematic steps we can follow in order to make innovation a habit instead of an occasional happy accident.

Take Action Now

- Think of a source of opportunity for innovation in pharmacy.
- Share your thoughts in the Pharmovator Community.

Next, we'll spend some time looking at the difference between entrepreneurship and intrapreneurship. Never heard of intrapreneurship? That's ok, in the next few pages you'll know what it is, the benefits it offers, how it can be implemented in your organization, and the common barriers we encounter with implementation.

•••

Entrepreneurship & Intrapreneurship

In this section, we'll focus on...

- What are Entrepreneurship & Intrapreneurship?
- Benefits of Intrapreneurship
- Implementation of Intrapreneurship
- Barriers to Intrapreneurship

What are Entrepreneurship & Intrapreneurship?

Let's begin with the more commonly known entrepreneur. **An entrepreneur is a person who organizes and manages any enterprise, especially a business, usually with considerable initiative and risk**.[9]

And while an entrepreneurial spirit is something to applaud and admire, many people are unable to become entrepreneurs due to lack of funding, manpower, strong backing, or branding. Or simply, fear. The truth is that most employees work and will continue to work in corporations. The question is: how can we support the entrepreneurial mindset and spirit within organizations? The answer is "Intrapreneurship."

An intrapreneur is a person within a large corporation who takes direct responsibility for turning an idea into a profitable finished product through assertive risk taking and innovation.[10] This is often an employee of a large corporation who is given freedom and financial support to create new products, services, systems, etc, and does not have to follow the corporation's usual routines or protocols. It's the system wherein the principles of entrepreneurship are practiced within the boundaries of the firm. Other terms commonly used are internal entrepreneur, entrepreneur on the job, and corporate entrepreneurship.

Looking at it historically, we see that intrapreneurship is not a new idea but is increasing in popularity as an important component of business. A famous early example is the Post-It note from 3M. A metaphorical "intrapreneurial home run" from 1974. Then in 1978, Gifford Pinchot created and coined this term as "dreamers, who do. Those who take the hands-on responsibility for creating innovation of any kind within a business."[11] In the mid-80s *Time Magazine* published an article titled "Here Come the Intrapreneurs" and Steve Jobs started an intrapreneurship team to create the Macintosh. Then in 1992 the word was added to the *American Heritage Dictionary*. In '94, Ken Kutaragi's intrapreneurial venture led to the development and launch of the Sony PlayStation and by 2014 Forbes declared intrapreneurs to be the most valuable employees of an organization. As of 2015, 28% of multinational corporations had intrapreneurial initiatives.

This is not a new idea and not a dying trend. Intrapreneurs are here to stay. But let's further differentiate entrepreneurs from intrapreneurs in the areas of status, independence, ownership, capital, resources, risk, operation, orientation, profit, and norms and rules.

Differences	Entrepreneur	Intrapreneur
Status	Owner of business	Employee
Independence	Works independently	Semi-independent, depends on organization governance
Ownership	Ownership of the business/firm	Only manages the business
Capital	Raises the requisite capital themselves	Does not raise any money
Resources	Must find all necessary resources	Access to core business resources, but must leverage them
Risk	Assumes all business risk	Only some risk related to project
Operation	From outside the organization	Within the organization
Orientation	Sets up their own enterprise	Enterprise within organization
Profit	Entitled to returns/profits from business	Fixed salary, potential bonus
Norms & Rules	Frames norms & rules of business	Bound by organizational norms & rules

Entrepreneur & Intrapreneur Differentiation

Entrepreneurs are owners of their own businesses. They work independently and raise the requisite capital themselves. They must find all necessary resources on their own, assume all business risk, and set up their own enterprise. They must also decide how to operate the business and frame norms and culture within the business. In return, they're entitled to profits from the business as decided with other investors.

In contrast, an intrapreneur is an employee of an organization who works semi-independently depending on organizational governance. They only manage their project but have no ownership of the business. They don't have to raise any money, hunt down resources, or assume the entire risk of a project as they're supported by their company. They're also bound by the rules and norms of the organization they work within and continue to pull a fixed salary (although they may earn a bonus or raise!) after their initiative is complete.

To support you in identifying who the intrapreneurs are in your own organizations, assess them through the intrapreneurial grid. This clarifies the roles from a vision and action perspective.

Moving from left to right is the low to high action. And moving from top to bottom is low to high vision. Workers tend to have low vision and valuable workers tend to take more action. Now, moving up in the middle, your people with increasing vision tend to be higher in leadership roles, from supervisors to managers. Inventors possess the highest vision, they can become an intrapreneur when they grow in action.

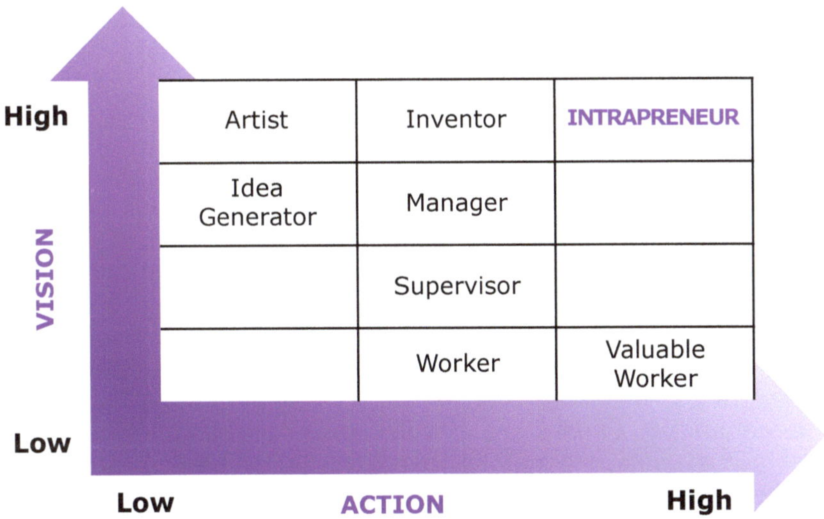

Intrapreneurial Grid[11]

An intrapreneur is someone with a high degree of vision and high ability to act. Some examples are Art Fry the inventor of the 3M Post-It Note mentioned above. He had a problem with his bookmark falling out of his choir book each Sunday morning and concluded that the non-permanent glue 3M had been developing at the time could be channeled for this use.

Or look at Jim Lynch, cleaning the gutters of his home in Massachusetts. It suddenly occurred to him that this was the perfect job to outsource to a robot and, since his company was in robotics, he asked his boss if he could work on this project as a side part of his job. The company supported him and now hosts a regular event called an “Idea Bake-Off” where employees get up to 10 minutes to present their pitches for new ideas or products.

It seems unnecessary to mention (and yet of course I will) Google at this point. They are a huge supporter of intrapreneurship within the organization, even earmarking 20% of their employees time to spend on creative projects outside their specific job titles. This investment has been well worth the time, benefiting the organization by creating Google Analytics, Gmail, Google AdWords and so much more.

This final example relates to healthcare — the Walmart Care Clinic. Alicia Ledlie was put in charge of this new venture to get it off the ground. While it wasn't specifically her idea, she did lead the charge to bring this idea into reality.

Now that we understand the difference between entrepreneurship and intrapreneurship, we will study its benefits.

Benefits of Intrapreneurship

If you're still asking the question "Why should my organization support intrapreneurship?" let me break it down even further. It's well known that intrapreneurship initiatives improve innovation, growth, and employee engagement, which are important to consider when a company is trying to grow.[12] Companies that foster innovation (through intrapreneurship) perform better. They also tend to have more products coming out and create more venture capital investments. Finally, intrapreneurship empowers and motivates employees, so they tend to be happier and more committed. Organizations with happier and committed employees are able to reduce staff turnover by 87%. Not to mention that up to 70% of successful entrepreneurs have come up with their business idea while working for a previous employer.[13]

By this logic, if companies supported intrapreneurship instead of stifling innovation, there are almost countless ideas their employees have for the organization (and world!) to benefit from. So many ideas could be the products of companies instead of new enterprises. Of course, we don't want to discourage people who have strong desires to be entrepreneurs, that drive should be supported. But when we think of how few people actually go off to become entrepreneurs, we can conclude that companies are losing access to a lot of great ideas still inside the organization simply by not being open to new ideas and insights.

Implementation of Intrapreneurship

Here are some key characteristics intrapreneurs and entrepreneurs have. They're not all encompassing, but they are something to look out for when trying to identify who might have this ability within your organization, or think about it for yourself.

Intrapreneurs are...

- Results Driven
- Action Oriented
- Creative
- Original
- Self-Confident
- Risk-Tolerant
- Ambitious
- Persistent
- Influencing
- High Energy
- Interpersonal
- Innovative

Next, I wanted to share some work that Gordon Pinchot did surrounding intrapreneurship.[14] These are known as...

The Intrapreneur's 10 Commandments:

1. Come to work each day willing to be fired.
2. Circumvent any orders aimed at stopping your dream.
3. Do any job needed to make your project work, regardless of your job description.
4. Find people to help you.
5. Follow your intuition about the people you choose and work only with the best.
6. Work underground as long as you can — publicity triggers the corporate immune mechanism.
7. Never bet on a race unless you are running in it.
8. Remember it is easier to ask for forgiveness than for permission.
9. Be true to your goals, but be realistic about the ways to achieve them.
10. Honor your sponsors.

Since publishing these, Pinchot has added a few additional commandments with added clarity,[14] which are...

- Ask for advice before asking for resources.
- Express gratitude.
- Build your team, intrapreneuring is not a solo activity.
- Share credit widely.
- Keep the best interests of the company and its customers in mind, especially when you have to bend the rules to circumvent the bureaucracy.
- Don't **ask** to be fired; even as you bend the rules and act without

permission, use all the political skill you and your sponsors can muster to move the project forward without making waves.

These rules and commandments make it clear that most people work within a culture that does NOT support intrapreneurship. It is an uphill battle and will likely be a difficult road to follow. Since this is the widespread general assumption, how can we build organizations that encourage and uplift intrapreneurs? Because the fact is that at least 25% of your employees are already intrapreneurs in terms of mindset and creativity. With some support and encouragement, these abilities can be tapped into for the benefit of the organization and the consumer.

Now that we know more about the individual intrapreneur characteristics, how can we make this part of our daily routines in our practices? Here are some key ways to build a culture of intrapreneurship.[15]

1. Show you mean business.
2. Include your entire organization.
3. Seek out the intrapreneurs already there.
4. Make time for innovation and creativity.
5. Actively promote the activities.
6. Make failure acceptable and reward success.

Remember that when you're venturing into these new areas you will likely be unsuccessful at first, but don't feel that this means you shouldn't try. In fact, you should model the spirit of intrapreneurship yourself by showing others that failure is acceptable. Many people say you want to fail fast so that you can move on and find the best solutions. Failure is simply part of the process of progress.

Intrapreneurship can be further enabled through the following. You can also foster a culture of intrapreneurship by empowering individuals and leadership that pro-actively embrace intrapreneurship. You can set clear definitions and metrics for what success means. Intrapreneurship is not a short game and intrapreneurs should not be sanctioned for failing. Additionally, internal collaboration is a must for intrapreneurship: bust the silos, break down the walls by creating spaces for interaction and collaboration, and launch internal professional social networks. You may also want to host innovation-driven events like boot camps or hackathons. These not only deliver great ideas with sound business potential, they also act as platforms for scouting talent. Beginner intrapreneurs usually have less developed entrepreneurial skills — support them by pairing with seasoned mentors to help navigate through difficulties and setbacks.

Barriers to Intrapreneurship

Be aware that there are many barriers to intrapreneurship in the following categories. Luckily, many of these barriers can be overcome with focused initiatives. I'll highlight just a few.

Barriers to Intrapreneurship[16]:

Systems

- Misdirected Reward and Evaluation Systems
- Oppressive Control Systems
- Inflexible Budgeting Systems
- Overly Rigid, Formal Planning Systems

Structures

- Too Many Hierarchical Levels
- Responsibility Without Authority
- Top-Down Management
- Lack of Accountability for Innovation & Change

Strategic Direction

- Absence of Innovation Goals
- No Formal Strategy for Entrepreneurship
- Lack of Commitment From Senior Executives
- No Entrepreneurial Role Models at the Top

Policies & Procedures

- Long, Complex Approval Cycles
- Extensive Red-Tape & Documentation Requirements
- Over-Reliance on Established Rules of Thumb
- Unrealistic Performance Criteria

People

- Fear of Failure
- Resistance to Change
- Parochial Bias
- "Turf" Protection
- Complacency
- Short-Term Orientation
- Inappropriate Skills and Talents for Managing Entrepreneurial Change

Culture

- Ill-Defined Values
- Lack of Consensus Over Value & Norm Priorities
- Lack of Fit of Values with Current Competitive Context
- Values Conflict with Innovativeness, Risk-Taking, and Proactiveness

In summary, intrapreneurship is practicing entrepreneurship within a corporation. It benefits ***both*** the company and the employee. Implementation occurs best within a structured approach. Barriers to implementation range from systems to culture but ***can*** be overcome.

Next, we'll look at the change and transformation necessary to innovate.

TAKE ACTION NOW

- Begin thinking about how intrapreneurship can be utilized in healthcare.
- Share your thoughts in the Pharmovator community.

•••

CHANGE & TRANSFORMATION

In this section, we'll focus on...

- What are Change & Transformation?
- Why is Change Important?
- Change Management

Change and transformation are foundational concepts and competencies related to Pharmovation.

"Change is the only constant."
—Heraclitus

What are Change & Transformation?

First, some definitions. To change is to make or become different.[17] It can also be to make things better as compared to the past. While Heraclitus aptly states that change is always happening, in an organization it's necessary to manage change so it does not overtake or overwhelm those it affects.[18] Whereas change management is the management of change and development within a business or similar organization. Transformation goes beyond typical change and can be defined as a thorough or dramatic change in form or appearance.[19] It's an act, process, or instance of transforming or being transformed.[19]

Transformation can also be seen as successfully reaching a new vision for the future.

Now that we've defined our terms, we'll spend some time understanding why this concept is important in our overall topic of pharmacy innovation and practice.

Let's look more closely at the difference between change and transformation. Change is typically thought of as a fix or improvement on what already exists. For example, iPhone 3 vs. iPhone 4 vs. iPhone 10 and so on. Transformation is a complete overhaul of the status quo, a new creation using present tools. This can be best illustrated through the caterpillar who transforms into the unrecognizable creature of a butterfly through metamorphosis.

Why is Change Important?

Within the concepts of innovation and intrapreneurship that we've already discussed are a lot of implied changes. Facilitating this change with grace and agility is paramount since innovation and intrapreneurship cannot happen without it. And yet, while change is inevitable, most humans are not very good at it. We must overcome many hurdles when facing change such as:

- **Change Fatigue**: Prior experiences with poorly managed change.
- **Lack of Skills**: Organizations may lack the necessary skills to properly manage change.
- **Lack of Ownership**: A certain style of leadership prefers a top-down approach where those enacting certain changes have no ownership over what's happening.

Now I'd like to share with you the Kubler-Ross Change Curve.[20]

This model describes the four stages that most people go through as they adjust to change. It's a well-known curve, and is unfortunately similar to the curve we see when people move through grief.

Now, when a change is first introduced, people's initial reaction may be shock or denial as they react to the challenge of their status quo. This is stage one of the change curve. Then, once the reality of change starts to hit people tend to react negatively, moving to stage two. They may fear the impact, feel angry, and actively resist or protest against the changes. Some will wrongly fear the negative consequences of change. Others will correctly identify real threats to their position.

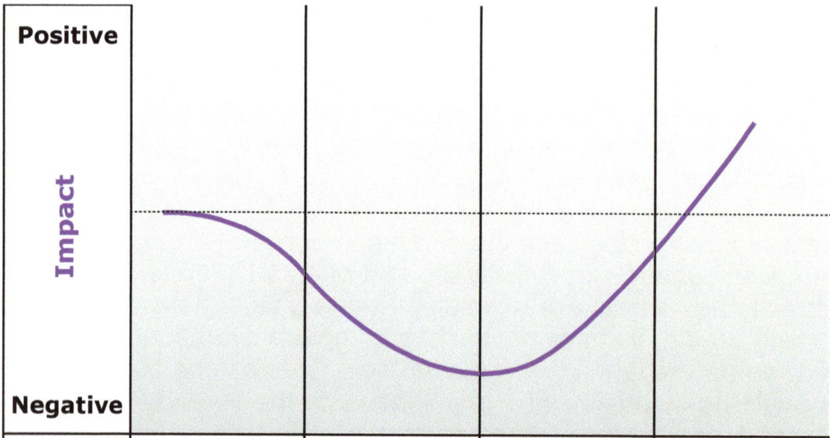

STAGE	1	2	3	4
STATE	Status Quo	Disruption	Exploration	Rebuilding
REACTION	Shock, Denial	Anger, Fear	Acceptance	Commitment

The Kubler-Ross Change Curve[20]

As a result, the organization experiences disruption, which if not carefully managed, can quickly spiral into chaos. Because, for as long as people resist the change and remain in stage two of the change curve, the change will be unsuccessful (at least for those who react in this way). And this is a stressful and unpleasant stage for everyone. It's much healthier to move to stage three of the change curve, where pessimism and resistance give way to some optimism and acceptance.

At stage three, people stop focusing on what they have lost. They start to let go and accept the changes. They begin testing and exploring what that change means for them. They learn the reality of what's good, what's not so good, and how they must adapt. Finally we arrive at stage four: rebuilding and commitment.

In stage four, people not only accept the changes, but start to embrace them. They rebuild their ways of working. Only when people get to this stage can the organization really start to reap the benefits of change.

Change Management

Managing change as a leader in your organization has many steps. You must understand the change that's about to take place, plan for it carefully, implement it thoughtfully, and communicate well about what's going to happen to those it will affect.

Two common frameworks for managing change in an organization are PROSCI-ADKAR[21] and Kotter's 8 steps.[22] We'll explore both in detail shortly.

Remember that however you choose to manage change, you'll want to incorporate planning for change as part of any project plan. Do not ignore the planning step. Through this process you'll be able to gauge the level of management needed based on the impact of the change or transformation. Planning will help you prepare to minimize the negative impact and improve the speed at which people adapt to the change. Your aim will be to reduce negative consequences by accelerating change. Give individuals the information and help they need. This will increase your likelihood of success.

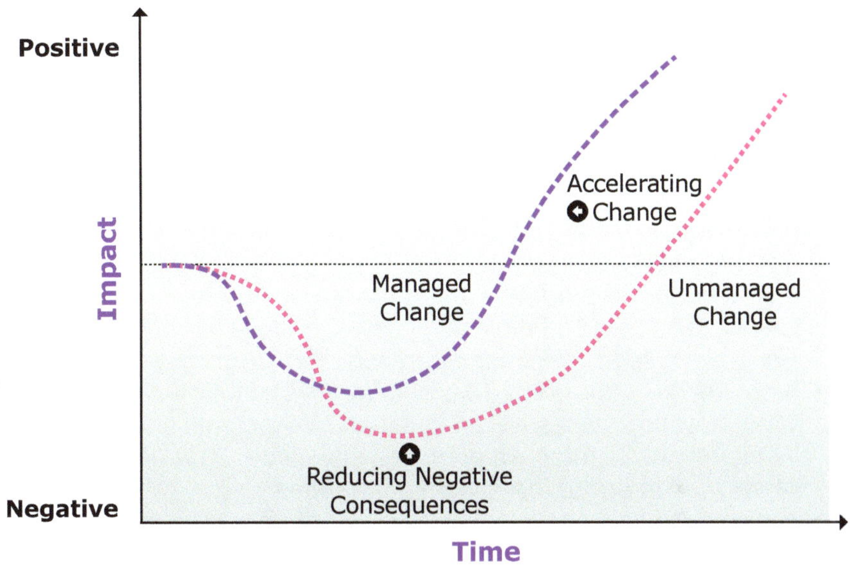

Using the Change Curve[20]

First let's discuss the PROSCI-ADKAR method of change management. ADKAR stands for[21]:

- **Awareness**: This step occurs as a pre-contemplation stage before plans are set in stone. You must be aware of what is and isn't working in your organizations. Research to find out what your options are. Communicate to others that there is a problem and focus attention on the most important reasons that a change must be made.
- **Desire**: This next stage is when you are contemplating what form of change you'll eventually implement. You must communicate benefits for the adoption of a new method of working (ex: Scrum).

Then you'll identify the risks involved in the impending change. Finally, you'll build momentum and excitement for what's to come as well as address fears by those this change will affect.
- **Knowledge**: Now you're preparing to enact change. You must use this time to learn new technical skills. Learn to think as a team, how to time box and share information. You should also set reasonable targets and goals during this phase.
- **Action**: Finally, it's time for action. During this phase you must employ a suitable governance framework and train team members on the basics. Make sure you start small and are communicating openly. Don't enact change through stealth. Adjust processes as necessary.
- **Reinforcement**: The last phase is maintenance, ensuring that the change you've implemented will continue to be part of future processes. In this phase you may wish to engage coaches or mentors, identify those who are adjusting to the change most effectively, and learn from your early mistakes.

Throughout the process of ADKAR, you'll want to ask different questions depending on which phase you're currently in. You'll also work with evolving objectives. Let's look deeper.[21]

- **Awareness**: What is the nature of the change? Why is change needed? What is the risk of not changing? *Objective: To have all involved understand why a change is necessary.*
- **Desire**: What's in it for me? Why should I choose this path? *Objective: For all involved to desire the particular forthcoming change.*
- **Knowledge**: How should we change? What training do we need? What new processes will be involved? What tools should we use? What new skills must we acquire? *Objective: That all involved will know how to adopt the imminent changes.*
- **Action**: What must I do to implement this change? What will show that the desired change has occurred? *Objective: For those involved to confidently be able to implement the change.*
- **Reinforcement**: What actions increase the likelihood that change will continue? What rewards and recognition should accompany those who excel in this new environment? *Objective: For the change to be permanent and successful.*

John Kotter offers another change management plan of action. He calls it the 8-step process for leading change. These 8 steps are broken down into three phases[22]: creating the climate for change, engaging and enabling the organization, and implementing and sustaining change.

They are[22]:

Creating the Climate for Change
1. Create Urgency
2. Form a Powerful Coalition
3. Create a Vision for Change

Engaging & Enabling the Organization
4. Communicate the Vision
5. Empower Action
6. Create Quick Wins

Implementing & Sustaining for Change
7. Build On the Change
8. Make It Stick

In my career, I've used both the PROSCI and Kotter methods within different organizations. I can confidently say from experience that they both work well. It's just a matter of choosing one, using it, and sticking to it. However, if you have a method your organization currently uses — go with that one. Keeping the same terminology your organization already understands will be in your favor. But, if your organization has no method to manage change now would be a good time to work with organizational developers and other leaders to start using one.

Tying these last few sections together, I'd like to share this quote:

> ***"The entrepreneur always searches for change, responds to it, and exploits it as an opportunity."***
> —Peter Drucker

As intrapreneuers, we have the opportunity to create innovation in our organizations by recognizing opportunities for change and putting a plan in place to address them.

In summary, we covered change and transformation are vital to the success of our organizations. The four-stage change curve can be long, but the negative impact can be minimized if you provide the appropriate communication. Change management can be facilitated through structured frameworks, such as ADKAR and Kotter.

We will revisit the topic of change management later in the chapter on execution, so you can put it into practice after you've planned for your new innovations. For now, let's move on to mindset.

•••

Mindset

In this section, we'll focus on...

- Importance of Mastering Mindset
- Common Mindsets
- Overcome Barriers to Effective Minds

Importance of Mastering Mindset

The term "mindset" often brings up other commonly associated words, such as attitude, and when thinking about mindset, we often focus on the positive aspects, such as optimism and purpose. Unfortunately, mindset can also have some negative connotations.

It is interesting that mindset can be defined in many different ways:

- A fixed mental attitude or disposition that predetermines a person's responses to and interpretations of situations.[23]
- A person's usual attitude or mental state is his or her mindset.[24]
- A mental inclination, tendency, or habit.[25]
- The established set of attitudes held by someone.[26]
- A person's way of thinking and their opinions.[27]

The most simplistic yet meaningful definition I have found is this:

*Mindset is a **habitual** or characteristic mental state that determines how you will interpret and respond to situations.*[24]

The word habitual is bold because I think it is so important with tying together what the definition really is. Habits are automatic, they just come to you naturally. And a great thing about a habit is it is something you can learn and practice.

We can think of mindset as a predictable loop. When we start with the mindset, it really is the basis for all of the resulting performance that we have. Moving from mindset, we have the resulting attitude,

Mindset Performance Loop

which is how we act and have our attitude portrayed to others. Other people can see the behaviors that we are actually doing. Then, people can see the physical actions we take and how they lead to the results we see and our overall performance. You can see how mindset is really the key to all of this. Now, you could end up with having poor actions and poor behaviors and still have a good mindset. But if you don't start with a good mindset, it's hard to have success throughout this path.

You've likely heard the famous quote from Henry Ford that I used at the beginning of this chapter: "Whether you think you can or you think you can't, you're right." And guess what? Henry Ford ***is*** right. The great news is that you can change your attitude and mindset just by deciding to. It is up to you. You don't need special skills or a charismatic personality to decide to think differently.

Mindset hugely impacts our reality and the importance of it in healthcare cannot be overstated. I'm sorry to remind you (as you likely already know) of the burnout epidemic in healthcare. I've been doing more and more research in this area and studies consistently show that up to 50% of physicians report symptoms of burnout while 30% of nurses seek new jobs within a year. Turnover is up and morale is down. The common trend is that stress leads to burnout which leads to higher turnover, higher levels of depression, low morale, anxiety, and unfortunately, increased rates of suicide.

Research from the Action Collaborative on Clinical Well-Being and Resilience reveals some startling statistics. High percentages of turnover, suicidal ideation and depression have become the norm.[28]

It's great that this organization exists, and they are starting to look at pharmacists as well. And burnout is becoming a regular phenomenon earlier and earlier in pharmacists' careers.[29] Research shows 64% of critical care pharmacists meet criteria for high degree of burnout, with higher frequencies at the start of many people's careers.[29] 50% of health system pharmacists in another study met criteria for a high degree burnout.[29]

While we don't have time to go into all the varied and detailed aspects of burnout, I do want to focus on one intervention strategy that has proven effective, and that is your mindset. There are many risk factors and intervention strategies to combat the burnout epidemic. Mindset is one of the most critical; how we approach stressful periods and situations is an important part of how we thrive in our careers and prevent burnout from taking hold.

It's important to remember that not all stress is bad. But sustained levels of stress are not good for our health. Additionally, how stress is perceived is just as important as the amount. Specifically, individuals who both perceived that stress affects their health and who reported a large amount of stress have a 43% increased risk of premature death. But those who can control that perceived level of stress based on how a more positive mindset can significantly reduce their risk.

Common Mindsets

While it's impossible to list all the types of mindsets a person may have. Here are a few common mindsets[30]:

Positively Perceived Mindsets

- Productive
- Short-term
- Creative
- Confident
- Social
- Growth
- Business
- Dreamer
- Gratitude

Negatively Perceived Mindsets

- Lazy
- Fixed
- Fear
- Envy
- Follower
- Greed

So, remember mindset is this habitual nature that can vary. You may have a more positive mindset in one area and more negative mindset in another area.

Carol Dweck, author of *Mindset: The New Psychology of Success* writes, "Mindset reveals how great parents, teachers, managers, and athletes can put this idea to use to foster outstanding accomplishment."[31]

From the myriad of options above, let's take a closer look at the idea of a fixed mindset vs. a growth mindset. **Beliefs** - A person with a fixed mindset believes that their abilities are fixed, and that intelligence is static while a growth mindset believes their abilities and intelligence can be developed. **Focus** - Those with a fixed mindset are focused on performance and outcomes. They don't want to look bad.

A growth mindset focuses on a desire to learn. **Challenges** - Fixed mindset folks avoid challenges while a growth mindset embraces them. **Obstacles** - When obstacles cross their paths, a fixed mindset is likely to give up easily while a growth mindset will likely persist. **Effort** - When it comes to effort, those with a fixed mindset view effort as fruitless while a growth mindset sees effort as the path to mastery. **Criticism** - A fixed mindset is likely to ignore criticism while a growth mindset attempts to learn from any criticism or feedback they receive. **Success of Others** - Finally, those with a fixed mindset are easily threatened by the success of others while others' success is inspiring to those with a growth mindset. **Result** - The result of these opposing mindsets is that those with fixed mindsets plateau early and achieve less than their full potential. Those with growth mindsets reach ever-higher levels of achievement because they put no limits on themselves.

So, can you see the obvious difference? Perhaps you see this in your own home or at work. Notice how your children or other family members approach challenges. Observe how your team members receive criticism. Find ways to foster a growth mindset in those you lead and teach

An important way to do this is by being aware of how we come across to others. This has a lot to do with mindset. The attitude we present and behaviors people see is their reality. If we show up negative and say things like, "Why does this happen to me? I can't do it. Life isn't fair." Then others will react negatively and follow suit. How can we overcome barriers to effective mindsets?

Overcome Barriers to Effective Mindsets

Here is a four step strategy to cultivate an effective mindset[31]:

1. **Listen to yourself**: The voice of a fixed mindset will stop you from following the path to success. You want to use your thought awareness to recognize negative thinking.
2. **Recognize you have a choice**: Simply put, you can control your mindset by making a decision. Only you can control it. No one else can do this for you.
3. **Challenge your fixed mindset**: If you begin to hear yourself thinking negative, fixed thoughts like, "I'm not smart enough/ good enough," remember that your abilities can be developed.
4. **Take action**: Practice growth mindset regularly. Encourage your team to do so as well. Support and coach them to encourage learning and open discussion.

In researching for this book, I came across something closely related to the burnout epidemic I'd love to unpack here. It's a program by the Institute for Healthcare Improvement (IHI) called "Improving Joy in Work", which is a specific type of framework.[32] They offer a new approach when looking at the challenge of burnout by flipping the focus to the positive aspects of work. Adopting positive attitudes in this manner has been identified as important to both wellness and resilience. And if you haven't figured it out, I'm definitely a big fan of positive attitude and its impact on our overall mindset.

Here are the specific framework steps for leaders[32]:

- Ask the staff, "What matters to you?"
- Identify unique impediments to joy in work in a local context.
- Commit to a systems approach to making joy in work a shared responsibility at all levels of the organization.
- Use improvement science to test approaches to improving joy in work in your organization (which is not surprising given this is IHI).

While we don't have space to go into all the aspects of this brilliant work, I'll pick out a few more highlights focused on the wellness and resilience piece of the puzzle. It's shown that health and wellness, self care, cultivating resilience and stress management, role modeling, having a system of appreciation for the whole person with work life balance, mental health, and depression and anxiety support has monumental impacts on an individual's ability to regularly find joy in work.[32] This is really where the positive mindset comes into play. Understanding the difference between harmful and positive stress, focusing on the positive, and finding balance for yourself and your team are all aspects that will serve you well in your Pharmovation journey.

Finally, I want to share with you two more traits that will help you develop a right mindset for this work. They are resilience and grit. **Grit** is perseverance and passion for long-term goals. It's the motivational drive that keeps you on a difficult task over a sustained period of time. **Resilience** involves the ability to get back up when you've been knocked down or to come back stronger after a loss. It's the optimism to continue when you've experienced some failures and times are tough.[33]

Now, when I am feeling down or concerned that I can't go on, I will tell myself a little internal mantra that goes, "I am resilient, and I can get through this; I am resilient and I can get through this." That's a little mantra that I say to myself in my head. I also say these kinds of things when I'm doing my nighttime meditation. If I'm having some negative thoughts then I move on to my typical meditation, which is to keep repeating the term "release, release, release." So to reaffirm all that we have discussed here, grit and resilience are just as important as the other traits that we've talked about for adopting an effective mindset.

It is my desire to see all mindsets and attitudes changed from more negative to more positive types:

From	→	**To**
Fixed	→	Growth
Closed	→	Open
Victim	→	Creator
Powerless	→	Empowered
Reactive	→	Proactive
Unaccountable	→	Accountable
Timid	→	Bold

For our profession, we have to move beyond reactive thinking and action. We need to stop thinking the onus is all on the physicians. As pharmacists, we need to be accountable for the entire medication use process. Being bold is really important for me as this was my word of the year and is necessary to achieve the transformation we desire.

In summary, I hope you now realize that mastering your mindset and supporting your team's mindset is vital in healthcare. While there are many different ways to describe mindset they can be summarized into two main categories: Fixed and Growth. While it's not easy to change your mindset, it is changeable, and the good news is it is entirely within your power. There are several steps you can take to overcome barriers to an effective mindset.

Take Action Now

- Complete the Mindset Worksheet in the Pharmovation Implementation Guide to assess your score and identify actions you might take.
- Share these actions in the Pharmovator Community.

I hope you will take the above actions towards cultivating the type of mindset that will serve you best as you move forward in your Pharmovation journey. Remember, it's YOUR time.

To support you incorporating the learnings from this chapter, access the Pharmovation Implementation Guide. Visit www.pharmovationguide.com or scan the QR code below for full access!

Chapter 2

Pharmovation OPPORTUNITY

"Pharmacy can do more with MORE."™
—Kimber Boothe

My husband, Richard, works in aviation. His entire career, even before college, has been spent at airports and working for international airlines. It is his passion, and he knows every aspect of the operations for his role as aircraft dispatcher and private pilot. While flying seems dangerous to the casual observer (you are in a steel cage barreling at hundreds of miles an hour through the sky after all) the processes in place to assure the safety of all involved are meticulous, well-planned, and followed to the letter every time a plane's wheels lift off the tarmac.

The safety processes in aviation are often looked to by healthcare leaders to draw comparisons and implement similar processes. This is not an uncommon conversation for us to have at the dinner table actually. There is an absolute necessity for processes and procedures as we have the safety of those in our care to consider. My husband's responsible for those on the plane and I, as a pharmacy leader, am responsible for the safety of every patient in our care. Unfortunately, aviation is doing a much better job ensuring the safety of those in their care. They have a myriad of checklists, processes, and procedures that are followed, without fail, each flight. When a safety event does occur, a massive investigation follows, procedures are updated, those responsible are held accountable and everything possible is done to ensure that a similar event doesn't happen again. Because when a plane goes down, hundreds of people are dead or injured, and it's a massive tragedy. It's a rare event. It's big news.

Yet in the healthcare system, if you look at patients who die or incur morbidity (undue pain and suffering) through human error it's like a plane crash every two weeks. EVERY TWO WEEKS. It's absurd. And it's a wholly unnecessary tragedy. The systems simply aren't in place to double check human error or hold those who make errors responsible. While technology is advancing, it isn't integrated in a way that helps reduce errors as much as possible. Sometimes this is because we have not built the knowledge to implement and other times it is because we have not advocated adding the needed technology. At the end of the day, technology can't be integrated without the people. And the people can't integrate technology appropriately without proper systems and frameworks in place to do so.

That's where Pharmovation comes in. How are we orchestrating the framework of our organizations to support lower levels of morbidity and mortality for patients while supporting our team members to perform their jobs with more confidence and joy?

In this chapter, we'll discuss why staying aware of the bigger picture (even while conducting daily tasks) is so vital. There is a huge need for well-trained and innovative pharmacists and technicians in the healthcare system. We'll unpack why that is, look at the need and opportunities available, explore the current landscape, and ultimately agree that there are many possibilities for pharmacy to increase involvement in disruptive innovation to improve patient care.

•••

Need & Opportunity

SECTION PREVIEW | SECTION PREVIEW |

In this section, we'll look at…

- Need
- Pharmacy Workforce
- Opportunity

Need

Let's start with the need. There are some important trends that are affecting pharmacy practice, including…

- Prescription Volume
- Drug Spending Increase
- Aging Population
- Complex Regimens
- Physician Shortage
- Transition to Value

Current trends show that there is increased spending on prescription drugs driven mostly because of a 21% increase in average drug price and a 5% increase in utilization since 2014.[34] Overall we see an increase in spending of 26% on prescriptions which is higher than in other sectors including inpatient care, outpatient care, and professional services which only rose 16%. The utilization across all of these areas is comparable between 3-5%. The only area we see a decrease in utilization is inpatient care as we transition more and more to outpatient procedures and care.[34]

The rise in prescription spending is driven by specialty medications at a higher price per unit and we will dive deeper into that trend coming up. Specialty drugs are more complex than most prescription medications and are used to treat patients with serious and often life-threatening conditions including cancer, hepatitis C, rheumatoid arthritis, HIV/AIDS, etc. While many can be taken orally, most require injection or infusion with special administration, storage, and delivery requirements. Their development leads to higher prices, and comprehensive care is required for education and monitoring.

It's important to note that prescription drugs account for about 10% of our overall national healthcare expenditures. Hospitals and other types of care account for much more, and we have shown in separate studies that prescription spending is helpful to reducing those other costs of care.[35]

A source I rely on to monitor current trends, growth, and development over time is the Kaiser Family Foundation (KFF) Health System Tracker. They keep track of average annual growth rates for select service types such as physicians, hospitals, and prescriptions. From their data, we see a steadying and more balanced growth of prescription spend over this past decade (~4%) as compared to the prior two decades (7-13%), where you see significant growth in prescription spending.[35]

What's also important to keep an eye on is spending on specialty drugs vs traditional drug trends. For instance, back in 2014, we saw a huge bump in the use of specialty medications and in their pricing, resulting in a 22% increase in per capita spending. But since 2014 we've seen this specialty drug spending decrease and come down to more mirror that of the other non-specialty spending.

The final piece of information from the Kaiser Health Family Foundation I want to draw your attention to is the annual change in per capita prescription drug spending compared to total healthcare spending. We again see another peak of specialty drugs prior to 2000. Then an increase in prescription spending that was above total healthcare spending around 2014. Unfortunately, this specific data has not been updated since 2017, but future projections indicate this coming decade will see pharmacy spending mirror total healthcare spending more closely.[36]

Related to prescription volume is the increased aging population in the United States. In fact, the aging population shows a 135% increase in those over 75 occurring by the year 2050.[37] The result will be a change in the elderly population over 65 from 35 million in 2000 to more than 80 million in 2050. Among this aging population (and other populations but most significantly with those over 75) there is an increase in the complexity of medication regimens.[38]

To add to the complex regimen trend, we must look at the drugs in the pipeline for development. Pharma, which represents the biopharmaceutical companies, compiles data on research pipelines and differentiate first in class drugs. First-in-class drugs tend to be those more unique medications that are not me-too drugs that are bringing significant advances to the market. The majority of drugs in our research pipelines are fitting the potentially first-in-class definition, which does lead to more complexity and need for more medication expertise.[38]

More expensive medication and complex medication regimes used by an aging population under no direct supervision combined with a shortage of providers represents a deeper emerging issue.

By the year 2030, the Association of American Medical Colleges (AAMC) projects a shortage of between 40,000 and 121,000 physicians.[39] The provider shortage is yet another area that is leading to a need for increase in pharmacy services. This shortage is then broken down by specific specialty areas as well as the determined retirement age of each physician. Each plays a role in determining the shortage. If primary care physicians choose to retire two years later, then we have about 20,000 physicians. Whereas the current status predicts that we will only have about 10,000 full-time equivalent physicians. But if physicians decide to retire earlier, we could be left with only about 2,500 primary care physicians. Another possibility falls somewhere in the middle, if physicians decline their hours instead of fully retiring, there will be a significant impact on surgical specialties especially, but all areas of the healthcare workforce will be impacted.

In the State of the Nation's Health Workforce, The Association of Academic Health Centers (AAHC) summarizes it like this: "The dysfunction in public and private health workforce policy and infrastructure is an outgrowth of decentralized decision-making in health workforce education, planning, development and policy making (out of order)... the costs and consequences of our collective failure to act effectively are accelerating due to looming socioeconomic forces that leave no time for further delay (out of time)."[40] So, you may have seen there have been some initiatives to help more people get into medical school and some debt forgiveness. Pharmacists can definitely play a role in repairing the dysfunction and filling gaps created by the shortage. Several of our national organizations have had conversations on how pharmacists can be included in the solution.

We must focus on the transition to value. This was laid out by the Institute for Healthcare Improvement some years ago and summarized by a triple aim for healthcare.[41] Subsequently a fourth area — provider engagement — has been added, but let us first explore the triple aims. These are: improving patient experience, achieving better health through improved outcomes, and managing and reducing costs. So when we think about our role as pharmacists in a struggling system, we must think about it holistically, with these three aims in mind.

We are seeing that the payers are moving from fee for service to more fee for value models. We'll cover this further in later chapters, but from a high level, when we look at some of the care models compared to the provider's financial risks, we do see a movement towards more complex models with significantly more financial risks put on the provider. For instance, the move from a shared savings model to bundled payments, to partial capitation, to global capitation, where you are expected to care for a patient with a set amount of money. This shift has moved us towards more clinically integrated networks, evidence-based coordinated care, and having more patient and population centers.[41]

Pharmacy Workforce

There are current concerns that our supply of pharmacists exceeds the demand, and I will argue that we should be able to increase the demand based on the factors we just discussed. The factors impacting the pharmacy workforce are complex and a comprehensive analysis is beyond the scope of this chapter. We will review the key data sources and metrics to shed light on the pharmacy workforce supply and demand.

Back in 2002, D.A. Knapp wrote an article projecting the need for pharmacists vs. the pharmacists available in 2020.[42] This is then broken down by different categories such as order fulfillment, primary services, secondary/tertiary services and then indirect or other services. While they projected a reduction in the need for pharmacists in order fulfillment, overall the projected need for total pharmacists was 417,000 with a supply of 260,000. Yet, the research estimated a shortage of about 157,000 pharmacists. Fortunately, we do have about 320,000 pharmacists practicing in the United States (nearly 60,000 more than Knapp predicted would be available), yet we still haven't reached the predicted level of demand for pharmacists and pharmacy services. With this increased demand for pharmacists, my hope is that more pharmacists will join the force to advance practice and help achieve the triple aim set out by the Institute for Healthcare Improvement.

Let's compare these projections with the current Bureau of Labor Statistics and its recent job Outlook 2019 to 2029. While pharmacist job growth is projected at -3% with 311,000 employed, technicians see double that in need, a projection of 4% with 438,000 employed.[43] For both professions this projection slowed compared to projections in 2016 and does not take into consideration retirements.[44] Either way the projections are far short of the 417,000 pharmacists projected by D.A. Knapp.

The Pharmacy Manpower Project, Inc. completed surveys to assess supply and demand of pharmacists in the workforce and reported in the Pharmacist Demand Indicator (PDI).[45] In short, the research showed that the supply of pharmacists was not meeting the demand from 2008-2015. Beginning in 2016 the PDI showed the demand was in balance with supply and the supply even exceeded demand in some regions. Specialized roles and management were in more demand than general or staff positions.[46]

Since the PDI, The Pharmacy Manpower Project was renamed to the Pharmacy Workforce Center, Inc. and they updated the report methodology to create the Pharmacy Demand Report (PDR). This information is intended to be utilized by the pharmacy profession and other stakeholders to assess and follow the trends for various career opportunities for pharmacists and pharmacy technicians on an individual state, region, and metropolitan area level. Positions across a multitude of different roles were considered, including clinical pharmacists, hospital pharmacists, other pharmacists, pharmacy directors, retail pharmacists as well as pharmacy technicians. This research helps us understand that demand for pharmacists is not simply one type of job posting or position, but a whole network of jobs and skills necessary to fulfill needs within the pharmacy network — from clinical pharmacists to technicians and everything in between. The posting quotient is the number of positions posted and normalized based on the number of pharmacists or technicians within the state. Let's look at a few examples comparing 2019 and 2020. In Alabama, there were 10 postings per thousand licensed pharmacists in 2019. And that was down to 4.5 in 2020. My state of Ohio is at 34 and it is maintained at 34. There are some states where there was an increase, like in Rhode Island, but for the most part, most states have declined in the number of postings per thousand pharmacists.

Now this differs from our technicians where for the most part we do see there is an increase in the number of technician postings per thousand technicians. And what's important also to notice is there are a lot more postings per thousand technicians than there are for pharmacists. For example, in Alabama, you see 232 positions posted per thousand technicians. And that actually did slightly decrease from 2019 to 2020. And again, if we jumped down to Ohio, where I live, we have 392, which increased to 453.

In fact, the demand for pharmacy technicians has increased dramatically over the past decade.[47] The good news is we do have more technicians becoming certified, which is very positive, and this is definitely an important part of practice advancement and will be an important part of considerations for Pharmovation execution. So this just shows the number of certified technicians across the country by state. And we do have a total of about 289,000 certified technicians.

A final benchmark I want to note here to bring home the need available for pharmacy professionals is the American Society of Health System Pharmacists (ASHP) national survey.[48] They conduct a survey every year to benchmark and discover how many pharmacists and technicians are staffed in hospitals across the country. This is normalized by dividing by every hundred occupied beds. The 2019 (most recent at the time of writing) survey showed approximately 19 pharmacists and 17 technicians per hundred beds.[48] This ratio has been increasing steadily, partially due to antimicrobial stewardship and medication history technician work, and likely due to some of the other elements we've discussed such as complexity of meds and higher acuity patients. Keep in mind that this metric is for acute care only and I am seeing similar trends in support of expanding ambulatory pharmacy services.

Part of the concern with the supply of pharmacists is pharmacy school enrollment and that the growth in the number of pharmacy schools has increased and outpaced other healthcare professions beginning in the early 2000s.[49] A challenge we see here is that students graduate with a significant amount of debt, which raises a question about a pharmacist's return on investment (ROI) from their schooling to their projected career. A study a few years back showed clearly that while pharmacists' salaries have increased steadily since 2002, it doesn't keep pace with the increase of schooling costs.[50]

With all this data, I don't see a good forecast to project the true quantified need for qualified pharmacists and technicians based on the vast needs related to medication use. Even today I see jobs go unfilled for months to a year all around the country. We have to find ways to be innovative about getting people in the right place. Given the trends presented here and shown in research, I still believe that pharmacy can do more with more. And we will need to advocate for more as we continue.

Let's put our pharmacy team members to good use in order to advance practice.

What to Watch for

I do not think we have a good forecast to predict the true quantified need for pharmacists given the trends presented.

Pharmacy Can Do More with More!
(And it looks like we have more)

Opportunity

Now that we've broadly outlined the need for qualified pharmacists, I'd like to quickly touch on the opportunities available and the role of pharmacists in expanding sectors. As we turn to examine this opportunity angle, I want to clarify that there's a role for pharmacists in so many sectors and that this is by no means meant to be all-inclusive.

Pharmacists have an opportunity to serve patients in many sectors including:

- Quality
- Patient Experience
- Electronic Health Record (EHR)
- Prescription Volume
- Aging Population
- Complex Medication
- Adverse Drug Events
- Physician Shortage
- Accountable Care Organization
- Opioids
- And MORE!

Role of Pharmacy
ACO: Accountable Care Organization
CBO: Congressional Budget Office
EHR: Electronic Health Record

Perhaps some of the above are sectors you'd not considered before. And we touch patients in so many areas across the continuum of care from ambulatory to acute care pharmacy, to specialty & outpatient pharmacy to clinic & home infusion. So these are just some of the main touch points where patients come into contact with pharmacies and our medication services.

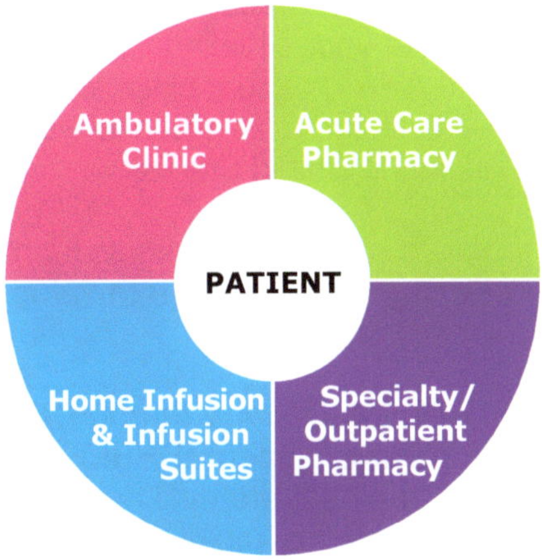

Pharmacy Continuity Touch Points

But as we further understand pharmacy's role within the healthcare enterprise, we'll see that pharmacy is an integrated system of business units with accountability for clinical and essential outcomes related to medication use across the continuum of care within a health system. This covers operations, acute care clinical services, ambulatory care, outpatient pharmacy and other managed pharmacy solutions and business services. There are so many aspects that the pharmacy enterprise of our health systems touch these days.

To sum up, there are several important trends that support the need for pharmacy. While the pharmacy workforce is trending to have a surplus of pharmacists graduating in the coming years there are significant gaps when it comes to utilizing these trained professionals to their utmost capacity. There are some great opportunities ahead for pharmacy to address recent trends and meet the needs of patients.

Let's continue by discussing the wider landscape of pharmacy and how this comes alongside disruptive innovations in the field.

•••

Landscape

In this section, we'll look at…

- Healthcare Landscape
- Pharmacy Landscape

Healthcare Landscape

Next, we'll be looking at some scans and forecasts for healthcare overall and pharmacy. In keeping with our theme of the chapter, these will continue to put the entire field in perspective — past, present and future — as we begin to strategize and plan for our own organizations' innovations.

First, let's discuss the American Hospital Association's (AHA) environmental scan from 2019.[51] Environmental scans will become an important part of what you'll be assessing as part of your situational analysis and strategic planning moving forward. The AHA is a great place to start since they publish this nearly every year — what they see as the forecast and key things that impact health systems in the United States.

In 2019, their top picks were consumerism, innovations (such as technological advances), chronic disease management, volume to value, social determinants of health, and new entrants to care.[51]

The AHA also partners with a few other organizations through the Society for Health Care & Strategy Market Development (SHSMD) to create a tool called Futurescan.[52] Summarized here are the key topics that the study predicted we should be considering moving forward. Included is disruptive innovation and the impact of new entrants on the future of healthcare, the dual transformation of healthcare and how that will be the key to sustainability moving forward. Also, the changing face of strategic health care partnerships, how to build a resilient health care organization, and technologies that are shaping the future of health and medicine. Additionally, we should consider that frictionless health care requires a connected healing ecosystem. In addressing the aging population in America (as mentioned before) they also offer a five part solution to healthy aging plus the assertion that innovation is key to the future viability of Medicaid.[52]

When we consider all of these, we see that they can easily integrate with pharmacy. There are obvious areas where pharmacy can make a positive impact and lend support and help to each of these areas.

Another excellent resource to consider is the American Council of Healthcare Executives (ACHE). It's an organization that goes beyond pharmacy to include other healthcare leaders and a perfect place for the necessary multidisciplinary conversations we should be having. Every year or two they aggregate research and release the top issues confronting hospitals. In 2019 they listed financial challenges, personnel shortages, behavioral health/addiction issues, government mandates, patient safety and quality, access to care, and patient satisfaction as the leading challenges to be addressed.[53] These are all important to keep in mind, again, not only to find ways that pharmacists can help to solve these issues and address concerns, but also when you're writing business plans and strategically pitching these plans to senior leaders. **Keep in mind that these are the things at the top of their to-do list. Anything you can do to help ease these specific burdens and stresses is highly beneficial to your plan getting approved.**

Pharmacy Landscape

Another forecast I always turn to is the American Society of Health System (ASHP) pharmacy forecast.[54] Each year, they publish a forecast that covers the next three years of trends. All of them are valuable. We'll be looking into this topic again in later chapters but it's important to introduce now as we discuss the landscape and disruptive innovation. Some of the top trends from 2020 were patient-centered care, pharmacy education and workforce, pharmacy leadership, evidence-based pharmacy practice, pharmacy supply chain, healthcare marketplace, healthcare reform, and black swan events — which ironically occurred in full force in 2020 with the pandemic.[54] Then, the 2021 pharmacy forecast included these topics: global supply chain, access to healthcare, analytics and big data, healthcare financing and delivery, patient safety, pharmacy enterprise and the pharmacy workforce.[55]

I want to tease this out a bit and look at a few specific details. Each of the sections of the forecast goes into some key recommendations for us to consider. This is what rises to the top after surveying pharmacy leaders as to what is likely to happen and what we need to act upon. Again, we'll revisit this as part of situational analysis later when you will score your organization, but I want to introduce some background now.

- **Global Supply Chain**: Global supply chain in particular highlights the scarcity of pharmacy resources. We want to help support the pandemic-related surge and follow up. Publicly reported quality measures are important here. Then, working on legislation we can help reduce some of the unnecessary spending on medications and help to improve the quality of the manufacturing processes.
- **Access to Healthcare**: We should be supporting telehealth and helping to implement and permanently put into place telepharmacy rules. Technicians need to be broadly and effectively utilized and move into enhanced technician training and roles. In short, we should make permanent any of the expanded scope of practice that was implemented in response to the pandemic. They want greater harmonization of formularies and formula decision-making processes, and they want policies related to non-FDA regulated therapies.
- **Analytics and Big Data**: Under analytics and big data, the forecast calls to recruit, resource, and expand the team of pharmacists in health informatics. We should begin to work more collaboratively and support the competence and capabilities of our team members around artificial intelligence. Then in turn, we can support all aspects of patient care across systems. In particular, analytics and patient outcomes should drive the strategic direction of our operations and clinical services. We need the data. We want to focus on improving our informatics, residency training programs and support, and have the data that we need. And finally, the last suggestion relates to the opportunities and limitations of our big data as we want to assure that we have outcomes that can be assessed.
- **Healthcare Financing and Delivery**: Collaborate with our government affairs teams and jointly establish a pharmacy policy platform. We want to monitor trends in drug contracting and fulfillment. Then, we want to have financial performance and positioning of the healthcare system that helps to cultivate strong relationships with our system financial leaders. Finally, we want to be able to evaluate every aspect of the pharmacy enterprise with respect to value offered to the patient and the system. This evaluation could mean both internally and built on external partnerships.
- **Patient Safety**: We want to have pharmacists placed in organization-wide roles related to patient safety. We want to be able to ask

provocative questions on how harm can be eliminated by getting all of that detail from our staff and team members. We want to engage in setting the health system and patient safety priorities beyond the medication use process. So as I like to say, anytime a medication is being considered, prescribed, ordered, or monitored, a pharmacist needs to be accountable for the process. We need to be aware of that and engage. We then want to have new patient safety measures and monitoring strategies. We want to make sure we have a formulary system to systematically identify the quality and quantity of our evidence. And we want to make sure we are addressing the wellbeing needs of our team.

- **Pharmacy Enterprise**: We want to look at expansion into ambulatory sites and telehealth settings, including the underserved and remote areas. We want to provide transitions of care medication services, medication reconciliation services, and documentation of our services is important. Finally, we need comprehensive medication management services for high risk and chronic patients, as well as for pharmacist, ambulatory, and population health management.
- **Pharmacy Workforce**: We want to work towards recognition of ambulatory care pharmacists as primary care providers within the health system. We should be looking at productivity and revenue generation benchmarks. Develop ambulatory care operational systems that: promote credentialing, billing, coding, and documentation for pharmacists' providers; achieve financial sustainability; align with the state and federal requirements for prescribing pharmacists. Then to have advanced technician roles and leadership positions and to assess auto verification adoption, and finally, to have an impact on the decreasing pharmacy student numbers. So while we've talked about the projected increase in surplus, there is significant concern that a shortage could be coming as we have less students going into pharmacy school and what impact that could have in the near term of the services that student pharmacists provide during their internships, rotations, as well as during residency programs.

In these forecasts, you can see a rising trend toward transitions of care, where historically health systems have been acute-care-focused. Now we ask, what are the innovations available and what innovations should we be looking to foster in order to address the above forecasted issues?

In summary, we learned that the broader healthcare landscape and pharmacy landscape is primed for innovation to advance practice and solve the unmet needs identified in these environmental scans.

Disruptive Innovation

In this section, we'll look at...

- What is Disruptive Innovation?
- Market Forces
- Healthcare Disruptive Innovation

What is Disruptive Innovation?

Here is where we begin our conversation about disruptive innovation in the pharmacy industry. First, I want to remind us of what our innovation descriptions are.[56]

The outcome of any innovation is a new or improved product, service, platform, or process. The degree of innovativeness or novelty can be categorized as[56]:

- **Incremental or Evolutionary**: Innovation that is an expected improvement on an existing product.
- **Radical or Revolutionary**: This is unexpected but does not affect existing markets.

Finally, we have the degree of change to consider. This is broken into two categories. First, sustaining change, which does not significantly affect existing markets. And second, disruptive change which creates a new market by providing a different set of values. This ultimately and unexpectedly overtakes an existing market.

Ok, with these definitions in place, let's take a look at some of the disruptive innovations currently happening to pinpoint where it already occurs frequently. Clayton Christensen is a well-known author on this topic, who's written a disruptive solution for healthcare called *The Innovator's Prescription*.[57] He coined the phrase ***disruptive innovation*** as an "Innovation that creates a new market and value network and eventually disrupts an existing market and value network, displacing established market-leading firms, products, and alliances."[57]

So, we can look at disruptive innovation as scary or as a potential positive, either way we need to be aware of it. Since we've already discussed disruptive innovation in the previous chapter, I don't want to spend too much time on it here. But bring back to mind examples like Apple, Uber, Amazon, and Google.

Market Forces

Over the last few years, there have been significant market forces that have impacted healthcare. One such force was the creation of new healthcare companies with large organizations like Amazon, Berkshire Hathaway, and JP Morgan, which was subsequently disbanded. We see a lot of vertical integration happening with insurance companies. We have Amazon acquiring PillPack and other organizations who banded together and created their own generic drug company because of drug supply issues. There are significant disruptive innovations occurring in the market today. Some of them are exciting and some of them haven't yet achieved their full plan.

We also see market forces with government influence where, over these last few years, The Department of Health and Human Services (HHS) is significantly trying to move forward. There is now a blueprint they created around prescription pricing, including improved competition, better negotiation incentives for lower list price and lowering of out-of-pocket costs. While most of this has not yet come to fruition because of the complexity of the system, you can see that it is at the forefront.[58]

Healthcare Disruptive Innovation

Now let's dive into where disruptive innovation shows itself in the healthcare industry. The AHA Center for Health Innovation studies these trends and noted that 2018 in particular was a year of unprecedented disruptive innovation.[59] These disruptions included: Apple announcing an iPhone health records feature; Amazon, Berkshire Hathaway, and JP Morgan Chase enter a healthcare partnership; Apple to roll out AC wellness on-site clinics for employees; Uber Health to help health care providers get patients to their appointments, Cigna Express Scripts announces a merger; Google offshoot launches a virtual diabetes clinic; Apple patents could make iPhones a medical device; Amazon's Alexa division adds a healthcare team; Walgreens and Humana to start in-store senior health care clinics; Amazon buys the online pharmacy, PillPack; Humana private equity firms close Kindred Curo deals; Tech giants partner on developing common EHR standards; Cigna-Express Scripts merger moves forward with conditions.

We see examples from nearly every month that change the way healthcare operates in significant ways. More and more of these disruptive innovations begin to touch on medication and medicines, where pharmacists have both a vested interest and a responsibility to be involved at the top levels. We see large companies merging and partnering on a regular basis. We must be aware. We must pay attention. And we must be part of these changes to ensure patient safety.

I have highlighted several of the innovative companies that are touching medications. For example, we have Amazon shown with some of the various things that they're doing around healthcare, such as their purchasing of PillPack and getting closer to patients with that acquisition. They are also creating virtual care pilots, investing in machine learning, and betting on blockchain. We have CVS Healthcare, obviously expanding beyond pharmacy to health hubs, stepping into in-home dialysis, and addressing social determinants of health. We see the same thing with Walgreens, which is also expanding and doing some innovative, disruptive things such as establishing medicare service centers, expanding digital marketplace. Their clinic strategy is evolving as they close most of the in-store health clinics while keeping those run by local health systems and expand partnership in senior clinics.[59]

Another element we must keep in mind akin to partnerships and mergers are the vertical integrations we increasingly see. United Healthcare, Aetna, Cigna, Anthem, Humana and BlueCross BlueShield all own their own pharmacies and pharmacy benefit managers.[60] The vertical integration includes the insurance companies at the top, the PBM owned by the insurer, the specialty and mail order pharmacy they own or integrate with, and even the provider services run by the insurer separate from the health systems. This integration is something to watch as a lack of transparency and steering can happen when these payers also have their own providers and pharmacies. We must advocate for patients at these levels, making sure we serve them as well as possible.

From the ASHP Forecast we see the following recommendations to watch out for as disruptive forces.[61]

- **Dismantling the Affordable Care Act**: Pharmacists should provide data that describe efforts to improve patient care. Of course, that did not end up happening. The affordable care act is still in place, but that was a significant issue and continues to be a need again for us to provide documentation of our value.
- **Pricing of Pharmaceuticals and Transparency**: Pharmacists must advocate publicly for patients suffering from egregiously high drug prices. We should endorse transparency in drug pricing due to contracts and arrangements by manufacturers, pharmacy benefits managers, and wholesalers should be demanded.
- **Drug Manufacturing by Health Systems**: Assessed as unlikely outside of one entry and Group Purchasing Organization.
- **Nontraditional Participants in Healthcare Delivery**: Find ways to partner and develop new strategies for care.
- **Additional Forces to Consider**: Change management to make bold changes with flawless execution.

In summary, with all of this information that's ever-changing, mind you, we cannot deny that keeping a view on the big picture of the healthcare system and pharmacy's place within that system is an important responsibility for pharmacy leaders. When developing strategy, we can see how it's imperative to keep an eye on environmental scans and forecasts. We must be aware of this and discuss how to navigate recent disruptive innovations as they provide both challenges and opportunities.

As we come towards the end of this chapter, you can see how the background regarding need, opportunity, landscape, and disruptive innovation will finally weave together into the overarching framework of the pharmacy enterprise today. It's time for our mantra friends...

Pharmacy can do more with more.

- More knowledge, more advocates, more funding, more strategies, better services, better leadership, well-integrated technology, and excellent execution.
- In short, pharmacy can do more with innovation. You might even say: *Pharmovation*. See what I did there?

With this background of the current and ever-evolving state of pharmacy, we will, in the rest of this book, discuss how we can affect change for the better in our industry. **In the coming pages you'll learn exactly what to do to advocate for resources, advance pharmacy practice, and accelerate your career, to bring joy to your work while improving patient outcomes.**

To support you incorporating the learnings from this chapter, access the Pharmovation Implementation Guide. Visit www.pharmovationguide.com or scan the QR code below for full access!

Chapter 3

Pharmovation ENTERPRISE

"Health is a state of complete physical, mental, and social well being and not merely the absence of disease or infirmity."
—World Health Organization

I attended the University of Connecticut for my undergraduate degree. My freshman year, I knew I wanted to be a pharmacist. I thought I knew what that entailed. But I was about to get a rude awakening. I was extremely naive to the health system as a whole. Because then, more so than now, the health system was extremely disparate and disconnected.

When I came home during spring break, my parents told me that my mother had been diagnosed with lung cancer. They had received the diagnosis a few weeks earlier but waited to tell me in person. She began treatment right away for metastatic lung cancer. That summer, I drove her to appointments and helped her navigate through the labyrinth of the healthcare system. Healthcare is a system I thought I knew something about, but negotiating it personally is still so difficult. While my mother had wonderful members on her treatment team, we had limited opportunities to speak to a pharmacist about her medications. As a pharmacy student at the time, I recognized this as a huge missed opportunity.

An additional difficulty was traversing through the many different points of care. My mother had chemo at one place, radiation at another location, her primary care physician's office down the road, and her oncology specialist at a separate complex. It was a maze to say the least. On top of which, I had to print her medical records from one hospital to take to her next appointment. There was simply no continuity of care. And still, with all these separate locations, there was no pharmacist on her team. Not at the oncologist, the primary care office, or anywhere. No one oversaw her total care. No one understood or considered how separately prescribed medications might interact or interfere with one another.

While at one of her radiation treatments, she began to complain of acute pain; she was unable to move her legs. What we didn't know at the time was the cancer had spread to her bones as well. Her leg had broken just walking to the car. I called an ambulance. She was rushed into surgery, and we thought she'd be able to recover and then we'd refocus on treating the cancer. Ultimately, she never left the hospital.

Unfortunately, this story is all too common. Many of us have had similar experiences with family members or loved ones. I don't know how, or if, my mother's outcome could have been changed, but I do know that there was no one overseeing the whole process of her treatment. No one to ensure a safe continuity of care. She had so many places to go to get the treatment she needed. So many touch points along the way. Nothing was integrated. No one comprehensively reconciled her medications, or considered how they might affect each other.

Better hand-offs can happen within a system. Now, the hospital where she received treatment has a comprehensive cancer center. A lot of aspects have improved drastically since 1993, but there's still a need to watch patient touchpoints closely. Many hospitals still provide oncology medications without a pharmacist involved. This must be changed to ensure patient safety, not just in oncology, but across the board.

In this chapter, the objective is to capitalize on the value of the integration and reach of the pharmacy enterprise. We'll start by looking at the big picture of healthcare, which will help us step back and think about where pharmacy fits into that picture. Next, we will think about the business of healthcare and answer the question or whether healthcare is a business. This will help us start to think about return on investment and how we create our strategic plans. Further, we will explore the history of pharmacy enterprise: where the term comes from, how it is used, and how it encompasses the larger and more important role within the health system. We'll also explore the vast scope of the pharmacy enterprise and you'll begin to assess your own organization with the useful Pharmovation Implementation Guide.

•••

The Big Picture

SECTION PREVIEW | SECTION PREVIEW

In this section, we'll look at...

- What are Health & Healthcare?
- US Healthcare Status
- Role of Health Systems
- How Does Pharmacy Fit In?

Since we've already spent some time covering healthcare landscape trends and disruptive innovations in previous chapters, it's time to take another step back and look at the big picture of healthcare. Understanding our why will help us to connect the dots to our Mission and Vision as we prepare to create our strategy.

What are Health & Healthcare?

We'll start by attempting to answer the question "What is health, and what is healthcare?" all while taking the pulse of the US healthcare status on the whole. We will be looking at the role of health systems and discovering how pharmacy fits within it all.

As I mentioned at the beginning of the chapter, according to the World Health Organization (WHO), "Health is a state of complete physical, mental, and social well being and not merely the absence of disease or infirmity." And yet, we usually consider healthcare to be only the treatment of disease or malfunction. We look to doctors and hospitals when something goes wrong.

Let's instead give healthcare a broader and more encompassing definition that includes preventative care.

Healthcare:

- The **organized** provision of **medical care** to individuals or a community.[62]
- The field concerned with the **maintenance or restoration** of the health of the **body or mind**.[63]
- The **prevention, treatment, and management** of illness and the **preservation of mental and physical well being** through the services offered by the medical and allied health professions.[64]

Now, let's look at the healthcare constituents. We often think about the patient as the center of our healthcare continuum, but that's not necessarily the case. In truth, there are four major constituents. We have the patients (the consumers), the payers (usually government employers or individuals), providers (including hospitals, doctors, and pharmacists), as well as the government.[65] Considering all these components, we see that healthcare is provided through exchange of payments and insurance coverage, while the government plays a role providing regulations to both payers and providers.

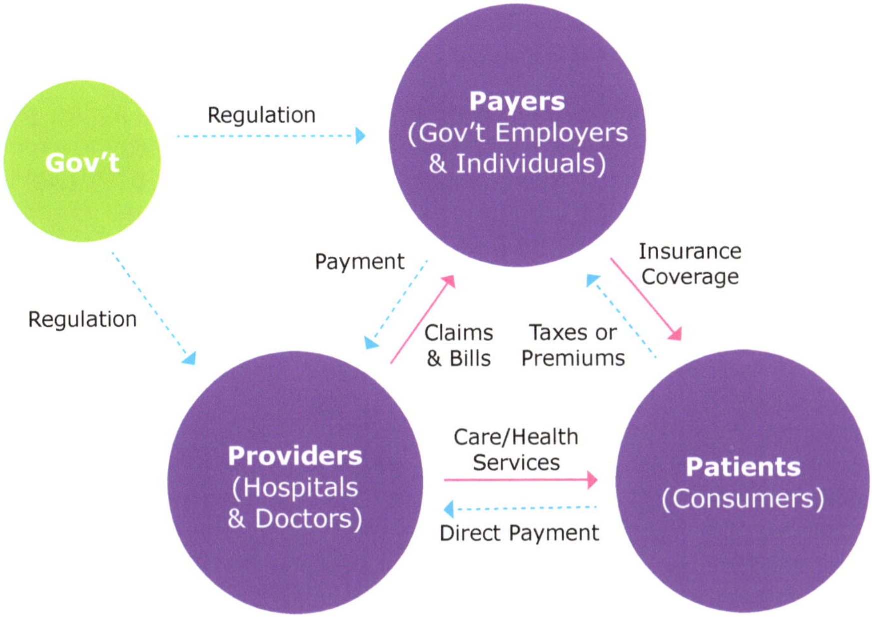

Healthcare Constituents[65]

US Healthcare Status

Let's jump into the status of US healthcare. The OECD or the Organization for Economic Cooperation and Development, is a global organization of many countries who get together and assess different metrics impartially. One of the frameworks they've created is for health system performance. In this case, we're not talking about health systems like we think of in the United States, but the broader concept of health care. They've created a framework that illustrates comparisons between countries which shows the health status of populations and health system performance. They use indicator by indicator analysis and snapshots to compare performance in five key areas: health status, risk factors for health, access to care, quality of care, and healthcare resources.[66]

Now, luckily, most countries have universal healthcare coverage. This promotes equitable access for needed health care services, and quality of care has generally been improving. But, this has come at a cost with health spending now accounting for about 9% of the gross domestic product for the average country.[66]

Now, I want to dig in and discuss a few comparisons across these domains. Shown here are the health status risk factors for health access to care and quality of care, comparing the OECD average to that of the

United States. If you're interested in the specifics of other countries, it's all available via their website. See the references for more details.

When we look at life expectancy, this has remained fairly flat for the US. We line up pretty much with the OECD average.[66] However, when we dive deeper into these statistics, we see that with both avoidable mortality (deaths per hundred thousand people), and chronic disease morbidity (diabetes prevalence), the US is doing worse than the OECD average.[66]

We do a bit better when it comes to overall self-related health issues, like risk factors for health and smoking. We have fewer than average smokers, which is good. Alcohol consumption is about on average, while we're significantly worse than the OECD average when it comes to obesity.[66] This is interesting because they've recently lowered the BMI target from 30 to 25, so either way the US is doing poorly in this category. Moving on to access to care, the US population that's eligible for core services related to insurance coverage and financial protection is much worse than the OECD average. Although this has gotten better over the last eight years when we've expanded health insurance with US financial protections.[66] Also again, we're significantly worse when it comes to primary care because we have many uninsured or under-insured individuals. The last measure to highlight is that of quality of care. Here, the US is on average with effective primary care and avoidable admissions for asthma or COPD. We're also on par with the average effective secondary care, which is shown as a 30-day mortality following an acute myocardial infarction. Finally, regarding effective cancer care, using a breast cancer five-year net survival rate, we are doing better than average. As you can see, there are clearly areas for improvement and our healthcare system is far from perfect.

Next, I want to discuss life expectancy. The OECD also has extensive research on this topic showing the life expectancy growth between 1970 and 2017. Japan has the highest life expectancy of 84.2 years, above the OECD average life expectancy of 80.7 years.[66] Again, the US comes nowhere near the top, with an average life expectancy of only 78.6 years, which is behind Chile, Slovenia, and Greece (among other countries).

The last big measure OECD considers are the health resources used. We look here at health spending and see that the US is significantly higher than other countries. We also have the highest health spending at 16.9% of GDP compared to a world average of only 9%.[66] We are spending more money than other countries and have a lower life expectancy, higher obesity, and higher rates of avoidable deaths per hundred thousand people to show for it. All in all, not great.

Now, before moving on, I do want to consider pharmacists. While I can't tie any direct correlations to this, I find it interesting to compare and understand how many practicing pharmacists there are. The OECD average is 83 pharmacists per 100,000 people in a population, and most countries have seen an increase in practicing pharmacists over the past two decades. With this metric, the US is above average with 95 pharmacists per 100,000, which has increased slightly from 2000 to 2017.[66]

Role of Health Systems

Let's shift now and look at the health system inside the US. The Agency for Healthcare Research and Quality (AHRQ) created the Comparative Health System Performance (CHSP) Initiative to study how healthcare systems promote evidence-based practices in delivering care. They then disseminate findings broadly across health systems nationally. To me, this is quite interesting because there isn't as much direct research being done around the specific effort of how health systems are performing. These initiatives have been around for a while, and there are a few key data points that I want to share with you.

Specifically, here are their listed objectives[67]:

- Classify and characterize types of health systems and compare their performance in terms of clinical and cost outcomes.
- Identify characteristics of high performing health systems.
- Evaluate the role of patient-centered outcomes research (PCOR) in health system performance.
- Disseminate findings broadly to help diffuse PCOR evidence across health systems nationally.

When we look at doing this type of research, of course, it's important to first define what a health system is before we can actually compare health systems.

So first, what is a healthcare system?

In the United States, a health care system is...

- An organization that includes **at least one hospital** and **at least one group of physicians** that provides comprehensive care (including primary and specialty care) who are **connected** with each other and with the hospital through **common ownership** or joint management.[68]
- An accountable care organization is not, by itself, indicative of joint management.[68]

So, now we've got a definition to work with. Let's look at some of the statistics of the health systems in the United States.

A lot of vertical integration has occurred even over just the past five years. In 2018, at least half of physicians were practicing as part of health systems instead of independently, which is up from 40% in 2016.[66] In looking at the number of hospitals and hospital beds, 70% and nearly 90% respectively are affiliated with a health system. The number of systems is growing as well. In 2016 there were 626 systems, which grew to 637 in 2018. The overwhelming majority are still nonprofit organizations. This will be an important point to remember when we start discussing healthcare as a business.[67] Of note, the average health system in the US has over 900 beds.

While we'll go more into detail with statistics later in our Strategy chapter, I want to briefly mention how healthcare systems measure performance. Typically, they measure clinical quality, cost, access, equity, patient experience, and patient safety (among others). They'll also consider organizational responsiveness, care coordination, community service, physician work-life satisfaction, governance, and innovation.[67] There are also performance measure sets currently in use including: Commonwealth Fund's State Scorecard on Health Systems Performance, CMS Hospital Compare, Minimum Data Set, The National Health Service (United Kingdom), Star Rating System, The Hospital Consumer Assessment of Healthcare Providers and Systems (HCAHPS) Survey, Baldrige criteria, National Committee for Quality Assurance's Healthcare Effectiveness Data and Information Set (HEDIS). Other combinations include adherence to clinical practice guidelines, in hospital mortality rates to measure quality, and costs per episode of care, or hospital operating performance. It's helpful to understand what measures health care systems are looking at when we begin to put together strategies we'd like to implement for our teams. We cannot justify resources unless we understand what's important to the system, and how we can improve these metrics. How can you strategize within the system?

How Does Pharmacy Fit In?

Now we ask, how does pharmacy fit into this system? We know that medicines play a crucial role in controlling future healthcare costs. It's important for us to know this and help others (particularly those who aren't pharmacists) understand it as well. We can shift the paradigm here by helping others (CEOs or CFOs for example) see the savings associated with properly administered medications. Medicines, if used correctly, help patients live longer, healthier lives, and are one of the most cost-effective therapies that we can deploy.

Of course, I firmly believe that allowing a pharmacist to optimize the use of medications and medication outcomes is critical to healthcare quality. In fact, data shows that medicine plays a huge role in controlling future healthcare costs where we can shift the paradigm to preventative care. For every dollar spent on a certain type of medication, this results in $3-10 of savings in reductions of hospitalization and emergency room visits. Properly administered medication shows a 10% reduction in the cancer death rates, which totals approximately $4.4 trillion in overall economic value.[69] We also see governmental organizations, like the congressional budget office, crediting the Medicare Part D program with savings on other medicinal costs. When the government considers the investment they made when paying for Medicare Part D, it ultimately resulted in surprising savings in other places in the healthcare budget. In short — investing in medication proved to be an excellent choice.

Another example is the cure rate for Hepatitis C, which is now above 90%. This dramatically decreases the burden of disease within the US healthcare system and the overall economy.[69] Just a few examples to show how medications fit into the overall health of the healthcare system. Now let's talk about where pharmacists fit in themselves.

> ***"Patients achieve optimal health and medication outcomes with pharmacists as essential and accountable providers within patient-centered, team-based healthcare."***
> —Joint Commission of Pharmacy Practitioners (JCPP)

I love the Joint Commission of Pharmacy Practitioners (JCPP) and this statement that touts the value of pharmacists improving patient outcomes. But, luckily, we also have non-pharmacy related organizations supporting this claim.[70,71,72] The Patient Centered Primary Care Collaborative supported the role of pharmacists in the "Patient-Centered Medical Home: Integrating Comprehensive Medication Management to Optimize Patient Outcomes" document. We also have the US Surgeon General's report from 2011, which talks about "Improving Patient and Health System Outcomes through Advanced Pharmacy Practice." And we have "The Expanding Role of Pharmacists in a Transformed Health Care System," which is from the National Governors Association (NGA). I highly recommend reading each of these papers.

In summary, as pharmacists our ultimate "WHY" is to support health — a state of complete physical, mental and social well being. We do this within the context of the US healthcare system being about average as compared to other countries — we are not above and beyond those practicing around the globe. We also see that the role of health systems is increasing and understand we must find ways to work within those systems. We can feel confident in our choice of profession knowing that pharmacy is the perfect profession to be in, if we wish to improve medication outcomes. We have a unique opportunity to support the health and well being of our patients.

•••

Business of Healthcare

In this section, we'll learn about...

- Business vs. Right
- Healthcare Reimbursement

Business vs. Right

Is healthcare a business or a right? This debate is almost unique to the United States, as most other countries provide healthcare through universal healthcare coverage. But, this coverage does come at a cost and with significant government intervention.

Let's begin with assuming healthcare is a right. Then, we have to look at our constitution. In our constitution, it is not mentioned specifically, however many advocates for healthcare as a right point to the 9th amendment, which protects all of the rights of the people that are not mentioned specifically elsewhere in the constitution. And yet, many interpret the 9th amendment to mean that the government cannot intervene in your personal life.

Let's now look at the possibility that it's a business[73]:

- An organization or economic system where goods and services are exchanged for one another, or for money.
- Every business requires some form of investment and enough customers to whom its output can be sold on a consistent basis in order to make a profit.
- Businesses can be privately owned, not-for-profit, or state-owned.

Looking at these definitions of business and the current state of healthcare in the United States, it seems clear that it fits the descriptions on the previous page. Healthcare is a type of business. Let's go a little bit further though, because I would love for healthcare to be a right. And, I want everyone to have equal access. It's a free market after all. Wait, is it a free market? That's another question to answer.

A free market...

- Is an economic system in which prices are determined by unrestricted competition between privately owned businesses.
- Leads to optimized supply and demand, reduced costs, and innovation.

Healthcare does not exist in a free market. It is under a lot of regulation, has high barriers to entry (licensure, training, etc.), and requires participants to utilize certain providers. Remember the constituents of healthcare we discussed in the previous chapter: patients (consumers), payers (government, employers, individuals), providers (hospitals, doctors), and the government (regulating the payers and providers). We see that healthcare cannot exist as a free market enterprise where there is simply business and consumer, supply and demand. In fact, usually the consumer is not the one paying directly for the goods/services received. There are other intermediaries involved. Healthcare may be more like a business than a universal right in the United States, but it's a very complicated system to say the least.

Healthcare Reimbursement

Let's look now at how healthcare is reimbursed. Traditional payment models are based on your location of care, with nuances related to how each payment is calculated and are documented in the respective Medicare Prospective Payment System (PPS). Physicians are reimbursed based on relative value units. Outpatient hospitals and surgery centers are paid based on an average patient visit charge called an Ambulatory Payment Classification (APC). Then inpatient acute care and long-term acute care (LTAC) is paid based on an MS-DRG or a diagnosis related group. And skilled nursing facilities (SNF)and home health are paid differently based on Resource Utilization Group (RUG).

We have evolving models of reimbursement along a scale of risk.

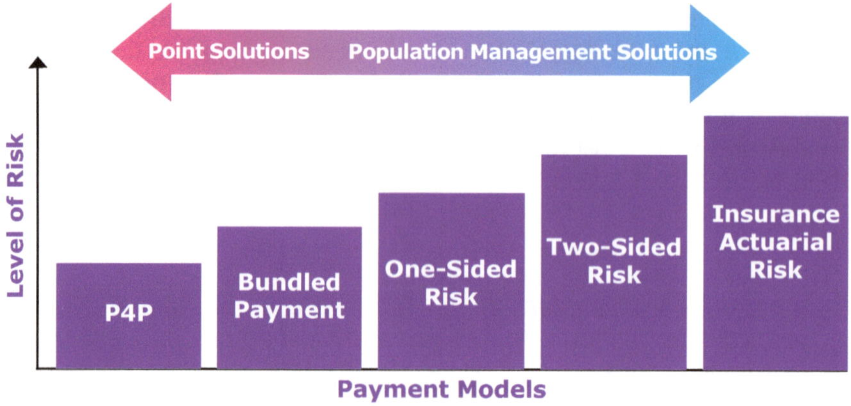

Evolving Reimbursement Models[74]

We see here lower levels of risk to newer payment models. These increase the risk and move towards more patient population management solutions, moving from P4P (pay for performance) to bundle payments. In a bundled payment, you're paid for a group of activities, such as being paid for 30 days after a transplant patient, regardless of what happens to that patient. Then we have a one- sided risk model and a two-sided risk model, where both the payer and the provider have risks to additional actuarial risk.

	2008	2010	2012	2014	2015	2018	2019
Legislation Passed	MIPPA	ACA		PAMA	MACRA		
Program Implemented			ESRD-QIP, HVBP, HRRP	HAC	VM	SNF-VBP	APMs, MIPS

Legislation

- ACA: Affordable Care Act
- MACRA: Medicare Access & CHIP Reauthorization Act of 2015
- MIPPA: Medicare Improvements for Patients & Providers Act
- PAMA: Protecting Access to Medicare Act

Program

- APMs: Alternative Payment Models
- ESRD-QIP: End-Stage Renal Disease Quality Incentive Program
- HACRP: Hospital-Aquired Condition Reduction Program
- HRRP: Hospital Readmissions Reduction Program
- HVBP: Hospital Value-Based Purchasing Program
- MIPS: Merit-Based Incentive Payment System
- VM: Value Modifier, or Physician Value-Based Modifier (PVBM)
- SNFVBP: Skilled Nursing Facility Value-Based Purchasing Program

CMS Value-Based Programs[74]

CMS is the leader in this area of transitioning to value-based programs. And of course, as the big payer with our Medicare patients, they often lead the way and many other insurance companies follow suit. Shown here are the changes over time in the various CMS value-based program models. Various initiatives have occurred over time, and we are now in the era of these alternative payment models (APM), and the merit-based incentive payment system (MIPS).

Now, I'd like to touch on the Quality Payment Program (QPP) through CMS.[75] This program began on January 1, 2017. Prior to QPP, payment increases for Medicare services were set by the Sustainable Growth Rate (SGR) law. This capped spending increases according to the growth in the Medicare population and had a modest allowance for inflation. However, as clinicians increased their utilization of services, the reimbursement for each unit of service had to be adjusted downward to hold costs constant. In practice, the SGR would have resulted in large decreases in the Physician Fee Schedule, which was not sustainable. To avoid these decreases in reimbursement, Congress had to pass a new law (every year) authorizing the current fee schedule and a small increase for inflation. With the Medicare Access and CHIP Reauthorization Act of 2015 (MACRA), CMS did away with the SGR.

Now we are able to reward high-value, high-quality Medicare clinicians with payment increases — while at the same time reducing payments to those clinicians who aren't meeting performance standards. CMS seeks to improve Medicare by helping clinicians focus on caring for their patients, rather than filling out paperwork. CMS will continue to listen and take steps towards reducing burdens for clinicians and improving health outcomes for Medicare patients. Clinicians have two tracks to choose from in the Quality Payment Program based on their practice size, specialty, location, or patient population: Merit-based Incentive Payment System (MIPS) or Advanced Alternative Payment Models.[75]

It's important to understand why we are trying to do this research to get to better payment models, because there are definitely strengths and weaknesses of the current payment models. Take a look at the graph on the next page. Shown there in the middle arrow, along the y-axis, you can move from a high risk of overtreatment to a higher risk of undertreatment. Along the center x-axis, moving from right to left, you can move from a low to high accountability for outcomes and costs.

Ok, so why does this matter? It matters because when you look at other forms of payment, such as the typical fee for service (you do a service, I pay you), you have a significantly higher chance of overtreatment because people are incentivized to get paid more for additional services. Unfortunately, things like this happen and there's no way really to measure accountability or patient-centered care with that. So, then we moved more toward quality pay for performance, but you then still have the risk of overtreatment, or even undertreatment. When a payor is only paying a certain amount of money, such as with a capitation, you can risk undertreating because of how the provider will be reimbursed.

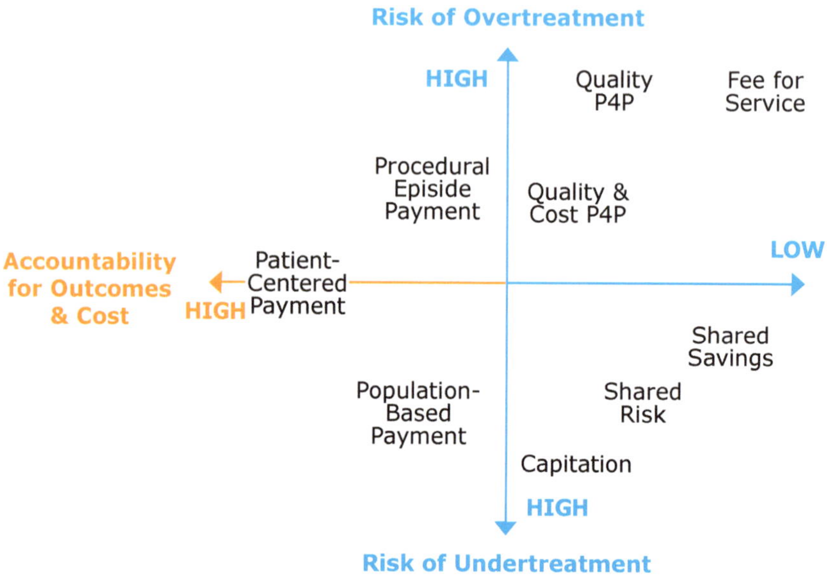

Strengths & Weaknesses of Payment Models[76]

So, then we move toward population-based payments, or procedural episodes, which did improve upon patient-centeredness, but these also have risk of overtreatment. We're trying to move toward a patient-centered payment model in order to have the best fit of a balanced and correct amount of treatment while also maintaining the highest amount of accountability for both cost and outcome. It's an uphill battle and not an easy puzzle to solve.

Here are a few innovative model categories that healthcare organizations are starting to work with in order to find a solution[77]:

- **Accountable Care**: Accountable Care Organizations and similar care models are designed to incentivize health care providers to become accountable for a patient population and to invest in infrastructure and redesigned care processes that provide for coordinated care, and high quality, efficient service delivery.
- **Episode-based Payment Initiatives**: Under these models, health care providers are held accountable for the cost and

quality of care beneficiaries receive during an episode of care, which usually begins with a triggering health care event (such as a hospitalization or chemotherapy administration) and extends for a limited period of time thereafter.

- **Primary Care Transformation**: Primary care providers are a key point of contact for patients' health care needs. Strengthening and increasing access to primary care is critical to promoting health and reducing overall health care costs. Advanced primary care practices — also called "medical homes" — utilize a team-based approach, while emphasizing prevention, health information technology, care coordination, and shared decision making among patients and their providers.
- **Initiatives Focused on the Medicaid and CHIP Population**: Medicaid and the Children's Health Insurance Program (CHIP) are administered by the states but are jointly funded by the federal government and states. Initiatives in this category are administered by the participating states.
- **Initiatives Focused on the Medicare-Medicaid Enrollees**: The Medicare and Medicaid programs were designed with distinct purposes. Individuals enrolled in both Medicare and Medicaid (the "dual eligibles") account for a disproportionate share of the programs' expenditures. A fully integrated, person-centered system of care that ensures that all their needs are met could better serve this population in a high quality, cost effective manner.
- **Initiatives to Accelerate the Development and Testing of New Payment and Service Delivery Models**: Many of the innovations necessary to improve the health care system will come from local communities and health care leaders across the entire country. By partnering with these local and regional stakeholders, CMS can help accelerate the testing of models today that may be the next breakthrough tomorrow.
- **Initiatives to Speed the Adoption of Best Practices**: Recent studies indicate that it takes nearly 17 years on average before best practices — backed by research — are incorporated into widespread clinical practice. Even then, the application of the knowledge is very uneven. The Innovation Center is partnering with a broad range of health care providers, federal agencies, professional societies, and other experts and stakeholders to test new models for disseminating evidence-based best practices and significantly increasing the speed of adoption.

Implementation of these innovative models is really research happening actively where these models are not available in every state or in every region. I encourage you to see what's available or in transition in your local area at **https://innovation.cms.gov.**

I want to touch a bit on medication reimbursement and medication-specific quality measures before we round out this section. Medications are reimbursed differently in different settings. This isn't always known to care providers. They don't always understand the impact of medications or the cost that will incur. For example, on the inpatient side, medication costs are included in the overall DRG (or diagnosis-related group) payment. So if a hospital is reimbursed $5,000 for an admission, and the medication costs $100 or $1,000, the hospital is still reimbursed the same amount. But on the outpatient side, most medications are reimbursed at an average manufacturer's price (AMP) with a discount, with a small dispensing fee on top. At our infusion centers, for example, medications are reimbursed with an average sales price (ASP), plus 6% or -22.5% for 340B medications. And, there's usually an added procedural code which covers administrative costs. Our goal should always be to reduce the total cost of care. And as we have talked about the value of medications, it's usually worth spending the money on medications, but it's important to really understand the total cost.

We'll talk more about this in the Strategy chapter coming up, but the Pharmacy Quality Alliance (PQA) is an organization that spends a lot of time looking at this. It supports a variety of sectors within the overall healthcare marketplace from accreditation programs to the pharmacy paid performance measure and more. They create measures such as performance measures on adherence, appropriate medication use, medication safety, medication therapy, management, and monitoring measures. Plus, they've also created quality improvement indicators. Again, we'll come back to this in a bit, but I wanted to make you aware of this organization as it does have a vested interest in medication costs for both the healthcare system and the patient.

In summary, we've discerned that at this present time, healthcare operates more as a business than a right in the United States, healthcare reimbursement is complex and changing, and the pharmacist must understand how we can impact value and manage medication costs as well as reimbursement.

•••

History of the Pharmacy Enterprise

In this section, we'll explore...

- What is the Pharmacy Enterprise?
- The History
- The Chief Pharmacy Officer

Let's now take a look at the history of the pharmacy enterprise. Personally, I love discussing the pharmacy enterprise. I find that when we're looking at ways to innovate pharmacy practice, thinking about the scope of this enterprise is an important opportunity for us in terms of how we define our services.

What is the Pharmacy Enterprise?

So, what is the pharmacy enterprise? Maybe you've heard of it. Maybe you haven't. This phrase is a fairly recent addition to the pharmacy lexicon that has been used commonly since 2006. The pharmacy enterprise is "an integrated system of business units with accountability for clinical and financial outcomes related to medication use across the continuum of care in a health system."[78] The term pharmacy enterprise was created to encompass the concept that pharmacy is much bigger and more important to the success of our health systems than the term pharmacy department implied.

The History

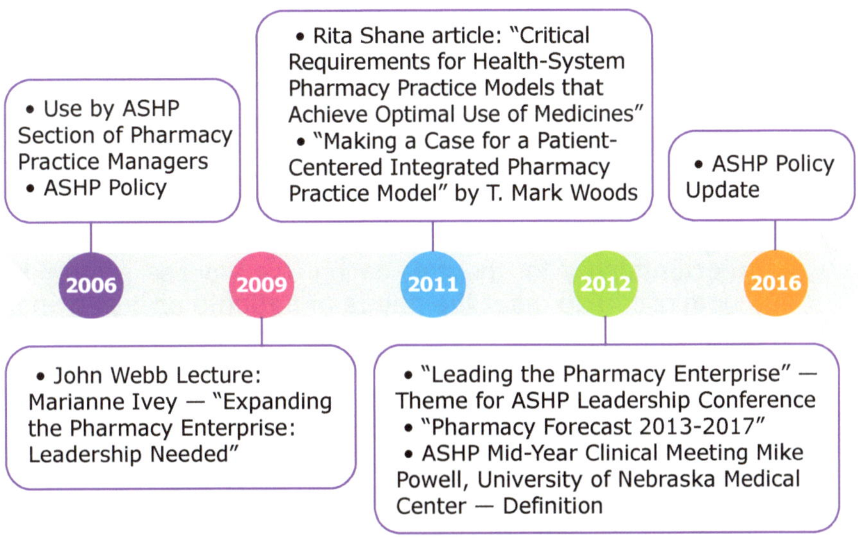

History of the Pharmacy Enterprise[78,79]

As we said, this term began its journey back in 2006 as part of the ASHP section of pharmacy practice managers. At that time, it was also used within ASHP policy. Then, in 2009, a John Webb lecture given by Marianne Ivey was titled, "Expanding the Pharmacy Enterprise: Leadership Needed." In 2011 two articles were published to give this new term credence: Rita Shane wrote "Critical Requirements for

Health-System Pharmacy Practice Models That Achieve Optimal Use of Medicines" and T. Mark Woods wrote "Making a Case for a Patient-Centered Integrated Pharmacy Practice Model." 2012 was a busy year for the history of the pharmacy enterprise. The ASHP Leadership Conference theme was "Leading the Pharmacy Enterprise," the Pharmacy Forecast 2013-2017 included recommendations with the term, and finally Mike Powell provided an expanded definition at the Midyear Clinical Meeting. Most recently, in 2016, the ASHP updated their policies to reflect the phrase as it's understood.

The first ASHP Policy in 2006 described the pharmacy enterprise as an outlet for pharmacists to advocate for a high level of **coordination** of all **components** of the **pharmacy experience** in hospitals and health systems for the purpose of optimizing the value of drug therapy and medication use safely. Further, ASHP encourages pharmacy department leaders to develop and maintain **patient-centered practice models** and integrate these practices into their team. The components of the pharmacy enterprise include general and specialized **clinical practice, drug use policy, product acquisition and inventory control, product preparation and distribution, medication use safety**, and other **quality initiatives**.[80]

But what exactly does it mean to lead a pharmacy enterprise?

We have this definition from Mike Powell in 2012 which is a helpful place to begin[81]:

- An **integrated** system of **pharmacy business units** organized with **accountability** for the medication use process across the continuum of care to **meet the needs of patients** as they **transition** from different levels of the health care delivery system.
- The pharmacy enterprise is organized to **innovate** to meet the **needs of the health care delivery system and patients,** and to **assure continuity of care, assuring medication adherence**, favorable medication use **outcomes**, and **new revenue streams**.
- The pharmacy operates with both **clinical and business goals** in support of the broader health care delivery system.
- This definition implies **accountability for the medication-use process across the continuum of care**.

I love this definition. It's thorough and all-inclusive. But it's a bit long to remember at the drop of a hat, which is why we also have the more succinct definition we used before: the pharmacy enterprise is "an integrated system of business units with accountability for clinical and financial outcomes related to medication use across the continuum of care in a health system".[78]

We now have some pharmacy enterprise history, we'll focus on the role of Chief Pharmacy Officer.

The Chief Pharmacy Officer

Keeping these in mind, it was becoming clear to the wider healthcare enterprise that pharmacy had an important overall role to play within the system. Thus was born the concept of chief pharmacy officer. The first published appeal for hospitals to create the role of chief pharmacy officer comes from Harold Godwin, who had retired from the University of Kansas Medical Center after 35 years. While there, he was also a professor and chair of pharmacy practice. In 2000, in a commentary in the *American Journal of Health System Pharmacy* (AJHP) he wrote, "it would seem that a health system also needs to have a chief pharmacy officer who has recognition and organizational parody with the other O's in the hospital."

The CPO should be responsible for drug use control policies throughout the organization. In order to implement a cohesive, consolidated enterprise approach, pharmacy must be supported by the appropriate organizational structure and leadership positioning at an executive level. By 2005, this idea gained further traction in the article "Rationale for Having a Chief Pharmacy Officer in a Healthcare Organization."[82] By 2019 the ASHP was fully on board, and began recommending that health systems capitalize on the strategic business and patient care strengths of pharmacists by proactively recruiting them into C-suite positions.[78]

To sum up, the term pharmacy enterprise encompasses the concept that pharmacy is much bigger and more important to the success of our health systems than the term pharmacy department implies. Pharmacy must be supported at the appropriate organizational level, ideally in the C-suite.

•••

Pharmacy Enterprise Scope

SECTION PREVIEW | SECTION PREVIEW |

In this section, we'll look at…

- Benefits of the Pharmacy Enterprise
- Pharmacy Enterprise Scope
- Assessment

Benefits of the Pharmacy Enterprise

Here are a few examples of potential benefits to the pharmacy enterprise system[78]:

- "If medications are managed appropriately, we will control costs, improve outcomes, and not only eliminate readmissions, but prevent many admissions in the first place."
- "...without managing the entire medication continuum, we cannot achieve the operational, quality, and safety efficiencies required for success in the world of accountable care."

So the big picture idea is that the pharmacy enterprise allows us, as pharmacy leaders, to tie together the entire continuum of care and reach pharmacy's full value. As an organization builds on a pharmacy enterprise platform to deliver increasing internal value to the organization, it provides value even to their external markets. Four strategies in particular to realize full value.

First, the pharmacy enterprise works to **counteract inflationary price pressures**. This is an ongoing challenge for our organizations, and pharmacy is well suited to negotiate with suppliers and respond to price and supply fluctuations, managing drug shortages, switching products, and working clinically to use the best, most available, and cost-effective product.

Next, the pharmacy enterprise works to **hard-wire high value prescribing**. We know that from what I like to call "formulary stewardship," that we can influence and use the appropriate cost-effective medications and create guardrails for high-cost medication use. These are great aspects to consider for innovation, and pharmacy is well-positioned to find new ways to do this.

Third, the pharmacy enterprise can **leverage pharmacy assets to reduce total cost of care**. We have opportunities to manage our employee drug benefits, potentially through our in-house pharmacies. And, we can develop sustainable pharmacy care management programs, where we add value such as reducing readmissions and improving value based payments.

Finally, the pharmacy enterprise creates a **principled pharmacy business strategy**. This is where we can have the opportunity to really look at the whole enterprise and formalize our business status. We can systemize script capture through our pharmacies and potentially scale and diversify our operating model into new, innovative solutions, which we'll also talk about in the upcoming chapters. When you tie this all together, there is potentially a huge impact on the margin there.[83]

When you consider typical pharmacy performance, and then add in the potential margin impact of the initiatives outlined above for best-in-class performance, what we see is that a high performing health system can improve around that total margin by 2.8%.[83] While that percentage doesn't sound particularly high, this can be the entire margin of an organization with the average of 2-3%. Let's look at it in real budgetary terms showing cost avoidance/expense reduction and growth through revenue generation.

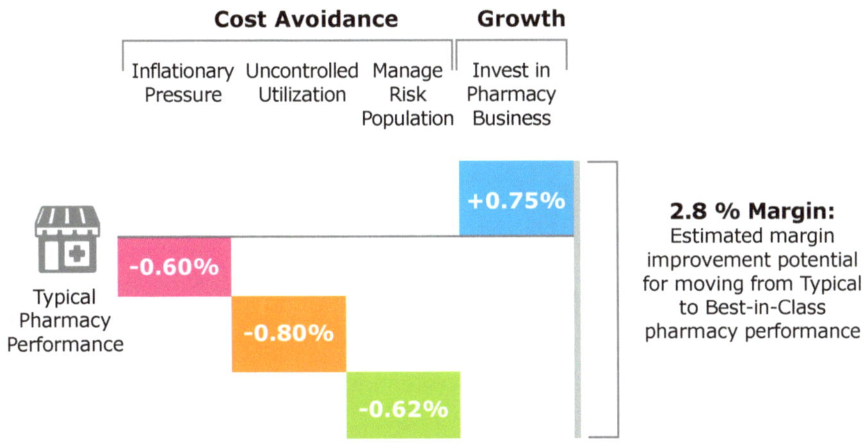

Enterprise Margin Potential[83]

Here are some specific examples of enterprise initiative success. Over a span of seven years, the Johns Hopkins Hospital Antibiotic Stewardship Program saw a savings of $17 million. Intermountain Health's centralized supply chain center found new approaches to reduce expenses and saved $1.2 million in one budgetary year. University of Chicago Medicine saw improved ambulatory access and decreased copays per patient on specialty drugs by identifying medication assistance and savings programs. This amounted to patient savings of 77.2%. Finally, Novant Health's launch of a system-wide outpatient pharmacy business allowed them to diversify their income streams and bring in an additional $50 million of capital.[84] These four examples addressed expense and revenue by minimizing unwarranted clinical variation, finding new approaches to reduce expense, improving ambulatory excess, and exploring diversified revenue streams respectively.

Pharmacy Enterprise Scope

We've spoken about the pharmacy enterprise as an integrated system of business units with accountability for clinical and financial outcomes related to medication use across the continuum of care in a health system. And we've talked about a few of the "buckets" that I see in terms of service lines, but I'd like to clearly list them here.

Pharmacy enterprise activities can — and should — be related to…

- Operations
- Acute Care Clinical Service
- Ambulatory Care
- Outpatient Pharmacy
- Business & Managed Pharmacy Solutions

Operations	Acute Care Clinical Service	Outpatient Pharmacy	Ambulatory Care	Business & Managed Pharmacy Solutions
Dispensing & Workflow	Clinical Practice Model	Outpatient/ Retail	Clinic-Based Clinical Pharmacy Services	340B Program
IT & Robotics	Clinical Practice Standards/ Stewardship	Mail Order/ Home Delivery	Clinic-Based Pharmacy Visits	Payer Population Health
Supply Chain & Procurement	Formulary Management/ Stewardship	Discharge Medication Delivery	Centralized Virtual Clinical Services	Payer Relationships
Inventory Management	Pharmoeconomics	Specialty Pharmacy	Telehealth	Business Development
Centralized Compounding & Repackaging	Medication Safety	MTM/ Vaccines	Population Health	Pharmacy Benefit Manager (PBM) Shared or Integrated Models
Sterile Compounding 797/800	Pharmacy Informatics/ Clinical Decision Support	Home Infusion 503A	Pharmoeconomics	
Provider Clinic & Urgent Care Med Fulfillment	Pharmacy Education & Residency	Bulk Compounding 503B	Employee Health/ Wellness Programs	
Diversion Management	Quality & VBP Goals	Patient Advocacy/ Medication Assistance		
Infusion Centers	Research			

Scope of the Pharmacy Enterprise

Let's look at this in a little more detail. What is shown below is kind of a checklist, of the key components in each of the service line areas for pharmacy. It includes the most common things to consider, as well as some new and innovative topics. We'll go further into detail in the services and technology chapters, but this is a great place to start for these foundational pieces of the pharmacy enterprise.

We'll now transition from the scope of enterprise to working on assessment.

Assessment

For your own work, you'll find the Pharmacy Enterprise Assessment available for download in the Pharmovation Implementation Guide.

Under each column you'll do two things:

1. List known activities currently available as related to the category.
2. Grade your organization on how it's integrating these innovations.

You'll grade on a scale from 1-5.

1. Fully Implemented/Optimized
2. Partially Implemented
3. Known Opportunity
4. Needs to Evaluate Further
5. Not Interested (or doesn't apply to my organization)

For example, you'll use a number one or color in green if that is something that is fully integrated. So, if you have already optimized your dispensing and workflow technology within your organization, you would put a number one right next to that. If you've partially implemented your clinical practice model, you can make it a two. Remember, this is your internal document that you have a chance to utilize, so don't hold back. Be honest with yourself. It's okay.

I'm looking forward to hearing your known opportunities you identified in our online Pharmovator Community. This can be an extremely useful tool in moving forward with strategy in the coming chapters.

In summary, the approach to the pharmacy department as an enterprise has many benefits. The scope of enterprise is vast and growing. We are learning and really thinking about innovation opportunities where pharmacy can play a roll. An enterprise assessment can be a useful tool in strategic planning, and it becomes a very good visual to share as you navigate and talk to your leaders to justify and advocate for those resources.

Take Action Now

- Fill out the pharmacy enterprise assessment in the Pharmovation Implementation Guide (available through the link/QR code below).
- Share in the Pharmovator Community your top 3 known opportunities.

To support you incorporating the learnings from this chapter, access the Pharmovation Implementation Guide. Visit www.pharmovationguide.com or scan the QR code below for full access!

Chapter 4

Pharmovation STRATEGY

"If you do not know where you are going, every road will get you nowhere."
—Henry A. Kissinger

In the winter of 2016, I signed up for an event called a Hackathon hosted by MIT and Yale in Connecticut. Over a long weekend, a harsh winter storm stranded several dozen of us together for a focused period of time, so we put our heads together and tried, under pressure, to come up with a fully fleshed out idea to pitch at the end of 72 hours. It was madness.

What's a Hackathon? It's like a pressure cooker for innovation. Dozens of people come together and are divided up into teams. Each team comes up with an idea and a business proposal to pitch to venture capitalists at the end of a designated time (ours was a long weekend). One idea wins the event and may even get seed money to create a prototype. It's pretty exciting. You're with energized and innovative thinkers, and you're all working toward a common goal.

I was there to work on medication reconciliation. As I've shared, it's a particular passion of mine and an area of pharmacy that could absolutely benefit from innovation. I had an idea to create an app where patients could take pictures of their medications to integrate their photos with the electronic health record. We were divided into groups, and I pitched my med reconciliation idea. My team was interested, so we ran it by the organizers, who, unfortunately, didn't receive it well. They said med rec was too challenging, and everyone they've seen try to tackle it in this type of environment fails. I was frustrated. I knew med rec needed innovation and I thought this was the perfect opportunity to create something new. We needed a fully interoperable list for patients that translated between platforms and followed patients wherever they went to receive care.

But, I wasn't working alone. There were other ideas on the table, so we switched directions to focus on newborns who were born to women struggling with substance abuse. These babies were going through substance withdrawal from the moment they were born. We created a blanket that would soothe the newborns with vibrations and sounds while also mimicking being held and swaddled.

And... we won! We created a business plan. We even created a prototype. It was very exciting and an interesting experience to look back on. My med rec idea, even though it was innovative and would have been helpful to hospitals across the country, wouldn't have won that competition.

In that environment, suffering babies were easy to sell. I don't mean that in a callous way, but strategically. When you only have a few minutes to pitch to a group of venture capitalists *Shark Tank*-style, it was easier to explain the need for these blankets than to go into all the detail needed for someone to understand the necessity for full medication reconciliation. This blanket was a much better product for this type of environment.

You are on a lifelong journey to justify resources. As a pharmacy leader it's one of your many responsibilities to constantly advocate for resources that improve the safety of patients and the quality of care that your team can offer. It is not an easy journey. But with the right kind of strategy and systems in place, it is manageable, and you can be extremely successful.

In this chapter we'll discuss how you can justify resources for both small and large needs through strategic planning — situational analysis, strategies/tactics, business plans, and sources for return on investment (ROI). So, let's jump in.

• • •

Journey to Justify Resources

SECTION PREVIEW | SECTION PREVIEW

In this section, we'll look at...

- Where Justifying Resources Fits In with Strategy
- Steps In the Journey

Where Justifying Resources Fits In with Strategy

Justifying resources — to yourself, your team, and the decision makers who approve purchasing and budgets — is a key part of our overall strategy. Let's look at this within the context of what I like to call our Connector Framework™. The framework shows how to connect the dots from your mission and vision through your strategic and tactical plan, ultimately to execution and excellence. We'll come back to this throughout the book.

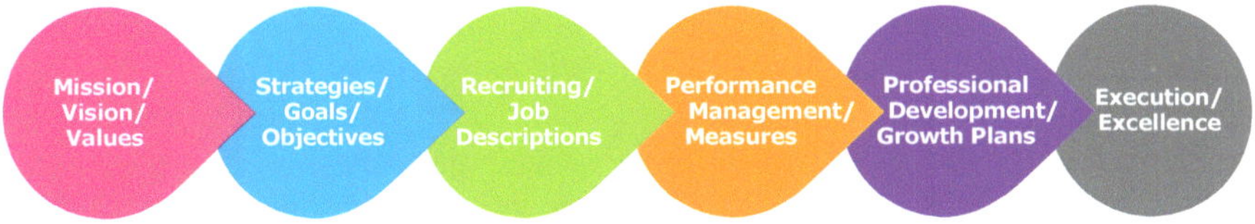

Connector Framework™

Everything begins with your organization's mission, vision and values. With those firmly in place and understood by your team, you move toward strategic goals and objectives. It's important to align your recruiting job descriptions, performance management measures, and professional development and growth planning. It's imperative that your strategic goals and objectives are informed by your organization's mission, vision, and values.

An organization's **mission** declares who we are, what business we're in, what is the purpose of our organization and why we do what we do. The **vision** of an organization builds upon the mission by articulating what an organization wants to become. It's a vision for the future. The **values** explain how an organization plans to operate. How do we want to be? In what way will we go about achieving our mission and vision? What values guide us along the way?

Mission, vision, and values are an excellent foundation for justifying resources. You may be tempted to create your own department level mission and vision, but I encourage you to write a department commitment statement that demonstrates how the department will support the overall organization. If you decide to do this, however, make sure your team's mission, vision and values align with the organization's.

Strategic Plan
Resource Options

Now, strategy can be implemented and resourced in three different ways:

1. Use existing resources if there is capacity
2. Reallocation of resources
3. Justify new resources through business plans

We will focus primarily on justifying new resources through business plans as this is the path to doing more with more. But it's important to understand that, if possible, you want to find creative ways to use existing resources and reallocate as much as possible. For example, I've put together business plans where we've reallocated a physician position to fund medication history technicians.

Steps in the Journey

Journey to Justify Resources

I created this five step process to summarize the journey to justify resources:

1. **Strategic Planning**: This step begins with an in depth situational analysis, the starting point for developing your strategy. This step is crucial for understanding and gaining insight into the present situation and external forces. During this step, which we'll cover in detail later on in this chapter, you'll articulate how you will achieve your vision. You'll also outline goals that must be achieved along the way and state objectives. Objectives must be concrete and measurable milestones along the way to achieving your goals.
2. **FTE Analysis**: This is the Full Time Equivalent (FTE) analysis of current resources. It's a crucial step to evaluate existing FTE capacity and allocation before committing to new initiatives. A few things you'll want to consider are labor and productivity metrics, recent services, non-productive time (paid time off (PTO)), training (Continuing Education (CE) Days), on-call needs, vacancy and turnover, medical leave, and current benchmarks.
3. **Business Plans**: Later on we'll go into more detail regarding business plans (yes, there's a template you'll be able to download at the end of this chapter!). This step should always come after planning and full FTE analysis. It's important with any business plan to have an executive summary. That should be your first page. You want to have your bottom line upfront summarizing your business plan. And then you can go into more details to supplement.
4. **ROI (return on investment)**: Your ROI analysis is a crucial element of both your business plan and gaining final approval. We'll go into more detail looking at soft dollars vs. hard dollars. Soft dollars come from things that are difficult to measure like intangible productivity that may lead to reducing or reallocating

resources. Hard dollars are measurable amounts of money like expense reduction, savings, or traditional revenue.

5. **Approval**: The approval process looks slightly different at every organization, so it's critical that you understand your organization's specific process, committees, and stakeholders. This process often consists of steps such as engaging stakeholders and sponsors, meeting with the department financial controller, presenting your business plan before the appropriate committees, and a review by FTE or vacancy committee.

Along this journey, keep in mind that engaging stakeholders and sponsors is critical to business plan approval. An excellent way to do this is to practice an elevator "strategic pitch" so conversations about your plan occur when informal opportunities arise. You're going to want to share this with everyone you see, and be strategic about networking with the key stakeholders on the committees within the process.

What to Watch For

Engaging stakeholders and sponsors is critical to business plan approval. Practice an Elevator "Strategic Pitch."

Your elevator strategic pitch is a quick 30-60 second overview of a service, project or proposal. It's perfect for communicating new initiatives to others outside of pharmacy. An example of how to structure this would be:

- **Opportunity**: Did you know that admission related safety events continue to occur at a rate of x% and cost $4,530 per event?
- **Proposal**: I'm hoping to expand dedicated pharmacy resources and standardized processes to reduce this.
- **Benefits**: Ultimately it will help us see higher rates of safety and quality, improve patient experience, and increase provider engagement and efficiency.
- **Resources**: We're looking at pharmacy FTEs like medication history technicians (MHT), pharmacists, and residents to bring this plan together.

Practicing this elevator strategic pitch will not only make others aware of your plans, but it will build your confidence when you're finally presenting your formal business plan. You'll have had so much practice along the way!

Some key points to consider when on the journey to justify resources:

- Know your **process** and **budget cycle**.
    - Trying to request resources outside of the budget cycle will usually fail because budgets have already been confirmed. Knowing when your budget cycle starts and ends will save you time and energy.
- Standardize your business plan **template**.
    - You will want to use your own organization's template if one exists. If not, you can use the one that I've provided in the Pharmovation Implementation Guide.
- **Be there** to present your case.
    - Some organizations have the business plan presented by the financial controller, but it's important for the pharmacy leader to be there in person if possible. Because we know our story better than anyone, we will provide more value and be able to answer more questions.
- **Packaging**/grouping plans is effective.
    - Future examples will demonstrate how this works. Suffice to say that combining a positive ROI plan with a negative ROI plan will allow both to be approved if the other reasons for approval are still valid.
- Use **hospital-specific data**, not just literature.
    - While it is a pet peeve of mind from a data perspective to demonstrate that every practice advancement works locally, I have been asked more times than not to show this. Additionally, the financial team members in your organization will want to see where this is hitting the bottom line.
- Insert pharmacy resources into larger **hospital growth business plans**.
    - For example, if the organization is already building a center of excellence for neurology or the cancer center, it is much easier to put those FTEs within those business plans than to create your own separate pharmacy department business plan. Make sure you're included in those conversations early in the process.

In summary, justifying resources will support your overall strategy when you don't have resource capacity or the ability to reallocate. The steps to accomplishing this include strategic planning, FTE analysis, business plans, ROI, and ultimately, approval. There are many opportunities along the way to be innovative and proactive in this journey.

Strategic Planning: Situational Analysis

In this section, we'll focus on…
- Methods
- Sources
- Creating Situational Analysis

As advertised, we'll now go more in depth regarding the initial steps of your justification journey. We'll explore methods and sources to create an in-depth situational analysis.

Methods

Situational analysis is the starting point for developing an effective strategy. It's crucial to understanding both the present situation and gaining insight into the future. There are several frameworks used to conduct situational analysis, but the basic three steps are collect data, conduct a systematic assessment, and compile your findings into a situational analysis framework. After this, you'll move onto your strategies, goals, and objectives.

Here are some commonly used situational analysis frameworks:

- **SWOT**: Strengths, Weaknesses, Opportunities, and Threats. This is a typical beginning analysis in many departments. Whatever situational analysis framework you complete, these factors should be considered either formally or informally.
- **Perspectives**: Financial, customer, internal process, organizational capacity. In this framework, you want to take different perspectives and analyze them. What's the financial situation? What are your customer's perspectives? What are the internal processes? How large is the organizational capacity? Organizational capacity certainly ties into that FTE analysis we've already discussed, so often these can go hand in hand.
- **PESTLE**: Political, Economic, Social, Technological, Legal, and Environmental. This method assesses different areas as they pertain to your organization's needs.
- **Porter's Five Forces**: Competitive rivalry, threat of new entrants, threat of substitution, power of customers, power of suppliers. Porter's five forces can be helpful when marketing new equipment or other types of merchandise. It's not used quite as often in healthcare, but when considering possible innovations it's important to be aware of.

- **5 C's**: Company, Customer, Collaborators, Competition, Context.
- **Organization-Specific Method**: There may be an organization-specific method of conducting situational analysis that you should include in your formal business proposal. Be sure to keep this in mind when beginning any new journey to justify resources.

In the downloadable template, you'll see that I've organized this section using a SWOT analysis and pharmacy healthcare specific analyses, but remember that other strategic framework analyses can be beneficial for different topics within pharmacy. So keep these other options in mind when you're doing your assessment.

Sources

So, what are the common pharmacy sources that you will use? You'll take advantage of **internal data and benchmarks** such as organizational metrics of quality, volumes, productivity and financial performance. You'll also consider these same metrics from your own department. If your department or organization isn't already tracking these metrics, it's time to start. It's important to know where you are before you can effectively plan for the future. Additionally, you'll want to get internal feedback from your stakeholders and staff to understand how your department is being perceived.

Next, you'll conduct a **systematic assessment**, for which you'll need to obtain your organization's strategic plan. This isn't just your department's plan, but the overall organization's strategic plan. You'll want to conduct the pharmacy enterprise assessment we've discussed in previous chapters and pull that into your situational analysis as well. You'll want to use forecasts such as the ASHP and AHA forecasts. You'll take inventory of quality measures, medical specialties and conduct a PAI self assessment.

Create a Situational Analysis

Let's look in more detail at your situational analysis. I recommend compiling your analysis in one document, which you can find a template for in the Pharmovation Implementation Guide. It is a spreadsheet with each source having its own tab. As discussed, the sources include: SWOT, Data/Metrics, Organization Plan, Enterprise Assessment, ASHP Forecast, Healthcare Forecasts, Measure Inventory, Medical Specialties, and PAI Self Assessment.

I want to draw your attention to the assessment you'll be doing on each of these sources. On the next page is an example of what each tab will look like.

Applicable to My Organization	Assessment	Add to Strategic Plan	Year to Add	Comment
Yes	1 - Fully Implemented	Yes		
No	2 - Partially Implemented	No		
	3 - Known Opportunity			
	4 - Need to Evaluate			
	5 - Not Interested			

Situational Analysis Worksheet

You begin with a yes or no choice — is this goal or situation applicable to my organization? Then, as you did with the enterprise assessment, you'll choose whether it's…

1. Fully Implemented
2. Partially Implemented
3. Known Opportunity
4. Need to Evaluate
5. Not Interested

Then decide whether or not you'd like to add it to your strategic plan. Make note of the current year, as you may wish to implement something now, but end up needing to revisit it in the future. Sometimes we get a little overzealous with what we're capable of doing in a short amount of time. You know I'm all about pharmacy doing more with more, but in the end we come up against limited resources and have to make tough decisions. There is a saying that we often overestimate what we can do in a year and underestimate what we can do in five — so put those big ideas in your plan for future years and take small steps to get there. Keep your notes from previous situational analyses and strategic planning for the future.

Looking at the **organization's strategic plan**. You want to capture and understand the organization's strategy, as well as the years in which they are planning to implement those strategies. Then you'll complete the same assessment that we just reviewed. You'll also want to revisit the status of your own current **pharmacy department strategic plan**. Remember that this is a chance to really be innovative about pharmacy. It's a huge opportunity. Many times our organizations don't have pharmacy-related items within their strategic plan at a high level, which of course relates to why pharmacists need to be part of the C suite as we discussed previously. When pharmacy has a spot at the table, it's often found that what pharmacy does ties directly into the organization's strategic plan. We just need to figure out how to connect the dots.

Now, you may have already completed your **Pharmacy Enterprise Assessment**, but you can use the template (available at the end of this chapter) to incorporate it into the situational analysis and help further clarify when you'll be working on your prioritized goals.

The next step is to do the assessment of the **ASHP Forecast**. I know we reviewed this in previous chapters, but during your strategic planning would be a good time to take specific recommendations from the most recent ASHP forecasts. Again, decide whether or not particulars are applicable to your organization. You won't be able to add everything (unless you have an unlimited budget, you lucky thing) so you'll need to prioritize and narrow down what you'll be requesting during this particular proposal. While you're unlikely to include everything, this is still a wonderful resource to include in your proposal and something that senior leaders should be aware of.

Here are the details below:

Section	ASHP Recommendation 2019	Applicable to My Organization	Assessment	Add to Strategic Plan	Year to Add	Comment
Future of Pharmacy Education and Workforce	Completion of a PGY1 residency must be the standard for entry into health-system pharmacy practice; ASHP along with health systems must continue the trend of increasing the number of PGY1 residency programs available					
	Health systems must capitalize on the strategic business and patient care strengths of pharmacists by proactively recruiting them into C-suite positions					
	Certificate training is critical to the effective use of pharmacy technicians, and remote over-sight of pharmacy technicians and other incentives may address the pharmacist shortage in rural and underserved areas					
	Pharmacy leadership should define advance practice roles for pharmacy technicians, establish appropriate training and competency standards for these activities, and provide incentives to technicians who perform expanded patient care roles					
	Schools and colleges of pharmacy must reduce class size to align with workforce needs, and the pharmacy community needs to redouble efforts to push forward federal provider status					
	ASHP must immediately invest in research on burnout among clinical pharmacists to educate pharmacists to educate pharmacists about this issue and provide solutions while minimizing any negative impact on patient care					
Medications Are Key Drivers of Healthcare Finance and Care Delivery	Pharmacists in health systems should take the lead in developing and implementing new models of care that take advantage of emerging vertical integration					
	In order to achieve the anticipated operational, clinical, financial, and risk benefits of disparate healthcare organizations coming together as systems, pharmacy leaders must have a formal strategic plan to assist the health system in achieving these goals					
	Pharmacists should take ownership for the optimal performance of all aspects of the medication-use system, including centralized prior-authorization management					
	Pharmacists must recognize how the costs and margins of biosimilars drive financial outcomes and respond accordingly to protect their institution's financial performance					
	Pharmacists should lead their health system's efforts around the 340B program to not only deliver the desired compliance results but also provide a clear delineation of exactly how 340B savings are deployed to provide care to vulnerable patient populations					
	Pharmacists must move beyond their traditional focus on disease treatment to become more-active participants in health-system community outreach programs					

ASHP Forecast Assessment

Other forecasts you'll want to consider are the AHA and ACHE forecasts, which can be found on the next page.

When you're considering innovative ways to accomplish these goals, you may want to look at the Center for Medicare/Medicaid Services (CMS). They have a lot of authorized programs and activities that focus on providing value.[77] You may be inspired by or even able to model after existing programs so you're not having to reinvent the wheel with your initiatives and proposals. Plus, this will demonstrate to your stakeholders that you're proposing a program or idea that's already proven successful elsewhere.

Report	Future Scan	Applicable to My Organization	Assessment	Add to Strategic Plan	Year to Add	Comment
FutureScan	**Opioid crisis:** Will emphasize non-pharmacological pain management to reduce opioid prescribing among employed physicians - 64%					
	Digital health: A major technology company, such as Google or Amazon, will emerge as a significant competitor for health care services - 73%					
	Bioelectronics: Will use "smart clothing" with embedded electronics for patient care, such as shirts that monitor heart rate and blood pressure - 50%					
	Workforce shortages: Will be one of the organization's three biggest challenges - 92%					
	Population health: Will increase by at least 20% the fiscal investment in population health strategies to address social determinants of health - 79%					
	Hospital/health system governance: Will have a strategic goal to increase the generational diversity of the governing board - 71%					
	Physician aggregation: Will significantly expand the organization's physician network - 76%					
	States' role in health care regulation: Will be subject to government regulation or oversight that affects commercial insurance rates - 74%					
AHA Environmental Scan	**Consumerism**					
	Innovations such as technological advancements					
	Chronic disease management					
	Volume to value					
	Social determinants of health					
	New entrants					
ACHE Top Issues	**Financial Challenges**					
	Governmental Mandates					
	Patient Safety and Quality					
	Personnel Shortages					
	Behavioral Health / Addiction Issues					
	Patient Satisfaction					
	Access to Care					

Healthcare Forecasts

Pharmacy Related	Measure Title	NQF Endorsement Status	Applicable to My Organization	Assessment	Add to Strategic Plan	Year to Add	Comment	NQF ID	Programs	Measure Type
Y	3-Item Care Transitions Measure (CTM-3)	Endorsed						0228,228	Hospital Compare (Implemente	Outcome
Y	ACE/ARB for LVSD	Endorsed						0137,137	Hospital Inpatient Quality Repo	Process
Y	Acute Otitis Externa (AOE): Systemic Antimicrobial Therapy - Avoidance of Ina	Endorsed						0654,654	Medicare Physician Quality Rep	Process
Y	Acute Otitis Externa (AOE): Topical Therapy	Endorsed						0653,653	Medicare Physician Quality Rep	Process
Y	Adjuvant Chemotherapy is Considered or Administered Within 4 Months (120	Endorsed						0223,223	Hospital Compare (Implemente	Process
Y	Adjuvant Hormonal Therapy	Endorsed						0220,220	Hospital Compare (Implemente	Process
?	Adult Major Depressive Disorder (MDD): Suicide Risk Assessment	Endorsed						0104,104	Medicare and Medicaid Electro	Process
?	Adult Major Depressive Disorder (MDD): Suicide Risk Assessment (eCQM)	Endorsed						0104,104	Medicaid Promoting Interopera	Process
?	Age Related Macular Degeneration (AMD): Dilated Macular Examination	Endorsed						0087,87	Medicare Physician Quality Rep	Process
Y	Alcohol & Other Drug Use Disorder Treatment at Discharge	Endorsed						1664	Inpatient Psychiatric Facility Qu	Process
Y	Alcohol & Other Drug Use Disorder Treatment Provided or Offered at Dischar	Endorsed						1664	Inpatient Psychiatric Facility Qu	Process
Y	All-cause Hospital Readmission	Endorsed						1789	Merit-Based Incentive Payment	Outcome
Y	American College of Surgeons Centers for Disease Control and Prevention (AC	Endorsed						0753,753	Hospital Compare (Implemente	Outcome

Steward	Contact	Measure Developer	Development Stage	Description	Numerator
University of Colorado Denver Anschutz Medical Campus			Fully Developed	The CTM-3 is a hospital level measure of performance tha	The numerator is the hospital level sum of CTM-3 scores for al
Centers for Medicare & Medicaid Services (CMS)			Fully Developed	Percentage of acute myocardial infarction (AMI) patients	AMI patients who are prescribed an ACEI or ARB at hospital di
American Academy of Otolaryngology - Head and Neck Surg		Centers for Medicare &	Fully Developed	Percentage of patients aged 2 years and older with a diag	Patients who were not prescribed systemic antimicrobial thera
American Academy of Otolaryngology - Head and Neck Surg		Centers for Medicare &	Fully Developed	Percentage of patients aged 2 years and older with a diag	Patients who were prescribed topical preparations
Commission on Cancer, American College of Surgeons		Commission on Cancer,	Fully Developed	Percentage of patients under the age of 80 with AJCC III (I	Chemotherapy is administered within 4 months (120 days) of
Commission on Cancer, American College of Surgeons		Commission on Cancer,	Fully Developed	Percentage of female patients, age >18 at diagnosis, who	Hormone therapy is administered within 1 year (365 days) of t
Physician Consortium for Performance Improvement - (PCP		Centers for Medicare &	Fully Developed	Percentage of patients aged 18 years and older with a dia	Patients with a suicide risk assessment completed during the
Physician Consortium for Performance Improvement Found		American Medical Asso	Fully Developed	Percentage of patients aged 18 years and older with a dia	Patients with a suicide risk assessment completed during the
American Academy of Ophthalmology		Centers for Medicare &	Fully Developed	Percentage of patients aged 50 years and older with a dia	Patients who had a dilated macular examination performed w
The Joint Commission			Fully Developed	This rate describes only those who receive a prescription	The number of patients who received a prescription at dischar
The Joint Commission			Fully Developed	This measure describes patients who are identified with a	The number of patients who received or refused at discharge

Quality Measures Inventory

Another tool I recommend borrowing from CMS is the **CMS Measures Inventory Tool**, which compiles various measures that are already in place and which organization created them. You will have an opportunity to prioritize which measures are applicable to your organization. I have added a column to indicate which measures are related to pharmacy and medication use. This is a comprehensive document, and I would call your attention to focus on the endorsed or implemented measures, as well as those that I have marked as being related to pharmacy. I would also encourage you to include your own organization's quality metrics — what quality measures are being publicly reported or are part of value-based contracts? Many of those will be in that organization's strategic plan that we talked about above, but sometimes the details may not be specified. So get a hold of your organization's quality plan and know what they're reporting on.

A final resource I recommend during this phase of planning is the PAI (Practice Advancement Initiative).[85] It provides 59 recommendations regarding optimal, safe, and effective medication use, focuses on aspirational guidance to serve as a roadmap for pharmacy practice advancement, and a future-focused set of concepts looking beyond today's barriers to change. A full discussion of PAI will be included in the Pharmovation Services chapter coming up.

Domain	Subdomain	ASHP PAI 2030 RECOMMENDATIONS	Applicable to My Organization	Assessment	Add to Strategic Plan	Year to Add	Comment
Patient Centered Care	Practice Focused	A1. Pharmacists should collaborate with patients, families, and caregivers to ensure that **treatment plans respect patients' beliefs, values, autonomy, and agency**.					
		A2. The pharmacy workforce should lead **medication reconciliation** processes during care transitions (e.g., emergency department, upon admission and discharge, ambulatory-care setting, community pharmacy, long term care).					
		A3. The pharmacy workforce should collaborate with patients, caregivers, payers, and healthcare professionals to establish consistent and sustainable models for **seamless transitions of care**.					
		A4. **Pharmacist documentation** related to patient care must be available to all members of the healthcare team, including patients, in all care settings.					
		A5. The pharmacy workforce should partner with patients and the interprofessional care team to identify, assess, and resolve **barriers to medication access, adherence, and health literacy**.					
		A6. Patients must have **access to a pharmacist** in all settings of care.					
	Organization Focused	A7. The pharmacy workforce, in all care settings, must have **access to complete patient medical records** and related health information.					
		A8. The pharmacy enterprise should be integrated and modeled to provide patient-centered care **across the continuum** (e.g., home and outpatient infusion, specialty pharmacy, community pharmacy, acute care).					
		A9. The pharmacy workforce should lead **medication education** for patients and caregivers that optimize outcomes, including in care transitions.					
		A10. Pharmacists should play an active role in ensuring that **ethical principles** drive clinical and business decisions related to medication use.					
		A11. Health systems must provide **24/7 pharmacy services** with advanced clinical capability.					
		A12. Health systems should support innovative models for providing a safe and appropriate level of pharmacy services for **small and rural hospitals or other alternative practice settings**.					
		A13. Pharmacy departments should take responsibility for appropriate medication use in the structuring of **external partnerships**.					
	Profession Focused	A14. Pharmacists should lead and advocate for **comprehensive medication management** in all healthcare settings.					
Pharmacist Role, Education, and Training	Practice Focused	B1. All pharmacists should have an **individualized continuing professional development plan**.					
		B2. Pharmacists should **leverage and expand their scope of practice**, including prescribing, to optimize patient care.					
		B3. Pharmacists should participate in and assume key roles on **emergency response teams**.					
	Organization Focused	B4. Health systems should require completion of ASHP-accredited **residency training** as a minimum credential for new pharmacist practitioners.					
		B5. Pharmacists should participate in organization-based **credentialing and privileging** processes to ensure competency within their scope of practice.					
		B6. Pharmacy practice leaders should ensure that their workforce has the necessary knowledge and competency to adapt to **emerging healthcare needs**.					
		B7. Pharmacists practicing in specialty areas should be **board-certified** through the Board of Pharmacy Specialties or other appropriate body.					
		B8. Pharmacy education, residency training, and continuing education should cover **healthcare reimbursement, payment, and business management** in all areas of practice.					
		B9. Pharmacists in all care settings should be included as **integral members of the healthcare team** and share accountability for patient outcomes and population health.					
		B10. The pharmacy workforce should be knowledgeable and have the resources to care for patients with **behavioral and mental health disorders**.					

ASHP PAI 2030 Situational Analysis

Besides these invaluable guidelines, PAI 2030 has also provided an online **PAI self assessment** tool to input the demographics and characteristics of your organization.[86] It allows you to create an assessment summary regarding different sectors of your organization and helps create a prioritized action list. I highly recommend completing this online assessment annually and using the score to guide your plans and show your progress based on the calculated score.

And you can copy your assessment right into your situational analysis spreadsheet. Easy breezy.

Now, let's get down to brass tacks. Your **SWOT** template will look like the one on the top of the next page.

Since it is the most common example of this type of analysis, let's walk through it a bit. There are some common mistakes made when conducting a SWOT analysis that I want to quickly address. The top section — strengths and weaknesses — is meant to be internal in origin. These are both the strengths (helpful to achieving your objectives) and weaknesses (harmful to achieving objectives) of your company. The bottom section, opportunities and threats, should be external in origin. They are not just the opposite of strengths and weaknesses. Opportunities and threats are unique.

	Helpful (to achieving the objective)	Harmful (to achieving the objective)
	STRENGTHS	WEAKNESSES
Internal Origin (attributes of the organization)		
	OPPORTUNITIES	THREATS
External Origin (attributes of the environment)		

SWOT Framework

Here's an example of what a SWOT framework might look like when filled in for a pharmacy department:

	Helpful (to achieving the objective)	Harmful (to achieving the objective)
	STRENGTHS	WEAKNESSES
Internal Origin (attributes of the organization)	-Dedicated/Seasoned Workforce -Single System Medical Board/P&T Committee -IT/Operations Alignment -Single EHR -Smart Pumps -Automated Dispensing Cabinets (ADC) -Sterile Compounding Software	-More Reactive than Proactive -Staffing Model Not Best Practice -# FTEs Below Average -Need More sSecialized Knowledge for Key Areas - Oncology, HVC, ED, Investigational -Non-Value Added Activities
	OPPORTUNITIES	THREATS
External Origin (attributes of the environment)	-Pay for Quality/Value Based Payment Expansion/Payer Contracting -Specialty Pharmacy Expansion -340B Expansion -Collaboratives -Pharmacist Provider Status	-Reduction in 340B Reimbursement -Healthcare Reform -Lock Out of Specialty Pharmacy Limited -Distribution Drugs or Payer Contracts

SWOT Example

After you've completed your SWOT analysis, identify which SWOT topics you'll incorporate into your strategic plan. Note that not all topics must be addressed but it's important to prioritize improving your strengths, addressing weaknesses, capitalizing on opportunities, and minimizing threats.

Also, beware of the danger of working in a siloed manner, away from outside opinions or influence. It's beneficial to collaborate with stakeholders and involve staff from an early point in the planning process

What to Watch for

Don't work in a silo. Collaborate with stakeholders and involve staff.

One of the most efficient methods for doing this during strategic planning is to conduct a **strategic planning workshop or retreat**. This can be done in two days. The first day will be spent on situational analysis. Collect data beforehand and use the time with your team to systematically assess this data and compile the situational analysis frameworks we've discussed. Day two will be spent developing the strategies and tactics of your strategic plan, which we'll discuss in more detail shortly. A strategic planning workshop or retreat is a wonderful opportunity to invite diverse attendees in addition to pharmacy leadership. This could be members from your department, including staff and residents, as well as people from other departments as your key stakeholders, such as physician leadership, nursing, and information technology. It can be extremely beneficial to hear outside opinions and have those voices in the room at this stage of the resource justification process.

To review, situational analysis consists of three steps: collect data, systematic assessment, compile situational analysis framework. While SWOT is one of the most common frameworks, organization and department specific frameworks are useful as well. Remember, you have a comprehensive situational analysis template available to download!

Take Action Now

- Complete the situational analysis in the Pharmovation Implementation Guide, available to download at the end of the chapter through QR code or link.

Strategic Planning: Strategies to Tactics

In this section, we'll focus on...
- 10 Step Process
- Utilize Worksheet Template

Now we'll go through the 10 step process that takes you from strategic planning to the tactics you'll need to employ. This process will utilize a template available to download, you guessed it, in the Pharmovation Implementation Guide.

10 Step Process

To refresh your memory, you've now completed your situational analysis, which is the starting point of developing strategy and gaining insight into your situation. Now, you'll create the strategies that are the high-level pillars to support your vision, and the goals that we must achieve to do so. Along the way you'll have objectives, which are concrete and measurable milestones. Let's look at it visually as well:

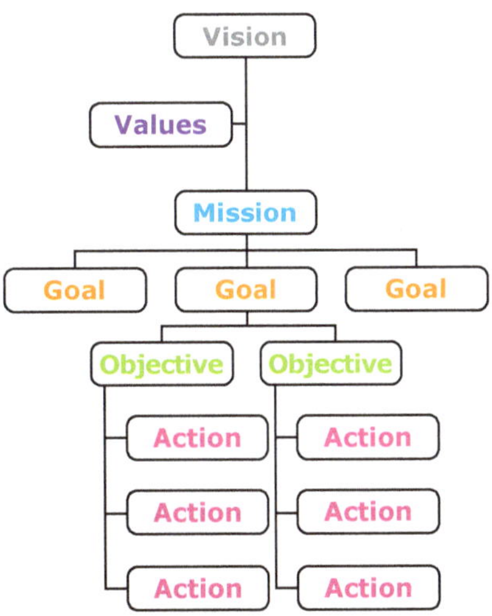

Strategic Plan Hierarchy

Within each objective you'll have small tactics or actions. There are planned, specific actions or tactics to help you achieve your objectives. They may also be grouped by strategies. Along the way you'll document metrics and data to measure your success.

Let's look at this 10 step process:

1. **Strategic Pillar**: First you'll choose which strategic pillars you will align with. Some people start with the pharmacy enterprise pillars, such as the ones we've discussed like acute care, clinical operations, etc. Others may wish to start with organizational pillars. Some of the common organizational pillars that

may exist within your group are quality and safety, patient experience, employee and provider engagement, or finances. Many organizations follow the same strategic pillars, but you can absolutely edit them to make it your own. No matter which way you start, you'll want to cross reference with other respective pillars to connect the dots. Remember, connecting your pharmacy plan to other groups within the organization can be extremely helpful in gaining approval.

2. **Goal Brainstorming**.
3. **Objective Brainstorming**: We'll talk about these next two steps together as they're pretty similar, but should remain two distinct steps in your overall strategizing. When brainstorming, you'll want to bring in previous strategic plans and situational analyses used in the past. These can help get ideas flowing for everyone in the room. You may also consider breaking into groups, each with a respective strategic pillar. Utilize a few different brainstorming techniques to allow for innovative ideas to enter the conversation. Finally, circle back and ensure that you systematically review the situational analysis, and make sure the ideas fit within the needs of your organization.
4. **Prioritization and Timeline**: Once you've decided which ideas you're considering, use a prioritization method, such as ranking. Have individuals select their top 5-10 choices. Then eliminate or delay goals with less selection. This process can also help you rank which needs are the most urgent and/or the most realistic. You can also use the scoring tool that is built into the spreadsheet to help you with this. If your organization has its own score, you can add that to this spreadsheet. It usually tends to be tied to your organization pillars. A third option is to create a priority matrix, analyzing the impact of each goal vs. the effort it takes to achieve it. Finally, you'll create a realistic timeline for accomplishing these goals. So what is the ideal number of strategies? There is not a magic number, so your results will be impacted by the effort involved and available resources. When choosing the number of goals and creating your timeline, be generous to yourself. It's not wise to schedule all the department time but to allow time for unscheduled projects and priorities. Choose 3-4 goals that will be the clear department priorities.
5. **SMART Objectives**: Ensure that your objectives are Specific, Measurable, Attainable/Achievable, Realistic/Relevant, and Time Bound.
6. **Metrics**: From each SMART objective, define what the specific quantitative target is, and how to determine when that target has been met or exceeded.
7. **Actions and Tactics**: It's common for tactics to be discussed

during strategic planning, but be sure to differentiate tactics and actions from goals and objectives. Make note of them, of course, but keep strategic planning time focused on high level goals and objectives. Details (AKA actions/ tactics) will be created in individual project plans per objective.

8. **Accountability**: You're all jacked up on planning and excited to change the organization now, but it's important to bring in accountability measures early on. This way, when the going gets tough you can continue to stay focused. You may wish to enlist a sponsor who can check on your progress or act as a sounding board when you need one. This would usually be a department director or high-level leader. Perhaps you form a committee to whom you can report progress and tracking to along the way. When choosing who you'd like to bring in the loop at this stage of the journey, consider the RACI framework. You need stakeholders who are…
    - **Responsible**: People or stakeholders who do the work. They must complete the task or objective or make the decision. Several people can be jointly responsible. Think staff and residents.
    - **Accountable**: Person or stakeholder who is the "owner" of the work. He or she must sign off or approve when the task, objective, or decision is complete. This person must make sure that responsibilities are assigned in the matrix for all related activities. Success requires that there is only one person accountable, which means that the buck stops there.
    - **Consulted**: People or stakeholders who need to give input before the work can be done and signed-off on. These people are "in the loop" and active participants.
    - **Informed**: People or stakeholders who need to be kept "in the picture." They need updates on progress or decisions, but they do not need to be formally consulted, nor do they contribute directly to the task or decision.
9. **Resource Needs**: Don't limit your brainstorming to tasks you can accomplish within existing resources. Think big! Identify needs for a business plan so you can advocate for these resources — Full Time Equivalents (FTEs) or capital (equipment/construction). Also, identify any IT resources your project may require and keep those in mind from the beginning of the process.
10. **Strategic Plan Summary**: Finally, you're ready to summarize your entire plan. Use the available download to organize your strategic plan for internal use. You'll also want to create a summary slide that can be communicated broadly. Make sure you include all pillars and goals, and potentially the objectives!

This 10 step process will take you from your strategic planning onto the tactics phase.

> **WHAT TO WATCH FOR**
>
> Not all department activities will be captured in a strategic plan. Use an operations plan and standard work to document those activities and reserve your strategic plan for new objectives and innovation.

Utilize Worksheet Template

Here are the template sections of your strategic plan spreadsheet and how they aligned to these different steps of your process.

1. Strategic Pillar
2. Goal Brainstorming
3. Objective Brainstorming

Strategic Pillar	Goal	Objectives (new line for each objective)

4. Prioritization & Timeline
5. SMART Objectives

				Pillar Alignment/Priority Score (1-10 each)							
FYXX	FYXX	FYXX	Organization Strategy Alignment	TOTAL	Quality/ Safety	Patient Experience	Employee Engagement	Financial	Efficiency	Regulatory/ Compliance	Effort /Difficulty

6. Metrics

Metric	
Target	Max/ Exceeds

7. Actions/Tactics

Key Tactics

8. Accountability — RACI

Project Team							
Sponsor	Committee	Accountable	Responsible	PGY1	PGY2	Student (Y/N)	Team Members

9. Resource Needs

Reources		
FTEs/ Busines Plan	Capital Business Plan	IT Project

10. Summary Plan Execution/ Status Tracker

Status				
Q1	Q2	Q3	Q4	Link to Project Folder

Strategic Plan Template Sections

Shown here is how you will capture the goals and objectives by strategic pillar and cross reference to the respective department or organization strategic plan. The goals are listed, and you can have several objectives for each of those goals. Many times, those objectives are what become the individual projects, but make sure your goal is specific enough and then support it with those individual objectives.

Strategic Pillar	Goal	Objectives (new line for each obj)	FYXX	FYXX	FYXX	Pharmacy Pillar Alignment
Safety/ Quality	G1	G1 O1:				
		G1 O2:				
	G2	G2 O1				
		G2 O2				
		G2 O3				
Patient Experience						
Employee/ Provider Engagement						
Finance						
Other						

Strategic Plan Pillar - Pharmacy Enterprise

Strategic Pillar	Goal	Objectives (new line for each obj)	FYXX	FYXX	FYXX	Organization Strategy Alignment
Operations	G1	G1 O1:				
		G1 O2:				
	G2	G2 O1				
		G2 O2				
		G2 O3				
Acute Care Clinical						
Ambulatory Care						
Outpatient/ Retail						
Business						
People						

Strategic Plan Pillar - Organization

As I mentioned, there are also some columns to the right of the spreadsheet to support tracking the plan status. Execution will be covered in chapter 9, where we will revisit the creation of project plans and reporting.

In summary, there are 10 steps in the Strategic Plan Strategy – Tactic Process: strategic pillar, goal brainstorming, objective brainstorming, prioritization and timeline, SMART objectives, metrics, actions/tactics, accountability RACI, resource needs, and plan summary.

Take Action Now

- Schedule a strategic plan retreat.
- Complete the strategic plan (available to download at the end of the chapter through QR code or link).

• • •

Business Plans

In this section, we'll learn about…
- Business Plan Components
- How To

Once you've got your strategic plan summary in place, it's onto the business portion of your proposal. We'll look at the essential components of a business plan and how to create one.

Business Plan Components

A business plan is a document outlining the services you want to provide for a potential business partner or stakeholder. It's a key tool utilized to justify a new clinical program, service, or personnel. It should be written for an audience. It's a document that explains the plan to an outsider and is not clinical or pharmacy specific.

Business Plan Components

A business plan should include the following components:

1. **Executive Summary**: This is a high-level overview that should be no longer than one page. Use lots of bullet points to make it readable and accessible. Include a sentence or two to propose your program, the benefits of this proposal (link this to organizational goals), a brief financial assessment of the situation, and an action plan. Don't include anything that's not in the rest of the material. Consider this page your abstract and know that it may be all someone reads of the plan. It should include everything, just quickly.
2. **Table of Contents**: An outline with page numbers of what's inside the rest of the plan.
3. **Background**: Include a key literature review, as well as an overview of current best practices as well as a gap analysis of where the organization currently stands. Include the current state of the organization as it relates to regulatory elements, quality and safety, as well as finances. Finally, end this section by explaining why this is important and including any data that supports the need for your proposal.
4. **Proposal**: In this section, you'll summarize the new clinical program, service, or personnel you're advocating for. Give a succinct statement of what you want to do and why. Make sure you focus on the target patient population or unit the proposal will affect. Also outline proposed activities and/or hours of service. Then you'll state which resources need to be committed to complete the project.
5. **Benefits**: Here you'll list and explain all the benefits of your wonderful proposal. Base these benefits on your organization's goals and look for win-win opportunities (things that benefit other departments besides pharmacy). These might include patient safety, patient satisfaction/experience, provider satisfaction, operational efficiency, cost savings, continuity of care, reduced readmission rates, revenue growth, reimbursement, patient outcomes, regulatory compliance, quality indicators, education/research, improved throughput and so on.
6. **Financial Assessment**: Here you'll outline what costs go into completing your proposal. What labor is necessary? What capital needs to be purchased or constructed? How about ongoing maintenance or operation costs? Also include any revenue the project will generate or savings it creates. Finally, you'll have a return on investment (ROI) analysis, which we'll explore in more detail in the following section.
7. **Action Plan**: Be specific in your action plan. Use Gantt charts and tables to show next steps so the information is easily accessible. Have clear actions and timelines plus measures of success to build credibility. What indicators will be used? Who is responsible

for auditing, measuring, and reporting? How often will data be collected and reported? How will the report be shared?

8. **Summary**: Here's your conclusion. Succinctly tell 'em what you told 'em. Review your proposal and benefits in particular. Remind the listener/reader of the organization's strategic plan and link back to that. An example might be: University of XXX Medical Center should implement a pharmacy managed medication reconciliation service which will reduce costs by $$$$/year, reduce adverse drug events, improve physician efficiency and satisfaction, and meet joint commission requirements.
9. **Appendix**: Finally, you'll include an appendix of additional detailed information should they want to look through it. This could be your ROI analysis, organizational literature review and/or detailed gap analysis, flow charts, pilot data details, detailed project plan, letter of support from key stakeholders, references, or acknowledgments.

The business plan template available to you in the Pharmovation Implementation Guide is a Word document that was adapted from resources through the ASHP PAI. I have seen organization business plan templates in Excel, PowerPoint, and even online forms.

How To

When you're creating this business plan, begin with innovative strategic planning, as we've discussed. But also know your organization's typical strategic planning process so you're familiar with how things have always been done. It's also a good idea to use an example business plan that's been approved previously in your organization or request a template from finance or your leader. Make sure you discuss your plan with your boss BEFORE you share it, you don't want them to be caught off guard. Additionally, you should get feedback from 3-5 trusted people before you formally give your proposal. Through this feedback you can develop FAQs and talking points to discuss after you've presented your plan. Also, within your plan, build in assumptions for growth. If it's a 5-year plan, for example, you want to ensure you have a ramp up to see results, but there may be elements you want to plan to revisit in a year or two to seek additional expansion.

Finally, you'll want to do an analysis of the stakeholders involved in any final decisions before you present. You'll want to know who has your back and who you can count on to support you in the room. Remember your elevator pitch? See the next page for an example.

Opportunity	Proposal	Benefits	Resources
• Admission-Related Safety Events Continue to Occur at a Rate of X% & Costs $4,530 per	• Expand Dedicated Pharmacy Resources & Standardized Process	• Safety/Quality • Patient Experience • Provider Engagement • Efficiency	• Pharmacy FTEs • Medication History Technicians (MHT) • Pharmacists/ Residents

Elevator "Strategic Pitch" Example

You'll want to practice this with as many stakeholders as you can leading up to your formal proposal. Have conversations in the hallway, lobby executives subtly along the way. Know how everyone is going to vote before the actual vote. To do that, you'll need to know who the decision makers are, so do your research. You can also get buy-in from key physicians in your organization to bolster your proposal.

A few presentation pearls to leave you with:

- Accompany your business plan with a PowerPoint presentation.
- Stay focused on facts and data.
- Use pictures where you can. A picture is worth a thousand words.
- Pick 3-5 key points and emphasize them throughout your presentation. Explain how your proposal supports organizational goals and initiatives.
- Be prepared to be challenged.
- Don't overplay the regulatory card.

Keeping these as well as your key business plan components in mind as you put together your proposal, will ensure that you put your best foot forward in the boardroom!

In summary, you learned the important components of a business plan, which are the executive summary, table of contents, background, the proposal, benefits, financial assessment, action plan, summary, and your appendix, and ultimately how to compile this all into a business plan.

Take Action Now

- Get started on the business plan (available to download at the end of the chapter through QR code or link).

Sources of Return on Investment (ROI)

In this section, we'll learn about...
- Sources of ROI
- How to Bundle to Achieve ROI

You're in the home stretch of strategy. Congratulations! In this section we'll cover different sources of ROI and ways to bundle them to achieve higher returns on your stakeholders' investment.

Sources of ROI

When we talk about value in healthcare, it's defined as quality over cost. Within that we have outcomes and patient experience divided by both the direct and indirect costs. Remember that, as much as we wish it didn't, healthcare functions as a business here in the United States. And that's always going to be top of mind for the stakeholders deciding whether or not to approve your proposals. No matter how brilliant they are, final decisions have to make fiscal sense. So when it comes to business planning and justifying resources, we can talk about value and how the plan helps to improve quality, but it will often come down to cost. So, finding the ROI for an initiative is critical to approval.

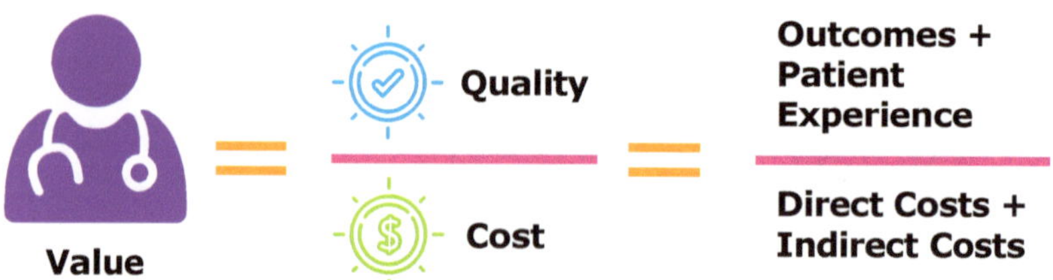

Healthcare Value[87]

There are two general sources you should look for regarding ROI: revenue and savings or expense reduction. Revenue includes real dollars you bill insurance. You need to consider the payer mix. Think of prescription volumes, billing for clinic visits, and value-based payments. Savings and expense reductions include decreased costs or a decreased pharmaceutical budget, as well as FTE reallocation. Also in the context of savings we have what we call soft dollars. These can be hard to track in a general ledger, but some examples are lower levels of adverse drug events and intangible productivity improvement.

The big opportunities for acute care services come in the form of cost management strategies.[88]

These can be[88]:

- Reimbursement and Charging
  - 340B Programs
  - CMS (DRG class)
  - Commercial Insurance (payer mix)
  - Outpatient Infusion Center
  - Coding and Processing
  - Indigent Care Programs
- Interdisciplinary Activities
  - Medication Utilization Program
    - Clinical Pharmacy Services
    - Assessment of Drug Costs
    - Medical Staff Support
    - Formulary Management
    - Therapeutic Interchange
    - Guideline or Protocol Development
    - Pharmacist Interventions
    - Plan Implementation and Analysis
- Pharmacy-Directed Activities
  - Purchasing
    - GPO Contracts
    - Facility Contracts
    - Wholesaler Contracts
  - Inventory Management
    - Wholesaler Ordering Programs
    - Storage
  - Waste Reduction
    - IV Product Waste
    - Returns

This list allows us the ability to look comprehensively at where we can find cost management strategies. I've found that many organizations don't optimize and manage formulary, for example, which I like to call formulary stewardship to use the most cost-effective therapies. This can be a great source of additional cost savings, which can fund the positions necessary to do these activities. Something like this can be a win-win when looking at an organization as a whole.

When it comes to soft dollars, we want to find ways to document and demonstrate the ROI potential here to our stakeholders as it's sometimes a bit ephemeral. On the next page is an example of the cost of medication reconciliation safety events, where we completed an internal assessment, which aligned closely with published literature, showing a cost increase of about $4,500 per patient event.

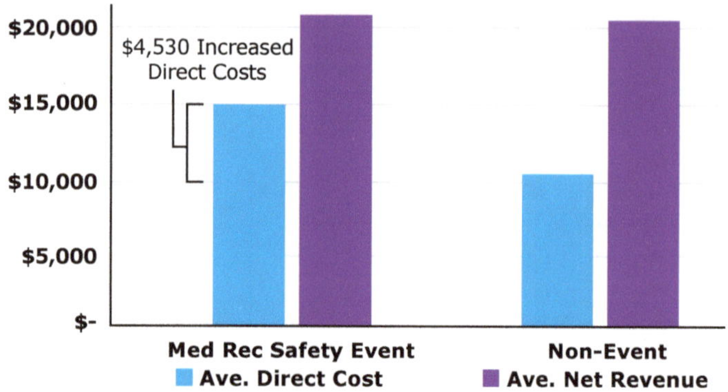

Cost of Medication Safety Event

The left bar graph shows the average direct and indirect costs for a patient that has had a safety event compared to a patient who did not have an event in the right bar graphs. And what you can see is the patients who had had a safety event on admission because incomplete medication reconciliation resulted in an additional cost to the organization of $4,500, which reduced the margin on those admissions. And we also saw a two-day increased length of stay, which directly correlated back to this cost.

On a related note, you may use this as an opportunity to create graphs and charts to help illustrate savings, as we spoke about previously. This helps soft dollar savings present in a more concrete way. You can say, "Oh we'll save money because we'll have fewer safety events with improved resources." Or you can show that you'll save $4,530 each time a safety event is avoided totaling $250,000. Which do you imagine will be more persuasive to stakeholders?

Now, again, these are still soft dollars, and we'll talk about why you cannot directly take this to the bank and say that you're going to save this money. Part of the reason is the savings ties back to patient days and length of stay reduction.

There are two common ways to look at your costs: indirect and direct. You have indirect costs, or overhead, and direct costs related to costs of a patient day. How much does it cost to keep a patient in your care for a single day? These costs relate to a nurse staffing budget, a nurse-to-patient ratio that must be maintained, and the amount of staff is adjusted based on the average daily census (ADC). When you have initiatives that are widespread, unfortunately they can have a small impact on individual units' average daily census. For example, medication reconciliation that we just talked about would only reduce the average length of stay by maybe one patient on a given unit. And that's not going to give you the ability to adjust the nursing staffing budget. But since we know nurses are overloaded generally, maybe one less patient can impact staffing stress levels and general well being. A goal can be to improve quality of care by reducing nurse workload. This would be considered soft savings. Within this, however, you'll have to consider reallocation of resources. Because if the finance department can decrease direct staff costs associated with your initiative, then there's potential for hard savings also.

Many organizations are successful at using length of stay reduction as hard dollar cost savings, but it's important to understand how your institution will account for this. Success is more common if the organization budgets at a higher level than the individual nursing units. Make sure you take the time to discuss your organizational protocol with someone in the financial department when putting together the ROI section for your business plan.

Let's turn our attention to the ambulatory setting to review some sources of both revenue and cost-saving. ROI ambulatory care pharmacy service sustainability can be achieved through revenue, pay-for-performance/value payments, cost savings and cost avoidance, specialty/outpatient pharmacy revenue, employee health self-insured savings, infusion center, and clinic administered medications. In addition, provider engagement and efficiency can be improved with the addition of a pharmacist on the care team.

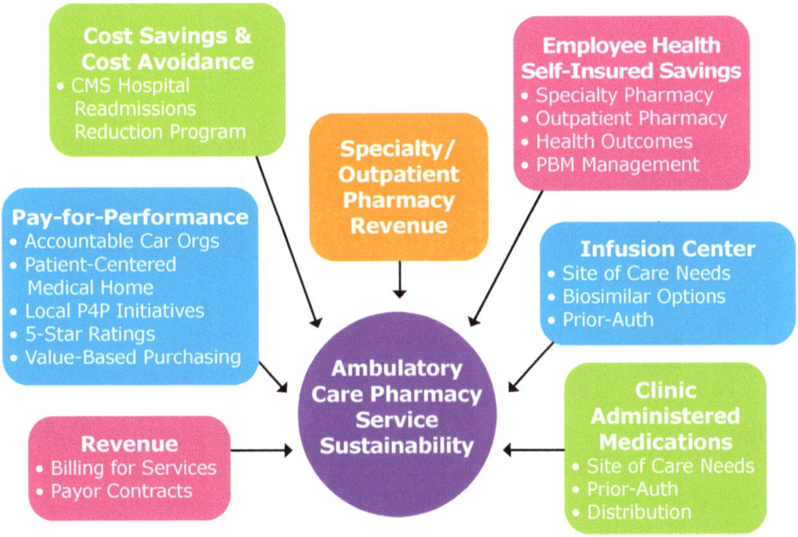

Ambulatory ROI

Now that we have the sources of ROI covered, let's jump into how to present this ROI, and more specifically, how to bundle plans.

How to Bundle to Achieve ROI

For the best chance of approval, a business plan needs to have a positive ROI — sometimes a 3-7 fold increase in ROI. As we discussed, that may not always be possible. Many initiatives are advanced for the good of the patient without a positive ROI, but another strategy I have employed is bundling of plans. I will show you examples from an academic medical center and a community health system where business plans were bundled to combine the ROI to advocate for resources across several initiatives.

	Resources									
Business Plans	RPH	Resident	Tech	Cost Savings	Revenue	Cost FY	Savings (Pharmacy Drug Budget Reduction)	Savings (Cost due to Length of Stay Reduction)	Total Savings/ Revenue	Net Savings Revenue
Medication Reconciliation	3.8	7	10	x		$$$,$$$		$$$,$$$	$$$,$$$	$$$,$$$
Antimicrobial Stwerdship	1	3.8		x		$$$,$$$	$$$,$$$	$$$,$$$	$$$,$$$	$$$,$$$
Drug Use Optimization	1		2.4	x		$$$,$$$	$$$,$$$		$$$,$$$	$$$,$$$
Oncology Pharmoeconomic	1			x		$$$,$$$	$$$,$$$		$$$,$$$	$$$,$$$
Perioperative Initiatives	1.4		1.4	x		$$$,$$$	$$$,$$$		$$$,$$$	$$$,$$$
TOTAL	8.2	8	13.8	x		$2,000,000	$2,500,000	$2,000,000	$4,500,000	$2,500,000

Academic Medical Center Bundled Business Plans

At the academic medical center, the individual business plan includes medication reconciliation, antimicrobial stewardship, drug use optimization, oncology pharmacoeconomic and perioperative initiatives. By bundling several different plans and requesting multiple FTEs, there were cost savings associated with many initiatives, but you can see some of the major cost savings were related to length of stay reduction. As discussed, those soft dollars can be difficult to document as true hard dollar savings, but it does significantly reduce the inpatient drug budget.

None of these plans were associated specifically with increased revenue, but there were separate business plans around ambulatory and outpatient work. For example, see above that the medication reconciliation program only has soft dollars associated with it. But, when you add up all these business plans with the reduction in the pharmacy drug budget achieved through other initiatives, we had enough additional savings to cover the cost of all the business plans, including medication reconciliation.

On the chart, you can see the total from all business plans combined. The cost is approximately $2 million. And the savings we would incur by reducing the drug budget was $2.5 million, so that paid for itself. Whereas if you were to choose the medication reconciliation business plan completely by itself, it would be harder to justify since there aren't hard dollar savings associated with it.

Business Plans	RPH	Resident	Tech	Cost Savings	Revenue	Cost FY	Savings (Pharmacy Drug Budget Reduction)	Savings (Cost due to Length of Stay Reduction)	Total Savings/ Revenue	Net Savings Revenue
Medication Reconciliation	8.2	8	13.8			$2,000,000	$2,500,000	$2,000,000	$4,500,000	$2,500,000
Antimicrobial Stweardship	10		7.4			$1,000,000	$300,000 Overtime Expense Reallocation		$$$,$$$	$$$,$$$
Drug Use Optimization	18.2	8	21.2			$3,000,000	$2,800,000	$2,000,000	$4,800,000	$1,800,000

Academic Medical Center Business Plan Summary with FTE Analysis

By taking it one step further, we did our FTE analysis and realized that we were not right-sized and we were trying to do more with less, when we know that pharmacy can do more with MORE. We did identify additional positions that were needed, and the savings that could be allocated to that included a reduction in overtime expense.

When we combined the plans, our total cost was $3 million, which was easily offset by a savings of $2.8 million. By combining the plans, we see about an equal ROI. Not a positive, but no negative in this bundled compilation. Because of this the business plan was approved because it achieved the additional quality and paid for itself.

Now I'd like to look at a case study from a community health system.

On the next page, you will find a similar acute care pharmacy business plan, which has added medication safety. There are also several ambulatory and outpatient plans as well. What you see on this plan is the plan name and the category, what the benefits are, and what source of ROI was used.

We'll begin at the bottom with acute care pharmacy looking at pharmacy practice advancement and medication safety. The goal here is to improve acute care patient to pharmacist ratio, improve admission medication reconciliation, and provide laptops for the decentralized shifts as well as other technology enhancements for the medication distribution system to improve safety. The ROI used here was formulary stewardship and cost management strategies.

Consolidated Plan Name	Category	Benefits	ROI
Ambulatory/ Outpatient Pharmacy	Specialty Pharmacy	Expand Services in Specialty Clinics	Specialty Prescription Revenue
	Ambulatory Clinical Pharmacy Services	Expand Services in Primary Care Clinics	Value-Based Contracts, Visit Revenue
	Associate Health/ Prescriptions	Add Outpatient Pharmacies	Prescription Revenue
Acute Care Pharmacy	Pharmacy Practice Advancement	Improve Acute Care Patient to Pharmacist Ratio Admission Medication Reconciliation Laptops for Decentralized Shifts	Formulary Stewardship/Cost Management Strategies
	Medication Safety	Technology Enhancement	

Community Health System Bundled Business Plans

Similarly, you can see the information related to the ambulatory and outpatient pharmacy plans. Originally, we did consider presenting these as one consolidated plan, but ultimately, because there was separate ROI for each of these, the plans were separated into three different plans to improve efficiency and timeliness of approval.

Cost Management Strategies	Savings	Pharmacy Restructure & Business Plan Allocation	Cost
Medication Use Optimization	$ XXX,XXX	Technician Market Analysis	$ XXX,XXX
Purchasing	$ XXX,XXX	Management Restructure	$ XXX,XXX
Inventory Management	$ XXX,XXX	Acute Care Business Plan FTEs & Tech	$ XXX,XXX
Waste Reduction	$ XXX,XXX	TOTAL	$ 3,000,000
Reimbursement	$ XXX,XXX	NET ROI	$ 1,500,00
Optimization	$ 4,500,00		

Community Health System Bundled Business Plan ROI

Here is an example of bundling your ROI for an acute care plan. You can see we committed to a $4.5M savings on our cost management strategies, which offset the total costs of the acute care business plans, which included the FTEs and management restructure as well as a technician market analysis, still resulting in a positive ROI to the organization of approximately $1.5M.

You can employ many cost management strategies to increase savings to offset the cost of your business plan.

When putting together this section of your business plan, make sure you're not giving up any hidden ROI. Assess and utilize all sources at your disposal to support bundling and grouping of plans. Who can you collaborate with? Who else can benefit from this plan? Rope in other departments and organizational needs as much as possible.

What to Watch For

Don't give up ROI. Assess and utilize all sources of ROI to support bundling/grouping of plans.

"Imagination is more important than knowledge"
-Albert Einstein

Again, be innovative. Think about how you can combine business plans to advocate for resources. At the end of the day, our goal is the same: to achieve our mission and vision for our organizations by improving patient care.

In summary, remember that, in the simplest terms, sources of ROI generally include decreasing expenses and increasing revenue. Bundling is an effective way to achieve ROI across multiple initiatives.

• • •

This chapter provides a lot of tools and templates to help you along your journey, so make sure you take advantage of that! Up next is the Pharmovation Services chapter, where we'll talk more about the opportunities and innovation that our colleagues are doing across this country to provide better services and improve patient outcomes.

To support you incorporating the learnings from this chapter, access the Pharmovation Implementation Guide. Visit www.pharmovationguide.com or scan the QR code below for full access!

Chapter 5
Pharmovation SERVICES

"We always overestimate the change that will occur in the next two years and underestimate the change that will occur in the next ten. Don't let yourself be lulled into inaction."
—Bill Gates

I have always been a fierce advocate for my team members to be able to practice at the top of their licenses. Technicians practicing at the top of their licenses support pharmacists to practice at the top of their licenses who in turn support physicians to practice at the top of their licenses. It's a ladder of support for the entire healthcare enterprise.

One of the ways I've seen this theory play out most effectively is through devoting time and resources to supporting technicians. Technicians are the structural foundation of the ladder of support. Yet, we tend to see a high (higher than average) level of turnover when it comes to technicians, due in part, to the fact that many pharmacy teams don't offer much, if any, upward mobility for them. Being a technician is often, sadly, a dead-end job with little career advancement available. Pharmacy leaders must find creative ways to maximize the potential of their technicians, who in turn, support the entire department. Because you cannot have a fulfilling career without advancement opportunities. Other strategies to support technician retention and engagement include competitive market pay adjustments, training & education, schedule flexibility, purposeful work, and manager support and attention.

To this end, I've included technician practice advancement and engagement strategies in each business plan I have proposed throughout my career. I created leadership opportunities, practice advancement options, and even advocated for director-level positions for technicians. These advancements not only support the development of individual technicians (which we'll discuss in depth later in the development chapter) but allows every member of your team the opportunity to practice at the top of their license, support the organization, and provide better quality services for patients.

And speaking of practicing at the top of your license, in this chapter we'll be looking at the needs and opportunities for pharmacists and technicians to be accountable and innovative with our roles and the services we provide. We'll discuss this generally, then look into different practice areas like acute care and ambulatory care innovation, plus some nontraditional innovation opportunities. Then we'll discuss ways to plan for acquiring the resources we need to offer these services and how we can track measures to show the value we're providing to our organizations. We'll then finish up with a specific case study from a community health system.

Remember the types of innovation we've discussed. It's not all about disruption. Innovation can also be about adopting ideas faster. This chapter won't be focused on disruptive innovation as much, as we'll see how we can implement all the known innovative services quickly so that pharmacy on the whole is able to practice at the top of it's capacity. This, in turn, allows us to practice at the top of our licenses so everyone is working smarter, not harder, and the patients benefit most of all.

Practice Advancement

In this section, we'll learn about...

- Why Practice Advancement is Important
- PAI History & Recommendations
- PAI & Innovation

To begin, we'll discuss pharmacy practice advancement and situate this within the broader world of the healthcare system. We'll discuss why practice advancement is important, the history of PAI and its links to innovation.

Why Practice Advancement is Important

Let's begin by grounding our discussion in the medication use process. You've heard me talk a lot about accountability. And when I think about accountability, I think about the entire medication use process. As we know, it looks like this: prescribing, documenting, dispensing, administering, and finally, monitoring. The process is supported by procurement of medications through the supply chain. If our team is practicing to their highest capacity, pharmacists will only be involved at the beginning and end of this cycle. Pharmacists will prescribe the medication, documenting it through technology, then technicians will dispense it and hand it off to nurses for administering. The pharmacist will hop back in to monitor the medication and its effectiveness, perhaps making tweaks in the prescription that starts the cycle over again. This is the ideal order of events:

Medication Use Process

This is only a model, and how this works in practice is not always the ideal process. But when we think about practice models and advancements this simply describes how a pharmacy department's resources are deployed to provide care. Obviously, one size will not fit all teams, but there are some standards we should ensure. These standards should include how pharmacists practice and provide care to patients as well as how technicians are involved to support care. Plus, of course, how we're leveraging automation and technology in the medication use system.

When we think about big advancements in pharmacy practice, we hop back in time to our prior practices and health systems. In the 1960's we provided unit dose medications, then in the 1990's we had the advent of pharmaceutical care coined by Helpler & Strand, then in the early 2000's we had technology such as bedside barcoding. This tool was a huge advancement in technology that greatly improved the safety of our patients. From 2002 to 2008 bedside barcoding was implemented by 66% of hospitals and organizations.[89] Shortly thereafter we have the advent of computerized physician order entry (CPOE) with clinical decision support, which increased to 54% by 2012 with the investments in the funds from the federal government.[89] Plus, we've seen an improvement from 10.4-17.5 FTE in the number of pharmacists per hundred beds from 2002-2012.[89] It's clear that we are increasing the resources provided in our health system.

When we think historically about those practice models, we've gone then, more from a drug distribution model to a clinical specialist centered model to a patient centered and integrated model of care. This is everything that I try to advance when it comes to pharmacy practice.

If a patient-centered integrated care model is the goal, it's only achievable by pharmacy being held accountable and collaborating with other departments. Of course, medication use touches a lot of other care providers, and we want to involve our patients in the process as much as possible.

So what is the rationale for practice advancement? It seems to happen naturally... Why should we push it? This conversation has been going on for decades. And while practice advancement and pharmacy is not a new thing, because we have yet to achieve full success, there are many reasons that keep this conversation at the forefront.

We'll divide the rationale for practice advancement into four categories: healthcare reform, technology, quality and outcomes, and other.

First, **healthcare reform**. With focused efforts on innovation the past few years have seen many advancements. We've grown our health systems, also known as integrated delivery networks (or IDN's), our accountable care organizations, and medical homes. We've seen the advent of medication therapy management (MTM), which has had massive success. But we still see many issues in rural health organizations being unable to integrate these advancements (and some urban health organizations as well.) Plus, we're always focused on that elusive quadruple aim: better care, better health, lower costs, and provider engagement.

Let's look at **quality and outcomes**. We've talked about the issues surrounding pay for performance in previous chapters, but it's worth remembering here. We've seen the formulation of the National Quality Forum (NQF) and other quality measures that are growing in importance for us to track and achieve. Keeping quality and outcomes at the forefront of practice advancement certainly helps move towards the quadruple aims mentioned above. Support of Risk Evaluation & Mitigation Strategies (REMS) for high-risk medications does as well. Plus, quality and outcomes is an area that has growing support for pharmacists' value within the healthcare enterprise. We're able to add value, as long as we're accountable, in a way that benefits the entire system.

Then we come to **technology**. Obviously we must use technology in a meaningful way, such as growing the electronic health record (EHR). We should also be advocating for required investments in areas like bar-coding, telepharmacy, and dispensing. But we'll cover this in more depth in our technology chapter later on.

Other reasons where we can advocate for practice advancement are the increased complexity of drug therapy, the known shortage of healthcare professionals, and integrating pharmacists as part of the care team to take on a direct role in patient care supported by the entry level PharmD and increasing residency training opportunities.

There is no shortage of areas for our practice to advance. At this point, I urge you not to feel overwhelmed by all the possibilities but see them as opportunities for future work and projects.

Remember you will not be working alone. We have the benefit and value of being part of the whole pharmacy enterprise. Speaking of which, let's discuss some of the benefits and value of that enterprise. There are many published improved processes and outcome measures.[90, 91, 92]

- **Mortality**: First, there's a direct impact on mortality. Rates decrease noticeably when a well-functioning pharmacy enterprise is part of a health care system.
- **Adverse Drug Events/Adverse Drug Reactions**: We've seen a quicker identification of frequency and severity of events, prevention of additional events, and fewer events requiring further treatment.
- **Health Services Use**: Lower rates of readmission, fewer patients transferred to intensive care, fewer emergency department/urgent care visits after discharge, shorter length of stay.
- **Therapeutic Management**: Anticoagulation drugs are more effective as well as pharmacokinetic dosing and drug monitoring.
- **Changes in Medication Regimen**: Fewer number of medications, increased rates of medication appropriateness, appropriately prescribed non-indicated medications.
- **Other Measures**: Better quality of life, higher patient satisfaction, higher rates of medication adherence, better knowledge of medication regimen, more cost effectiveness, and higher immunization rates.

Additional support for the advancement of practice comes from resources also discussed in Chapter 3: "The Patient-Centered Medical Home: Integrating Comprehensive Medication Management to Optimize Patient Outcomes"[93]; "Improving Patient and Health System Outcomes through Advanced Pharmacy Practice"[71]; and "National Governor's Association Center for Best Practices — The Expanding Role of Pharmacists in as Transformed Health Care System."[94] Depending on the leadership at your organization, having these sources available to draw from when advocating for services may be particularly helpful.

PAI History & Recommendations

Continuing our look at practice advancement, we must understand that this is not a new topic. While the name has changed throughout the years, there have historically been specific, well-documented initiatives where health systems have intentionally worked toward advancing practice. This began in 1985 with the **ASHP Hilton Head Conference**, followed up in 1989 with a **Pharmacy and the 21st**

Century Conference. Then in 1993, in Texas, we had "**Implementing Pharmaceutical Care**," where several pharmacy leaders came together to put recommendations in place. Then we have the **ASHP 2015** (initiated in 2003) and subsequent **2020 vision**. Throughout the years there have been a lot of efforts and initiatives happening and slowly coming together.

We also have the **Pharmacy Practice Model Initiative (PPMI)** working to advance care through a 2010 PPMI Summit and, in 2014, a summit focused specifically on ambulatory care. In 2015, the initiative itself underwent a metamorphosis, changing their name to **PAI (Practice Advancement Initiative),** then in 2019 PAI 2030 was born. All of these meetings and recommendations are profession-led initiatives to empower pharmacists to take responsibility for patient outcomes and increase accountability.

Why am I listing a bunch of conferences? Because it's important to understand that work like this isn't a new idea or something we're just thinking about now. It's a long-time effort that you're joining. Pharmacy leaders have been working to advance practice for decades, current technologies make this possible at a quicker rate than ever before, so it may seem like pharmacy advancement is the hot new thing, but we are building on the work of many who came before us.

If you aren't familiar with PAI (Practice Advancement Initiative), then let me put it into context. PAI is to pharmacists like Magnet Status is for nursing. It's an elective program through the American Nurses Credentialing Center (ANCC) that's dedicated to advancement of practice and excellence by fostering pharmacy leaders. To compare, the Magnet Recognition Program for nursing defines itself in the following ways[95]:

- Designates organizations worldwide where nursing leaders successfully align their nursing strategic goals to improve the organization's patient outcomes.
- Provides a road map to nursing excellence, which benefits the whole of an organization.
- To nurses, Magnet means education and development through every career stage, which leads to greater autonomy at the bedside.
- To patients, it means the very best care, delivered by nurses who are supported to be the very best that they can be.

Magnet is structured with sections on structural empowerment, exemplary professional practice, new knowledge, innovation and improvements, and transformational leadership, all supported with documentations of empirical outcomes. Because Magnet is recognized by many health systems, I often equate PAI to Magnet to emphasize the importance of improving our PAI score with attention and resources.

Since PAI was developed in 2010, let's take a look at some of the progress that has happened since then.

CARE TEAM INTEGRATION

2017	AVERAGE	
50%	57%	Hospitals that have processes to ensure medication-related continuity of care
66%	63%	Pharmacists in ambulatory settings who follow a standardized patient care process
93%	79%	Hospitals that have pharmacists who have taken a leadership role in an antimicrobial stewardship program
43%	42%	Hospitals that have collaborative practice agreements between pharmacists and other healthcare providers
36%	38%	Pharmacy departments that evaluated ways to improve the org's effectiveness as an ACO

CREDENTIALS & TRAINING

2017	AVERAGE	
49%	51%	Pharmacists who provide patient care services in ambulatory settings who are included in organization-based credentialing and privileging process
50%	51%	Hospitals that have pharmacy technicians certified by the Pharmacy Technician Certification Board (PTCB)
45%	36%	Hospitals that offer residency training compared to 30% in 2011
65%	58%	Hospitals that train pharmacy students on transitions of care in the medication-use process

AUTOMATION & TECHNOLOGY

2017	AVERAGE	
44%	26%	Hospitals that have barcode medication administration compared to 15% in 2011
46%	37%	Hospitals that use barcode technology during the inventory process
33%	24%	Hospitals that have pharmacist interventions automatically captured through the information system

LEADERSHIP IN MEDICATION USE

2017	AVERAGE	
70%	79%	Hospitals that have developed a strategic plan for implementing automation and technology designed to improve the safety and efficiency of medication use
80%	82%	Pharmacy leaders who engage in regular, direct communications with hospital administration and the board of directors about medication management systems performance
75%	73%	Ambulatory care practitioners who participate in initiatives aimed at medication safety, quality, and cost evaluation

LEVERAGING PHARMACY TECHNICIANS

2017	AVERAGE	
70%	61%	Ambulatory care systems that utilize pharmacy technicians or other supportive personnel to support pharmacist patient care services
76%	68%	Hospitals that have all distributive functions that do not require a pharmacist's clinical judgment assigned to pharmacy technicians
42%	39%	Medication preparation and distribution tasks are fully assigned to pharmacy technicians

National PAI Metrics: 2017 vs. Average (2011-2017)[96]

While I won't go through every detail of this chart, since you can go through it yourself, I want to point out that on the whole (with a few exceptions) the differences in 2017 are not significantly higher than the average calculated between 2011 and 2017. I find this a bit disappointing. And yet, I also find these metrics motivating. These results are a big factor in why I began teaching courses and putting together this book. Because there is so much potential and so many avenues for advancement that we're not yet taking full advantage of.

There have been some PAI pharmacy success stories, such as a 33% reduction in 30-day hospital readmissions when pharmacists provided comprehensive medication management, a 270% increase in residency positions from 2007-2019, and a 41% increase in pharmacist completion of comprehensive medication reviews with pharmacy technicians in clinical support roles.[97]

The goal for the most recent ASHP PAI Summit in 2019, titled **PAI 2030** was "to significantly advance the health and well-being of people by supporting patient-centered care delivery models that optimize the most effective use of pharmacists as direct patient care providers."[97] The domains recommended to focus on to achieve this audacious goal are:

- Patient Centered Care
- Pharmacy Technician Role, Education, and Training
- Pharmacist Role, Education, and Training
- Technology and Data Science
- Leadership in Medication Use and Safety

Within these sectors the summit included 59 streamlined and updated recommendations to promote optimal, safe, and effective medication use, expand pharmacist and technician roles, and implement the latest technologies. Above are the main domains, but we also have sub domains available that further categorize these aims.[97]

Additional subdomains included:

- **Practice-focused**: Recommendations that relate primarily to frontline pharmacy practice.
- **Organization-focused**: Recommendations that relate primarily to pharmacy departmental leadership or the policies or practices of the institution.
- **Profession-focused**: Recommendations that require profession-wide attention for implementation.

And a few themes for change that were outlined[97]:

- Optimize care via pharmacist-provided comprehensive medication management.
- Advance pharmacy technician roles.
- Harness data to improve patient health.
- Integrate pharmacy enterprise for convenient and cost-effective care.
- Adopt personalized, targeted therapies.
- Public health opportunities in social determinants, chronic illness, and addiction.

And the summit didn't stop here, they continued to go into deeper detail through the recommendation for each category as we can see in these charts. For ease, I have **bolded** the key word in each recommendation. These are also available for easy reference in the Situational Analysis tool in the Pharmovation Implementation Guide via the link at the end of the chapter.

- Patient Centered Care[97]:
  - Practice Focused
    - A1. Pharmacists should collaborate with patients, families, and caregivers to ensure **treatment plans respect patients' beliefs, values, autonomy, and agency**.
    - A2. The pharmacy workforce should lead **medication reconciliation** processes during care transitions (e.g., emergency department, upon admission and discharge, ambulatory-care setting, community pharmacy, long term care).
    - A3. The pharmacy workforce should collaborate with patients, caregivers, payers, and healthcare professionals to establish consistent and sustainable models for **seamless transitions of care**.
    - A4. **Pharmacist documentation** related to patient care must be available to all members of the healthcare team, including patients, in all care settings.
    - A5. The pharmacy workforce should partner with patients and the interprofessional care team to identify, assess, and resolve **barriers to medication access, adherence, and health literacy**.
    - A6. Patients must have **access to a pharmacist** in all settings of care.
  - Organization Focused
    - A7. The pharmacy workforce, in all care settings, must have **access to complete patient medical records** and related health information
    - A8. The pharmacy enterprise should be integrated and modeled to provide patient-centered care across **the**

continuum (e.g., home and outpatient infusion, specialty pharmacy, community pharmacy, acute care.)
    - A9. The pharmacy workforce should lead **medication education** for patients and caregivers that optimize outcomes, including care transitions.
    - A10. Pharmacists should play an active role in ensuring that **ethical principles** drive clinical and business decisions related to medication use.
    - A11. Health systems must provide **24/7 pharmacy services** with advanced clinical capability.
    - A12. Health systems should support innovative models for providing a safe and appropriate level of pharmacy services for **small and rural hospitals or other alternative practice settings**.
    - 13. Pharmacy departments should take responsibility for appropriate medication use in the structuring of **external partnerships**.
  - Profession Focused
    - A14. Pharmacists should lead and advocate for **comprehensive medication management** in all healthcare settings

- Pharmacist Role, Education, and Training[97]:
  - Practice Focused
    - B1. All pharmacists should have an **individualized continuing professional development plan**.
    - B2. Pharmacists should l**everage and expand their scope of practice**, including prescribing, to optimize patient care.
    - B3. Pharmacists should participate in and assume key roles on **emergency response teams**.
  - Organization Focused
    - B4. Health systems should require completion of ASHP-accredited **residency training** as a minimum credential for new pharmacist practitioners.
    - B5. Pharmacists should participate in organization-based **credentialing and privileging** processes to ensure competency within their scope of practice.
    - B6. Pharmacy practice leaders should ensure that their workforce has the necessary knowledge and competency to adapt to **emerging healthcare needs**.
    - B7. Pharmacists practicing in specialty areas should be **board-certified** through the Board of Pharmacy Specialties or other appropriate body.
  - Profession Focused
    - B8. Pharmacy education, residency training, and continuing education should cover **healthcare reimbursement, payment, and business management** in all areas of practice.

- B9. Pharmacists in all care settings should be included as **integral members of the healthcare team** and share accountability for patient outcomes and population health.
- B10. The pharmacy workforce should be knowledgeable and have the resources to care for patients with **behavioral and mental health disorders**.
- B11. Training and credentialing should exist to develop and recognize pharmacists who specialize in **health information technology**.
- B12. Credentialed ambulatory-care pharmacists should be considered **primary care providers**.
- B13. The profession should champion **multi-state or national licensure** for pharmacists.
- B14. Pharmacists, in collaboration with other key stakeholders, must work to increase **public, regulatory, and health professional understanding of pharmacists' roles and value**.

- Technology and Data Science[97]:
  - Practice Focused
    - C1. Pharmacists should **use health information technologies** to advance their role in patient care and population health.
    - C2. Pharmacy practice leaders should foster the development and application of **advanced analytics** (e.g., machine learning and artificial intelligence) in activities such as risk assessment, monitoring performance metrics, identifying patients in need of pharmacist care, optimizing medication use, and business management.
    - C3. Pharmacy practice leaders should be engaged in assessing **emerging patient care technologies** (e.g., mobile applications, monitoring devices, digital wearables or ingestibles, blockchain technology) to support optimal medication use outcomes.
    - C4. The pharmacy workforce should be competent in **health information technology** (including but not limited to analytics, automation, and clinical applications of technology) with ongoing education and training embedded at all stages and career developments.
  - Organization Focused
    - C5. **Virtual pharmacy services** (e.g., telepharmacy) should be deployed to optimize operational and clinical services that extend patient care services and enhance continuity of care.
    - C6. The pharmacy enterprise must have **sufficient resources** to develop, implement, and maintain

technology-related medication-use safety standards.
    - C7. Pharmacy departments should have **access to an analytics resource**, such as a data scientist, to collect, aggregate, measure, visualize, and disseminate data related to the financial and clinical performance of pharmacists.
    - C8. Pharmacy departments should use technology to ensure the **safe compounding of sterile products**.
  - Profession Focused
    - C9. Pharmacy should employ **high reliability principles** when designing and selecting health information technology.
    - C10. Pharmacy should advocate for information technology that is **inter-operable and transparent** with respect to usability, security, and functionality across the continuum of care.
    - C11. Pharmacy should establish standards for the application of **artificial intelligence (AI)** in the various steps of the medication-use process, including prescribing, reviewing, medication orders, and assessing medication-use patterns in populations.

- Pharmacy, Technical Role, Education, and Training[97]:
  - Practice Focused
    - D1. Pharmacy technicians should participate in **advanced roles** in all practice settings to promote efficiency and improve access to patient care.
    - D2. Pharmacy technicians should have **complete responsibility for advanced technical and supporting activities** (e.g., order fulfillment, tech-check-tech, regulatory compliance, supply chain management, diversion prevention, revenue cycle management, patient assistance programs).
  - Organization Focused
    - D3. All newly hired technicians should have completed an **ASHP/ACPE-accredited technician education and training program**.
    - D4. Health systems should **require technicians to be certified** by the Pharmacy Technician Certification Board.
    - D5. Pharmacy departments should foster the development of **professional career paths** for pharmacy technicians.
  - Profession Focused
    - D6. A **scope of practice including core competencies** should be developed and defined for pharmacy technicians in acute-care and ambulatory-care settings.

- Leadership in Medication Use and Safety[97]:
  - Practice Focused
    - E1. Pharmacists should advance the use of **pharmacogenomic information** for personalized medication treatment.

- E2. Pharmacists should assume **leadership roles in medication stewardship activities** at the local, state, and national levels.
- Organization Focused
    - E3. Pharmacy must be an active and accountable partner in the **financial stewardship** (e.g. minimizing waste, using cost-effective therapies, managing supply chain) of care delivered in all settings.
    - E4. Pharmacy practice leaders should ensure **evidence-based medication use** by continually analyzing and reporting use patterns and outcomes.
    - E5. Health systems should support **inter-professional innovation centers** designed to pursue breakthroughs in areas such as patient experience, medication use, clinical outcomes, operational efficiency, technology, and revenue generation.
    - E6. Health systems should support the **well-being and resiliency** of their staff.
    - E7. Pharmacy departments should strive to achieve **equity, diversity, and inclusion** in all technical, clinical, and leadership roles.
    - E8. The pharmacy enterprise should engage, employ, or develop expertise in areas such as **finance, analytics, business management, quality assurance, informatics, human resources, payer relations, and supply chain management**.
    - E9. Health systems should have a **pharmacist executive leader**, with a reporting structure consistent with other executive leaders, to oversee and influence enterprise-wide decision making related to medication use and technology.
    - E10. The pharmacy workforce should **assess and mitigate risk in medication-use systems** across all settings.
- Profession Focused
    - E11. Pharmacists should lead the development, implementation, and evaluation of medication-related **national quality indicators and accountability measures**.
    - E12. Pharmacists should be leaders in federal and state legislative and regulatory policy development related to improving **individual and population health outcomes**.
    - E13. Pharmacy should partner with inter-professional organizations to define and delineate **practice advances into state and federal laws** to optimize patient care.
    - E14. Pharmacy should leverage healthcare models that acknowledge **pharmacist value and align payment with quality of outcomes**.

Again, it's important to situate ourselves within the work that's already been done and the recommendations already available. There's no need to start from scratch or reinvent the wheel with pharmacy innovation, much of it is right here just begging to be properly implemented into healthcare systems.

And speaking of not reinventing the wheel, we also want to look at successful implementation of new pharmacy practice models. Luckily, The Consensus of the Pharmacy Practice Model Summit from 2011 provides us with just those examples.[98]

Successful Implementation of New Pharmacy Practice Models:

- E4a. Department of pharmacy administrative leadership.
- E4b. Clinical pharmacy leadership.
- E4c. Ensuring competence of current pharmacy staff to provide drug therapy management.
- E4d. Assignment of pharmacists to patient care units.
- E4e. Expansion of pharmacy technician responsibilities.
- E4f. Pharmacist electronic access to complete patient-specific data.
- E4g. Support from health care executives.
- E4h. Support from physicians.
- E4i. Support from medical staff leadership.
- E4j. Support from nursing leadership.
- E4k. Implementation of collaborative practice agreements.
- E4l. Establishment of pharmacist provider status under Medicare.
- E4m. Training for all pharmacy students on the roles of safety and quality in the process.
- E4n. Training for all pharmacy students on transitions of care.
- E4o. Increased number of residency-trained pharmacists.

I do want to touch briefly on the Joint Commission of Pharmacy Practitioners (JCPP) and their vision for pharmacy's future. This is a group of several professional pharmacy organizations who have agreed that "Patients achieve optimal health and medication outcomes with pharmacists as essential and accountable providers within patient-centered, team-based healthcare."[99]

The JCPP also provides us with a helpful definition for **Medication Management Services (MMS)** which states, "Medication management services are a spectrum of patient-centered, pharmacist provided, collaborative services that focus on medication appropriateness, effectiveness, safety, and adherence with the goal of improving health outcomes."[99] The complete pharmacists' patient care process was approved by JCPP organizations in May 2014 and is supported by 13 national pharmacy organizations. Medication management service includes the following elements[99]:

- Patient-centered approach to care — the service is individualized for a specific patient, focuses on the patient's needs and concerns, and involves the patient in the care process.
- Assessment of medication appropriateness, effectiveness, safety, and adherence.
- Consideration should be given to accessibility and cost of medications.
- Collaborative approach to care that involves the patient, caregiver(s), pharmacists, and other healthcare providers.
- Focus on health outcomes.

There's nothing here that conflicts with anything outlined or decided on in PAI's 2030 vision, but in terms of MMS we do see a more expanded definition, which can be helpful. Specific things to consider with medication accessibility and cost are brought into the conversation and a reminder to involve the patient in the care process. These are all things that may seem intuitive to pharmacy leaders like yourself, but nonetheless are vital to have documented in writing and as a working template to build systems on. Because unfortunately they won't be intuitive to everyone building the healthcare or pharmacy enterprise. Having this documentation along with the conviction that this is how things should and must be done is a powerful tool at your disposal.

Another powerful tool to be aware of is the work JCPP has done to clarify the pharmacists' patient care process.

Here we have a 5-step patient-centered care outline that is meant to collaborate, communicate, and document to the highest possible excellence.

Pharmacists' Patient Care Process[100]:

- **Collect**: The pharmacist assures the collection of the necessary subjective and objective information about the patient in order to understand the relevant medical/medication history and clinical status of the patient.
- **Assess**: The pharmacist assesses the information collected and analyzes the clinical effects of the patient's therapy in the context of the patient's overall health goals in order to identify and prioritize problems and achieve optimal care.
- **Plan**: The pharmacist develops an individualized patient-centered care plan, in collaboration with other healthcare professionals and the patient or caregiver that is evidence-based and cost-effective.
- **Implement**: The pharmacist implements the care plan in collaboration with other health care professionals and the patient or caregiver.

- **Follow-up**: Monitor and Evaluate. The pharmacist monitors and evaluates the effectiveness of the care plan and modifies the plan in collaboration with other healthcare professionals and the patient or caregiver as needed.

Another area we can support pharmacy practice advancement is within pharmacy training itself. There's been a push lately towards expanding residency opportunities and training that presents the opportunity for what I call a "quadruple win."

Residency expansion…

- Expands Resources for Practice Advancement
- Elevates Level of Practice of Staff/Preceptors
- Recruiting Support Fills Open Pharmacist Positions
- Fill Gap of More Residency Applicants than Positions Available

Additionally, we see that residency expansion can lower the pharmacist to patient ratio across the system, elevate expectations of pharmacy services, allow for increased research opportunities, support weekend staffing needs, and add revenue through CMS Pass-through funding to support additional training or conference attendance.

There are also mutual benefits for student pharmacists (experiential rotations & interns) and the organizations. Students benefit by receiving additional opportunities to manage drug therapy problems under supervision, strengthen critical thinking and problem solving skills, build confidence, and mature professionally. Plus, it benefits the institution by expanding the reach of clinical pharmacy services, having additional recruitment opportunities and providing rotation revenues. I know that's not always possible, but it's definitely been my goal for pharmacy students to have consistency in their availability because that's where it really can help support advanced practice.

PAI & Innovation

Now let's bring it all together with PAI and innovation. I mentioned earlier that this chapter would not be so much about disruptive innovation as incremental innovation. As we begin to wrap up this first section, I want to remind you that innovation points to the application of better solutions that meet new requirements, unarticulated needs, or existing market needs. We want to execute ideas which address specific changes and achieve value for both the company (health organization) and the customer (patient). Through all this, we are able to overcome the evidence-practice gap, one of the most preventable and frustrating things that exists within pharmacy (and many other) practices. When we have the evidence to support new practices, we must shorten the time it takes to implement and integrate those practices into common use.

Our goal is to provide opportunities for innovation and provide new products, services, or processes. We're not always talking about radical and revolutionary innovation; incremental and evolutionary innovation is just as meaningful. It's also important for us to retain the meaning of the word innovation so it doesn't lose its value and become just another buzzword.

There are growing needs and a lot of efforts being made around innovation for pharmacy services. If you'd like to continue your research, here are a few examples of innovation initiatives and resources you can explore:

- University of Maryland Center for Innovative Pharmacy Solutions[101]
- *Innovations in Pharmacy Journal*[102]
- Institute for Innovative Pharmacy Practice[103]
- Cedarville University Center for Pharmacy Innovation[104]
- VCU Center for Pharmacy Practice Innovation[105]
- APHA Foundation Practice Innovation[106]
- ASHP Innovation Center[107]

We will revisit some of these organizations' innovations in the coming sections. This last example, the ASHP Innovation Center is particularly interesting and has only been recently announced. We'll discuss more specifics around acute and ambulatory care shortly, but briefly the ASHP Innovation Center aims to build upon the innovative foundation in pharmacy as the profession looks to the future and embraces technologies that will improve the lives of our patients.[108] The center will focus on digital transformation, artificial intelligence, innovations in pharmacy practice, advanced data analytics, and big data. They're committed to investing in technologies including auto-verification, next-generation robotics and automation, virtual reality, and digital therapeutics. Plus, the center will dedicate resources to genomics and personalized medicine.[108] It's an exciting time to be a pharmacist!

What to Watch For

Keep other professional roles in mind and how pharmacy PAI will impact and benefit them.

As you begin to plot and plan ways to advance practice through innovation in your own organization, it is important to keep other professional roles in mind (those outside the pharmacy enterprise) and consider ways that pharmacy advancement will impact and, most importantly, benefit them as well. While I do want pharmacy to be accountable, we cannot be seen as non-collaborative because of the shared responsibility for these activities. Including these aspects in business proposals and budget meetings will ultimately help your work be more successful and easily accepted by the rest of the healthcare enterprise.

We can see clearly through the detailed work of those who've come before, that practice advancement is important for our profession and patient care. This statement is supported by external organizations beyond pharmacy leadership. Practice advancement is nothing new, it's broad and has been in progress for decades. I hope you'll spend additional time perusing the consolidated PAI 2030 recommendations and JCPP methods because they are an extremely useful source for innovation and practice advancement.

To summarize, we learned that practice advancement is important for our profession and patient care is supported by external organizations. Practice advancement is broad and has been in progress for decades. Consolidated PAI 2030 recommendations and JCCP methods are useful and great sources of innovation.

Take Action Now

- Read references on support for some advanced practice.
- Complete the PAI 2030 situational analysis assessment if not yet complete.

Acute Care Innovation

In this section, we'll look at...

- Examples of Acute Care Innovation

Examples of Acute Care Innovation

Next, we'll look at specific examples of acute care intervention. First, let's remember the continuity touchpoints for pharmacy practice.

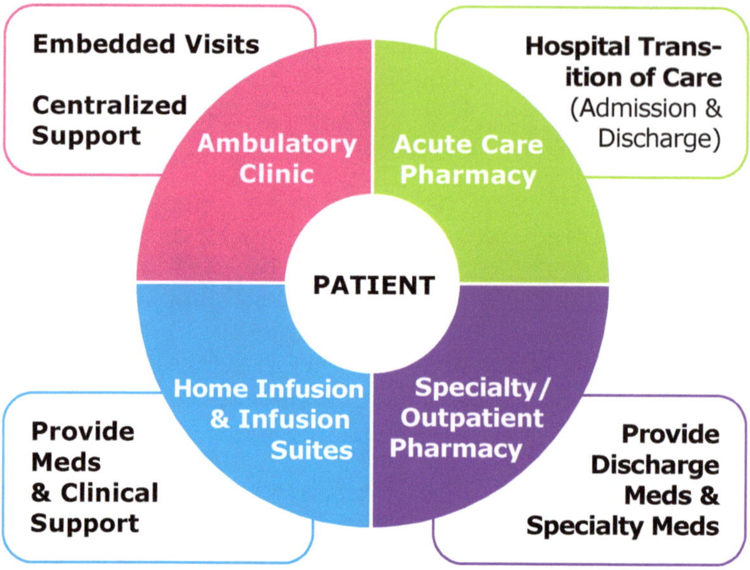

Pharmacy Continuity Touch Points

In this section, we're going to focus on the upper quadrant: Acute Care Pharmacy. This includes the hospital stay and transitions of care. This is a great preview of a few other touch points we'll focus on a bit later in the chapter, such as ambulatory services. Plus, it's good to keep in mind the touch points that don't have a place in this chapter like specialty and outpatient pharmacy, as well as infusion services.

We should always stay aware that pharmacy is accountable for patient safety across the continuum from acute care, during the transition to ambulatory care, and while under the care of ambulatory services.

During acute care, the areas for particular attention are:

- Medication Reconciliation (admission/transfer)
- Patient Care Rounds
- Patient Education
- Antimicrobial Stewardship
- Pain Stewardship
- Medication Dosing and Monitoring
- Rapid Response Teams
- Medication Expert Available to Team

During the transition from acute to ambulatory care, these areas should be top of mind:

- Medication Reconciliation (upon discharge)
- Patient Education
- Medication Affordability (prior insurance authorization or medication assistance programs)
- Discharge Medication Delivery

And within ambulatory care, areas of accountability concern are:

- Medication Reconciliation (see a theme here?)
- Disease State Management
- Population Health
- Annual Wellness Visits
- Refill Management
- Ongoing Patient Education
- Precision Medicine/Pharmacogenomics
- Medication Reimbursement

Operations	Acute Care Clinical Service
Dispensing & Workflow	Clinical Practice Model
IT & Robotics	Clinical Practice Standards/ Stewardship
Supply Chain & Procurement	Formulary Management/ Stewardship
Inventory Management	Pharmoeconomics
Centralized Compounding & Repackaging	Medication Safety
Sterile Compounding 797/800	Pharmacy Informatics/ Clinical Decision Support
Provider Clinic & Urgent Care Med Fulfillment	Pharmacy Education & Residency
Diversion Management	Quality & VBP Goals
Infusion Centers	Research

Scope of the Pharmacy Enterprise - Acute Care

While the focus of this particular section is services within acute care, keeping accountability in mind along the way will serve us well when discussing leadership and development in later chapters. Within acute care we'll spend time in both operations and clinical service opportunities. Here again is a good moment to remind ourselves of the scope of the pharmacy enterprise.

Within the pharmacy enterprise operations activities include dispensing and workflow, centralized compounding and repackaging, provider clinic and urgent care med fulfillment, as well as diversion management. Let's consider a possible innovation example for each of these areas. Remember that innovations can be either technology-related (which we'll cover in detail in a later chapter) or service-related.

So, when it comes to **dispensing and workflow**, the pharmacy enterprise can provide dedicated technicians to service nursing units and lighten their load with full services. Some health systems have nurses coming to the pharmacy to pick up meds or bring meds for labeling — is there a better way for pharmacy to take on this responsibility so nursing can focus on their areas. When we operate **centralized compounding and repackaging**, it will save time to create patient-specific doses so this doesn't need to be done later on in the workflow. Thinking beyond hospital clinics we can support provider clinics and **urgent care locations with med fulfillment**. We need to appropriately allocate our resources to service all clinics equally. This may mean having people on standby when unexpected requests arise. For **diversion management** we should advocate for pharmacy accountability in all things. We have a responsibility to lead reports and investigations as necessary. Another issue that often arises is **drug shortages**. In this we are positioned well to collaborate with physicians and other teams who this affects to find possible solutions.

Turning to clinical services, here are a few more examples of areas where pharmacy services have room for innovation:

- Clinical Services
  - Clinical Practice Model
  - Clinical Practice Standards and Stewardship
  - Formulary Management and Stewardship
  - Pharmacoeconomics
  - Pharmacogenomics
  - Medication Safety
  - Pharmacy Informatics and Clinical Decision Support
  - Pharmacy Education and Residency
  - Quality and Value Based Purchasing Goals
  - Research
  - Medication Reconciliation
- Roles
  - Pharmacists' Role
    - Insulin Management
    - Warfarin Dosing and Counseling
    - Refill Authorization
    - Pharmacogenomics
    - Emergency Department
  - Technicians' Role
    - Medication Histories
    - Sterile Products Room to Manage Final Check

The list could be endless, and we won't be able to go over every single possibility. But hopefully with these examples you can see how services and the services we can offer to support our organizations on the whole can be just as valuable as investing in technology. Offering and supporting through these services is yet another opportunity for our teams to be practicing at the top of their licenses.

When I think about pharmacy practice, there is also an opportunity for a **full model change**. As we talked earlier about what is a practice model, sometimes our model is not optimized. When we get to the right patient to pharmacist ratio, we don't necessarily need to worry about doing specific initiatives. Because we will have the right number of resources to maximize patient care for A to Z, soup to nuts, admission, to discharge — if we have the right number of team members to support that on the acute care side. Let's look at an example of full model transformation from Minnesota, at a large academic medical center. The hospital moved to a team-based integrated model where there was a lead for each kind of service line clinical team, a team of clinical pharmacists, as well as the decentralized techs that were responsible for all aspects of an individual patient's care. Whether it was order verification, med delivery, clinical services, drug information, formulary, regulatory, or quality, this team did it all. They'd created five clinical team leaders across their key service lines. This looks very positive and the nursing staff and providers at this hospital felt very supported. In this way pharmacy supports other clinical teams and both pharmacists and technicians have the opportunity to practice at the top of their license and challenge themselves daily.

Another topic that is important and, unfortunately, not yet maximized is **Age-Friendly Health Systems**. This is the term that's being used to promote this to patients and other team members. The American Hospital Association (AHA) has partnered with the Institute for Healthcare Improvement (IHI) and Catholic Health Association (CHA) to create an initiative around geriatrics and elder care support throughout our health systems.[109] Of course, medication is a primary topic around elder care so pharmacists should be involved with this initiative. There is a growing patient population that will be in need of these services as time moves on, and it is an initiative we should get ahead of so we don't arrive late to the party.

I want to wrap up this section around a few suggestions that ASHP has made for ways to extend the role of pharmacy students.[97] Within the Practice Advancement Initiative, it's recommended for pharmacy programs to allocate pharmacy student time to drug therapy management services, which can include antibiotic stewardship, anticoagulation monitoring, code blue participation, drug information, IV to PO conversion, fall consults, renal dose adjustments, therapeutic drug monitoring, and vaccine assessment and administration.

It's also recommended to include training for all pharmacy students on the roles of safety and quality in the medication-use process, which includes clarifying drug allergies, documenting adverse drug events, participating in quality improvement projects, performing audits, and conducting research. Finally, all pharmacy students should receive training regarding transitions of care that should cover medication history, medication reconciliation, patient counseling, meds-to-bed, prior authorization, discharge phone calls, and facilitating patient assistance programs. While it's difficult to complete all these changes at once, this should at least be on the minds of all our pharmacy training programs so they're moving in the right direction for training future pharmacists.

One last thing I'd like to point toward for your own future research is the recipients of PAI's Demonstration Grants. These folks were able to get grants through ASHP to document their initiatives and some are quite fascinating. Principal Investigator Pamela Moye, PharmD, worked on reducing the rate of hospital readmissions in heart failure patients, for example.[110] Other opportunities for pharmacy innovation are being explored by a journal titled Innovation in Pharmacy.[111] A few articles I've found of interest are those looking at integrating pharmacy students into marriage and family therapy, considering a pharmacist's role in a dental clinic, and the collaboration between emergency department doctors and pharmacists. I recommend the journal for further reading. Case studies in pharmacy innovation are available for you to read on your own time through the links available at the end of this chapter. It's important to spend time researching what's worked in other hospitals (and what challenges arose) to see what may be the best fit for your organization.

In summary, we learned there are many examples of acute care innovations to advance pharmacy practice. We can learn from all of these examples and how we might apply them to our practice.

Take Action Now

- Share in the Pharmovator Community what acute care innovation you're most interested in.

•••

Ambulatory Care Innovation

In this section, we'll learn about...
- Examples of Ambulatory Care Innovation

When we shift over to ambulatory care and reconsider the scope of pharmacy enterprise, we realize that it encompasses not only what we traditionally considered ambulatory care, but also touches on clinical services, some outpatient retail specialty pharmacy, and business and management pharmacy solutions. As we continue, keep in mind that these are interweaving elements that relate to ambulatory care.

Examples of Ambulatory Care Innovation

Outpatient Pharmacy	Ambulatory Care	Business & Managed Pharmacy Solutions
Outpatient/Retail	Clinic-Based Clinical Pharmacy Services	340B Program
Mail Order/Home Delivery	Clinic-Based Pharmacy Visits	Payer Population Health
Discharge Medication Delivery	Centralized Virtual Clinical Services	Payer Relationships
Specialty Pharmacy	Telehealth	Business Development
MTM/ Vaccines	Population Health	Pharmacy Benefit Manager (PBM) Shared or Integrated Models
Home Infusion - 503A	Pharmoeconomics	
Bulk Compounding - 503B	Employee Health/ Wellness Programs	
Patient Advocacy/ Medication Assistance		

Scope of the Pharmacy Enterprise - Ambulatory & Outpatient

While we'll spend most of our time dissecting ambulatory care clinical service innovation, there are definitely services that intersect and interact with other parts of a healthcare enterprise.

When I think about ambulatory models, I first consider the **service and delivery model** where we have both embedded pharmacist services like chronic disease management, joint medical appointments, target drug monitoring, medication reconciliation, and comprehensive medication reviews or **centralized pharmacist services**, which supports telemedicine, population health management, refill support, and medication assistance to name a few.

Another factor we need to consider in building out your ambulatory model is a numbers game. **Population and panel size**. We can think of it in two separate categories:

1. **Target populations**: For example, high risk patients, individual disease focus, specific medication focus, non-adherence to prescribed medications or poly-pharmacy. Each of these focuses may make sense for your team or your organization depending on what types of patients you see most. Consider all options.
2. **Patient Ratios or Panel Size**: What's typically possible now is approximately 1 pharmacist to every 3-7 providers, which is 8,000-25,000 possible patients, or 250-500 active patients/panel. Of course, we'd like these ratios to change for increased pharmacy coverage.

All of these aspects fit both within and without ambulatory care, so again, when we discuss ambulatory pharmacy, we should be mindful that strategies employed here could require collaboration with other departments or outside organizations.

In this discussion, we must also remember that our healthcare system primarily functions like a business. So when implementing innovative changes this must be part of how we present new services for approval.

The Ambulatory ROI chart on page 99 of this book lays out a myriad of ways to get creative with ways your services can start creating margin. Exploring these options will be particularly helpful on your journey to justify resources and create business plans supported by ROI. Services must be sustainable to continue to be offered, either on their own or through support from other services or departments. We can look at ways to save or avoid costs by reducing hospital readmissions, gain revenue by billing for new services, and so much more. While many people may see this as extra management, I look at opportunities like this as a win-win. Because what we're trying to do, ultimately, is find more ways to advance pharmacy practice through innovation. Remember, not every innovation has to be big and flashy!

Now, the APHA Foundation that we've discussed previously has a practice innovation website with a lot of initiatives that have been implemented over the years.[112] I want to make you aware of that resource as it's updated regularly and a great place to start so that again, you're not trying to reinvent the wheel. On the next page are some examples:

- Chronic Obstructive Pulmonary Disease
- Collaborative Practice Agreements
- Medication Therapy Management
- Oral Health Initiatives
- Osteoarthritis and Chronic Pain
- Patient Self-Management Credential
- PSMC and Value-Based Health Benefits Design Considerations in Patient-Centered Team-Based Care
- Pharmacogenomics
- Pharmacy's Appointment Based Model
- Project IMPACT: Immunizations
- IMPACT Care Transformation Institute

Luckily as well, there's also research to show the value of a pharmacist.[113,114] So it won't be difficult to prove your worth to those who may not already understand the worth of the pharmacy enterprise. Without going into too much detail I'll give you a few key places to start when you need backup and validation for your next initiatives. First are some examples from Virginia Commonwealth University, or VCU, where they provide initiatives and examples around their projects.

Virginia Commonwealth University (VCU) Center for Pharmacy Practice Innovation[105]:

- Project InnoVAte
    - Purpose: To design, test and evaluate evidence-based approaches to delivering clinical and community-based interventions aimed at reducing the risk, complications, and barriers to the prevention and control of diabetes and cardiovascular disease in underserved areas of Virginia
- Implementation and Evaluation of a 24-hour Ambulatory Blood Pressure Monitoring Service in Community Pharmacies
    - Purpose: To pilot a community pharmacy driven 24-hour ambulatory blood pressure monitoring service, develop a business model through which pharmacists are reimbursed for the service to ensure sustainability and reproducibility and explore patient, pharmacist, and physician perceptions of and satisfaction with the service
- Using Intervention Mapping to establish an outpatient Chronic Kidney Disease Anemia Clinic at VCU Health
    - Purpose: To develop and establish a pharmacist-run anemia clinic in the outpatient chronic kidney disease clinic at VCU Health using the Intervention Mapping framework

- Evaluating the impact of pharmacists on patient outcomes and quality of care provided in primary care clinics within the Bon Secours Medical Group
    - Purpose: To assess the impact of pharmacist services on patient outcomes and the achievement of quality measures in primary care clinics within the Bon Secours Medical Group
- Implementation of Outpatient Antibiotic Stewardship Core Elements in a Free Health Care Clinic
    - Purpose: To address inappropriate prescribing of antibiotics for urinary tract infections using a pharmacist-led antimicrobial stewardship program
- Pilot for a Community Pharmacy Incentivized-Care Model: Impact of Pharmacist Monitored Patient Blood Pressure Readings
    - Purpose: To improve ambulatory blood pressure measurement at a local community pharmacy using an incentivized care intervention.

Next are a few examples from the Institute for Innovative Pharmacy Practice out of Washington.

Institute for Innovative Pharmacy Practice (I2P2)[103]:

- The Gaps in Diabetes Care — Statins (GuIDE-S) Study
    - To compare the impact of usual care and a community pharmacist-led model of initiating and monitoring statin therapy.
- Project VACCINATE
    - Improve influenza, pneumococcal, pertussis, and herpes zoster immunization rates in adults.
- Direct Access Study
    - Pharmacist prescribing of hormonal contraceptives.

And finally, some examples out of Cedarville, where they have clinical pharmacist services and ambulatory care settings.

Innovation Research — Cedarville[104]:

- Project: Clinical pharmacist services in ambulatory care setting: Patients' and providers' satisfaction and impact on patient clinical outcomes
    - The long-term goal of this study is to support the continuing evolution of clinical pharmacist services. This project will assess both provider and patient satisfaction with clinical pharmacist services at a federally-qualified health center as well

as assess if there is a correlation between patient satisfaction of clinical pharmacist services and patient clinical outcomes related to services provided (diabetes, hypertension, hyperlipidemia, and anticoagulation). This assessment will provide an evaluation of pharmacist services and allow for improvement and expansion of services to best serve the clinic.

- Project: Opioid Pilot Project from the National Association of County and City Health Officials and the Centers for Disease Control and Prevention (NACCHO/CDC Opioid Pilot Project)
  - Dayton, Ohio, is at the epicenter of the current opioid crisis. While the state of this public health issue is constantly changing, changing prescription opioid prescribing patterns remains an important aim. In conjunction with Public Health of Dayton & Montgomery County, two student pharmacists were trained to provide academic detailing to physicians regarding evidence-based opioid prescribing practices. Following the training, the student pharmacists participated in piloting academic detailing calls and visits with physicians in Montgomery County, Ohio.
- Project: Regeneration — Preparing student pharmacists to educate youth about the dangers of prescription drug abuse
  - Given the opioid crisis and the need for pharmacists to address issues of abuse in the community, student pharmacists were trained using a team-based learning approach to educate youth on prescription drug abuse. Out of this training, student pharmacists then developed curriculum and went to schools and community groups to educate them on the dangers of prescription drug abuse.

In other words, there's an embarrassment of riches when it comes to how many opportunities for innovation we see in ambulatory care.

In summary, there are many examples of ambulatory care innovation to ensure continuity of care. Each of these examples will help us to better understand ambulatory care innovation.

Take Action Now

- Share in the Pharmovator Community what ambulatory care innovation you're most interested in.

•••

Non-Traditional Innovation

In this section, we'll learn about…
- Examples of Non-Traditional Innovation in Health Systems & Beyond

Before you start to make moves on your own project planning and idea brainstorming, I'd like to point to a few non-traditional innovation options. We'll consider non-traditional careers or unique roles that you may consider creating in your organization, some non-traditional services that you may wish to offer, or even non-pharmacy roles that can support the pharmacy enterprise.

Examples of Non-Traditional Innovation in Health Systems & Beyond

Here is an incomplete list of areas where pharmacists currently work in the United States from Pharmacy Times[115]:

- Academia: Clinical Practice
- Academia: Economic, Social, and Administrative Sciences (ESAS)
- Academia: Pharmacy Sciences
- Ambulatory Care
- **Association Management**
- Chain Community Pharmacy: Management
- Clinical Specialists
- **Community Health Center (CHC)**
- Compounding Pharmacy
- **Contract Research Organization**
- **Corporate Management**
- Government/Federal Pharmacy
- Home Health Care
- Health System Pharmacy: Inpatient
- Health System Pharmacy: Outpatient
- Independent Community Pharmacy
- Long Term Care
- Mail Service
- Managed Care
- Medical Communications/ Drug Information
- Nuclear Pharmacy
- **Office-based Medication Management**
- Pharmacy Industry: Medical Liaison
- Pharmacy Industry: Research and Development (R&D)
- Pharmacy Industry Sale and Marketing
- Pharmacy Benefit Management (PBM)
- **Pharmacy Law/Regulatory Affairs/Public Policy**
- Specialty Pharmacy
- **Entrepreneur**
- **Consultant**

Some of these may be familiar or obvious to you and some may be things you'd not considered before, and I've highlighted some more **non-traditional & unique roles**. For example, I currently work as a management consultant, helping pharmacy enterprises expand their vision and mindset and get what they need on a certain project. And if you choose an entrepreneur path you can work in a variety of settings. I even have a friend who works for NASA as a pharmacist. Not exactly where you'd expect a "Pharmacist Wanted" sign in the window, but there you have it. Pharmacists are needed and can serve in a variety of non-traditional roles across many sectors of the workforce. When we're thinking about how we can advocate for more pharmacy services, are these areas where we can expand and grow and then later have a bigger impact?

Let's also consider some **non-traditional services** a pharmacist or pharmacy enterprise might consider offering:

- Pharmacogenomics
- Nutrigenomics
- Functional Medicine
- Wellness Coach
- Health and Fitness Coach
- Medication Access
- Patient Advocate/care Navigator
- Public Health
- And more!

A big trend in these non-traditional services are in preventative care, health and wellness. While medications are cost effective, we ideally want to keep people off of medication and what better way to do that, then helping people be proactive in their health.

Or **non-pharmacy roles within the health systems**. Creating one or more of these roles within your team can bring in outsiders with a fresh perspective that may benefit the enterprise.

- Service Line Leader/Administrator
- Patient Safety/Quality/Healthcare Improvement
- Value/Care Transformation
- Patient Experience
- Information Technology
- Strategy & Innovation
- Business Development
- Integration - Mergers & Acquisitions
- Compliance/Regulatory
- Government Relations

- Education & Training
- Chief Operating Officer
- Research

There are countless examples and ideas of non-traditional innovation both within pharmacy and the pharmacy enterprise and outside of traditional health systems. Your next career move, and the sector which you serve is entirely up to you. The skills of a pharmacy leader are needed all over the place!

In summary, there are many examples of non-traditional innovation in health systems and beyond. It's worth exploring each one, the more information we have the better.

Take Action Now

- Brainstorm exciting non-traditional pharmacy roles.

Planning & Tracking

In this section, we'll look at...

- Planning for Services
- Tracking Implemented Services

Now we'll begin to move into the planning and tracking section of this chapter. We'll discuss planning for services that you wish to implement and the necessary tracking of those services once they're in place. Briefly, the tools you will use for planning & tracking by phase are:

- Planning for Services
  - Situational Analysis – New Services
  - Service Planning Worksheet – FTE & Business Plan Needs
- Implementation/Execution
  - Project Plan (See Chapter 9)
- Tracking Implemented Services
  - Project Plan Milestones
  - Choose Metrics
  - Create a Visual Scorecard for Reporting

Planning for Services

Before implementing any new services (or even significantly updating services already offered) there should come a planning period. You and your team need time for situational analysis and detailing what new services will be offered and how. Included at the end of this chapter is a link for extra resources which includes both a service planning worksheet and a scorecard, which I'll mention shortly. I offer them both as valuable tools for you to download and use to guide both the planning and tracking of new services in your organization. Here's what you'll find for the service planning resource:

Category	Service / Area	RPHs	Tech	ROI	Business Plan RX or IDN
Clinical Program Growth / Service Line Expansion					
Requested Pharmacy Services					
PAI / Pharmacy Initiated					
Internal FTE Analysis					
TOTAL					
Services to Stop		(-)	(-)		
		(-)	(-)		
NET TOTAL					

Service Planning Worksheet

The categories that I like to look at in terms of really understanding if you have enough resources to do something are shown on the left. You want to understand if your organization is growing and has planned **clinical program growth or service line expansion**. And in the case study next, we'll definitely walk through this in a specific example. A common example that we see these days is a lot of growth in oncology service lines or even neurology or geriatrics. And at the same time you want to understand where they may be closing down services as well, which you can capture at the bottom of the worksheet.

You then want to include areas of **requested pharmacy services**. This defines the services you have not been able to provide because of a lack of resources. For example, the Emergency Services would like a pharmacist on all shifts to be based in the emergency department.

Then there are those services that you have identified that are **practice advancement initiative** related or department initiated. Like you decide that there's a need based on all of the things we've talked about, maybe it's pharmacogenomics or a new area, opioid stewardship, maybe those are things that you have not been able to address.

Finally, you want to complete your **FTE analysis**. Are you right-sized? Do you have enough resources to address the needs of the populations that you're already serving? Or is there some room for excess? As we've talked about, when it comes to service planning, you want to think about whether you can reallocate resources that you have. Perhaps you have to stop doing something to create capacity and that can be captured at the bottom and subtract the FTE.

Perhaps you have found efficiencies within your practice, and you can add new services with existing capacity. You may also identify that you are not resourced for existing services and need to justify resources. That's why in this template, you'll capture all of these areas.

You'll then capture how many pharmacy techs and pharmacists that would be needed for the service. You'll indicate if there is a return on investment? Yes or no. And then whether or not you need a business plan and indicate if it's pharmacy or for the broader IDN scope. For example, if your health system is growing in the area of oncology, you can add pharmacy resources to that overall oncology business plan and you don't have to write your own separate business plan. That is key. And it's definitely a recommendation mentioned in the business planning section of Chapter 4.

The final step of the worksheet is to sum the resources required. The caveat here is that there may be economies of scale. For example, adding a pharmacy-initiated service that can also help with the service line expansion. Get the numbers on paper and then see where your resources can fill multiple needs, and especially look at the ROI in the business plan as they will more likely be approved.

Tracking Implemented Services

A part of the planning stage should also be choosing target metrics. You'll need to gather data on the current metrics that exist within your organization before implementing change so you're able to compare how the new services work vs. the previous services offered.

With these target metrics you can choose which metrics to report to leadership and staff. Some of them can be just for you. Not everything must be reported to higher ups as too many metrics can be overwhelming. It's best to collect more data than you need then choose what's beneficial to pass on. Keep in mind financial metrics, as you will likely need to include these in any business plans you put together.

Additionally, remember that it's often wise to suggest a ramp up of services over a period of time so that change is implemented in stages instead of all at once. The adjustment can be easier on team members, leadership, and patients this way. Keep this in mind and make sure not to over commit. You know, one of my mottoes is under promise and over deliver. Of course we want to be aggressive with our business plans. And of course we want to get things approved, but it does not help anybody if we can't achieve those targets. Keep this in mind and be realistic when ramping up.

These are some examples, again, of the common buckets we'll see in business plans from clinical practice:

- Clinical Pharmacy Practice
  - Patient to Pharmacist Ratio
  - Orders Verified Per Pharmacist Per Hour
  - Medication Reconciliation Capture and Discrepancies
  - PAI Score
- Medication Safety
  - Medication Error Reporting
  - % of Doses Compounding with IV Workflow Solution
- Human Resources
  - Associate Engagement
  - Technician Turnover
- Financial
  - Drug Expense Line Item Budget
  - Target Drug Budget
  - Drug Spend Per Bed Per Day
  - FTE Budget
  - Patient Visits and Billed Encounters

Use the Scorecard Worksheet to document the planned metrics for your business plan performance tracking. There is an example of what it will look like in the next page.

Because you can pretty much put any measure you want into this scorecard, it's a great way to capture metrics. While we don't have time to go into all the different types of dashboards and scorecards, I do want to point out how in this one you'll assign a threshold target and a maximum goal then color code within your various time frames to show where you are in relation to your goal. The chart above is also the one you can download for your own use with the link at the end of the chapter.

MEASURE	THRESHOLD	TARGET	MAX	20XX Q1	20XX Q2	20XX Q3	20XX Q4

Scorecard Worksheet

MEASURE	THRESHOLD	TARGET	MAX	20XX	20XX
Weekday	43:1	30:1	25:1		
Evening/Weekend					
Weekday	50	40	30		
Evening/Weekend	60	50	40		
% Units Covered	50%	75%	100%		
% Units Rounding/Team	25%	50%	75%		
% Units Covered	65%	75%	85%		
% Units Rounding/Team	25%	50%	75%		
% Units Rounding/Team	30%	40%	50%		

Key for Metric Result: Below Threshold | Threshold | Target | Max

Scorecard Worksheet - PAI Metrics Acute Care

Then, when presenting metrics to leadership you can choose to share this document directly or translate it into a graph. I often find graphs to be helpful for those who aren't in pharmacy and appreciate having the information translated into a familiar shape, like a bar or line graph. The key overall is to show how you compare to the targets planned. Just showing numbers is not a scorecard and is a big pet peeve of mine, as the reader does not know if the number is good or bad and if you are achieving your goal or not.

The chart on the bottom of the previous page is an example of how some PAI metrics for acute care services were recorded.

Now, what should the frequency of your reporting be? It will be a little bit based on the metric and the frequency that it changes. There may be things you have to track on a weekly basis and others that are best tracked monthly. Other metrics may only be gathered quarterly, or even bi-annually or annually, depending on your specific area. So whether it's the patient to pharmacist ratio, the orders verified per pharmacist, or looking at the actual self assessment score, you want to have those metrics captured, especially if you're comparing them to general metrics like the standards set by ASHP.

In summary, planning for services includes taking the situational analysis and service planning to identify FTEs and business plans needed. When tracking services that have been implemented this will include creating project plan milestones and putting identified metrics into a visual scorecard to communicate the success (hopefully!) of the new services to stakeholders.

Take Action Now

- Identify the metrics that you will commit to and monitor for the execution of your new service.

•••

Case Study

In this section, we'll explore a…
- Community Health System Case Study

Community Health System Case Study

As we bring this chapter to a close, I'd like to share a quick case study with you about the journey to justify resources for service practice advancement in a community health system.

The journey is in the five steps:

1. Strategic Planning
2. FTE Analysis
3. Business Plans
4. ROI
5. Approval!

1. Strategic Planning

Here is my Service Planning Worksheet in action:

Category	Service / Area	RPHs	Tech	ROI	Business Plan RX or IDN
Clinical Program Growth / Service Line Expansion	Oncology	3	3		IDN
	Cardiology	2	2		IDN
Requested Pharmacy Services	Medication Reconciliation	5	10	Soft	Rx
	Pharmacogenomics	1	1	TBD	IDN
PAI / Pharmacy Initiated	Formulary Stewardship	3	3	Yes	Rx
Internal FTE Analysis	Acute Care - Below Benchmarks	8	22		
	Ambulatory Care - Anticoagulation Only	TBD			
TOTAL					
Services to Stop	None	(-)	(-)		
NET TOTAL					

Service Planning Worksheet

In the clinical program growth and service line expansion category, not surprising, was oncology and cardiology. As a new pharmacy leader, I was requested to improve the med reconciliation process. Excitingly, the health system was also already working in the area of pharmacogenomic and requested support under the precision medicine initiative. From a PAI and pharmacy-initiated area, I was definitely looking at formulary stewardship. The formulary was open with limited cost containment and optimization. This area could be a great practice advancement and source of ROI.

The FTE analysis is documented here in the worksheet and the steps to determine this result are summarized next. Needs were identified for ambulatory care to expand services beyond anticoagulation, but it was decided to create a separate plan for that.

No services were identified to stop, and we were really just looking to add. When you add up the number of pharmacists and techs needed with the initiatives, it looks like a ton of resources. But there are definitely some economies of scale. For example, resources for Oncology would potentially help support the service needs for med reconciliation, et cetera. So, there is some overlaps, but ultimately there was still a big need.

And then the question was, was there return on investment for these? Med reconciliation is definitely a tough one. As we've talked about, it's a great topic, but your end points tend to be more soft in terms of your return on investment. It can be harder to tie a specific length of stay reduction or reduce readmission to these activities. Pharmacogenomics has a potential ROI through soft endpoints, but also through billable services for clinic encounters. There were savings for formulary stewardship related to optimizing the medications utilized.

From a business plan perspective, many of these initiatives were actually under the delivery network because they were expanding in these areas with oncology, cardiology as well as pharmacogenomics.

2. FTE Analysis

Then we looked at our internal FTE analysis on the acute care side. We were below benchmarks, so there was a need to add resources there. With these aims in mind, we moved forward with a more thorough systematic approach with PAI inputs. Our systematic assessment approach had five steps:

1. Complete Hospital Assessment
2. Review Assessment Result
3. Prioritize Action Items
4. Evaluate Peer Comparison
5. Formulate Action Plan
6. Implement Change

To support the process, we conducted a PAI workshop with staff which included a before and after survey on knowledge of PAI and a few breakout sessions so everyone on the team could help design the practice model change. The breakouts included workflow prioritization, practicing at the top of your license, practice model, and scheduling. This was extremely helpful for getting everyone on the same page and to understand the information and planning process behind the new model and services we planned to implement.

It's a mistake to wait until implementation to involve the entire team in a new service or other change (like we talked about in Change Management). This will catch people off-guard, make them feel ambushed, and generally feel negatively towards whatever is coming. Soften the blow, prepare the landing, involve people earlier on so their voices can be heard, and their opinions can be part of the decision-making process. This doesn't mean you have to take every suggestion from every first-year pharmacy tech on the team, but it does give the team a place to gather and unite around change instead of it seemingly springing up out of nowhere.

We continued on with our FTE analysis and time and motion study results, as you can see here:

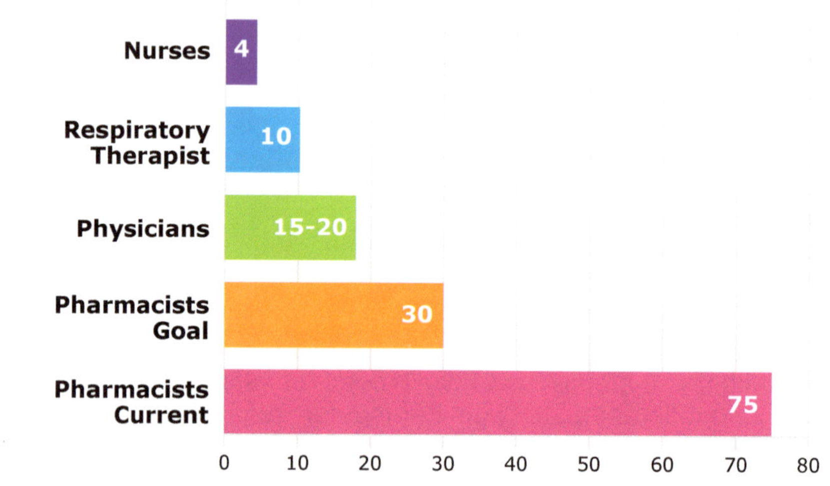

FTE Analysis Patient-Healthcare Provider Ratios[116]

This was a typical health system where each pharmacist was taking care of about 75 patients when our target would be closer to 30 to support comprehensive care. The labor benchmark compared to other health systems ranged from less than 25th-35th percentile. While lower can demonstrate major efficiency, it also can mean you don't have enough resources to do advanced services.

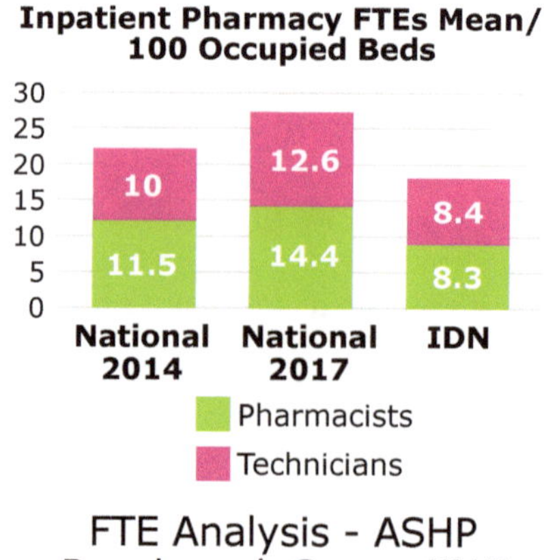

FTE Analysis - ASHP Benchmark Survey[116,117]

We also looked at the ASHP benchmark survey, which looks at the number of FTEs per hundred beds. It can be found on the bottom of the previous page. This IDN was below both surveys in terms of the number of pharmacists and technicians. I think it's important to note that the jump from 2015 to 2017 was postulated by the researchers to be due to advanced practice initiatives such as med reconciliation and antimicrobial stewardship.

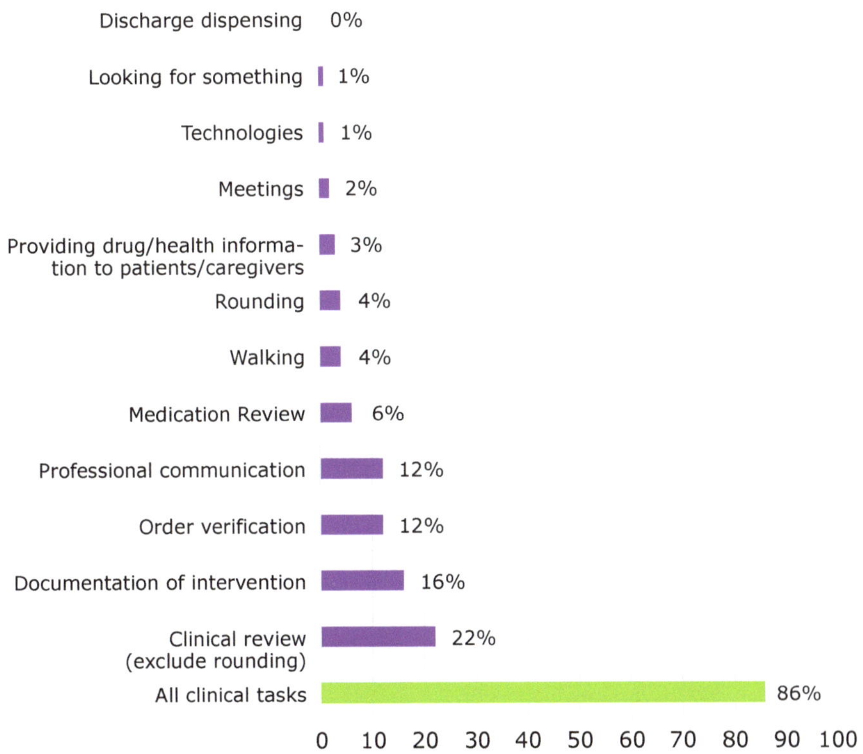

Time & Motion Study Results[118]

The time and motion study was conducted to really understand if there were opportunities for efficiencies and to ensure top of license practice and identify technology needs.

We then created a business plan using a practice model justification. It broke down into two buckets of things we'd like to implement: right size (nothing over the top) and practice advancement (moving in the right direction).

- Right Size:
    - Increase Order Volume & Patient Acuity

- Decrease Autoverification
- Indirect Days Not Budgeted
    - Education Days
    - Committee Involvement
- STD/FMLA
- Vacancy
- Overtime & Working Above Boarded Hours

- Practice Advancement:
    - Goals: to improve patient to pharmacist ratio, to allow pharmacists to be an integral part of the care team, and to be accountable for patient medication outcomes.
    - Additional Activities Possible
        - Medication Reconciliation
        - Team Rounds
        - Antimicrobial Stewardship
        - Counseling High Risk Patients
        - Available Resource to entire team
        - Unit Initiatives

So, these were our goals, we now have something concrete to work toward, but there's a long way to go yet before implementation. Getting to these specific goals requires us to look at a more general goal achievement plan that's applicable across the pharmacy enterprise.

Like this:

Getting to Goal

3. Business Plans

Using these guiding principles WITH the specifics we outlined above, a pharmacy business plan may look something like this:

Business Plan Name	Category	Description
Acute Care Pharmacy Business Plan	Pharmacy Practice Advancement & Service Line Support	Expand clinical practice model for pharmacists to be part of team & advance technology support
	Medication Reconciliation	Establish pharmacy assisted medication history and reconciliation
	Medication Cost Management	Med use optimization & formulary restrictions, Med Assistance Program
Ambulatory/ Outpatient Pharmacy Business Plan	Specialty Pharmacy	Establish accredited SP program and increase volume of RXs filled
	Ambulatory Clinical Pharmacy Services	Disease State Management / Population Health with face to face or telehealth visits with RPH
	Associate Health	Optimize medications to reduce admissions and decrease cost. PBM Analysis
HR Pharmacy Plans	Management Restructure	Restructure & align leadership team to support transformational pharmacy goals.
	Vacancy Coverage "Float Pool"	Expand FTE RPH & Tech to cover vacancy
	Technician Training Program	Establish an inhouse or partnership accredited tech training program.
Infusion Center	Infusion Center Optimization	
Innovative Growth Business Plans	Outpatient Pharmacy Expansion	
	Integrated Service Center (Mail Order, Home Infusion 503a)	

Pharmacy Business Plans

There's a business plan template available for you to download at the end of this chapter. When filling it out make sure to use the standard sections but also supplement with the additional sections desired by your organization that may include:

- Mission Alignment
- Market Analysis
- Risk of Adopting the Project
- Qualitative Analysis
- Assumptions
- Qualitative Score

Without any of these elements, remember that a business plan will be incomplete. You'll need to return to the research and planning stage.

4. ROI

Returning to the case study, during our research and planning phase, we considered more than 20 different strategies for medication cost management from ASHP, as discussed in ROI section of Chapter 4.

Presenting a myriad of strategies can be helpful to stakeholders so they understand that you're willing to approach an issue from several angles in order to make it successful. It also sets up expectations so it's understood that the first attempt may not be successful. But if at first you don't succeed — *say it with me* — try, try again!

5. Approval

We also, of course, included the ROI summary.

Cost Management	Savings	Pharmacy Restructure & Business Plan Allocation	Cost
Medication Use Optimization	**$XXX,XXX**	**Technician Market Analysis**	**$XXX,XXX**
Purchasing	**$XXX,XXX**	**Management Restructure**	**$XXX,XXX**
Inventory Management	**$XXX,XXX**	**Business Plan New Positions & Technology**	**$XXX,XXX**
Waste Reduction	**$XXX,XXX**		
Reimbursement	**$XXX,XXX**	**Total**	**$300,000**
Optimization	**$4,500,000**	**Net ROI**	**$1,500,000**

Acute Care Business Plan Return on Investment (ROI)

You see here that we've made it an obvious decision for the stakeholders to make. It's almost a no-brainer. When implementing our cost management strategies, we'll save $4.5 million and our project only costs $3 million. So it's an easy $1.5 million in return. You must spend planning time on finding ways to SAVE money in addition to pricing out how much changes you're planning will cost. Present a business plan with solutions, not with more problems for leadership to solve.

The Extra Step: Tracking

Upon approval, it is important you track and report your progress. We broke down the resource allocation of the 25 added FTEs and how they supported the identified needs and goals.

The fiscal benefits of a business plan will be a primary performance measure in most cases. Healthcare functions as a business. We can't forget that! For this plan, performance was monitored through

Support Category	Actions Taken
Expansion of Service Lines	Addition of 1 oncology coordinator and 2 emergency department pharmacists
Practice Model Optimization	Expansion of pharmacy residency program, from 6 PGY1s to 12 PGY1s and 5 PGY2s, to restructure for more optimal pharmacist-to-patient ratio. Dedicated resident run services.
Medication Reconciliation	Addition of Medication History Technicians to assist pharmacists in acute care transitions
Leadership Support	Leadership expansion with pharmacists coordinators and technician supervisors
System-wide Float Coverage	Addition of cross- site pharmacists and technicians for better Family and Medical Leave (FMLA) and education days coverage

Business Plan Resource Allocation[118]

reductions in the drug budget shown here as a normalized percentage of the drug budget. While FTE expenses increased by 2%, the additional drug budget reductions equated to 2.9%. This yielded a positive ROI while also advancing services.

As I mentioned in the strategic planning phase, PAI was our north star. These were at the top of our minds as we decided what we wanted to ask for and which direction the project should take. We not only looked within the organization for what their specific needs were, but also took guidance from the wider world of healthcare and the need for pharmacy advancement itself.

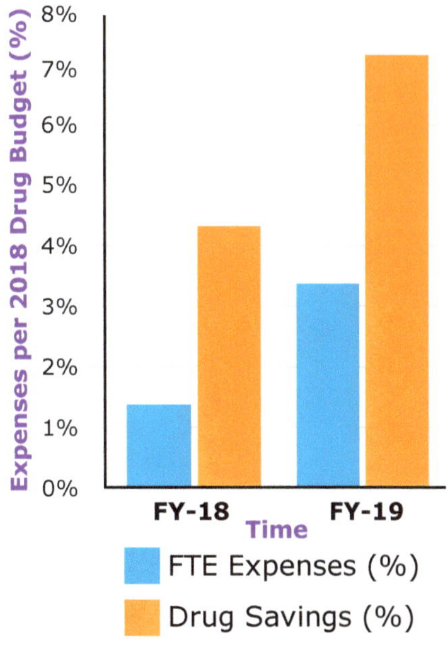

Net ROI[118]

Some of the specific PAI initiatives that this health system was able to implement as a result of their business plans are shown here:

Objectives	Tactics
Clinical Practice Standardization	-EHR Workflow/Documentation Standardization -Acuity Scoring -Activity Prioritization -Scheduling/Shift Optimization -Hospitalist Rounding
Service Line Support/ Expansion	-Oncology -Heart Failure/LVAD -Pulmonary/Adult ECMO -Emergency Departments -Primary Care & Specialty Clinics
Medication Reconciliation	-Admission -Discharge -Ambulatory
Residency Expansion	-PGY1 -PGY2
Students	-Intern Program -APPE Student Optimization Including Pend Function
Precision Medicine	-Pharmacogenomic Testing w/ EHR Integration -Pharmacogenomic Clinic -Precision Oncology
Patient Experience	-Quiet at Night -Medication Education
Operations PAI	-Staffing Workflow & Tech Check Tech

Department PAI Objectives & Tactics

In summary of this entire chapter — and it's been a big one! — it's important for us to know how to justify resources for service practice advancement. It may take time, but the results will advance your career as well as your pharmacy practice. The best and most effective way to do so is to use a systematic approach that encompasses the needs of both the pharmacy enterprise and the greater organization, as well as — of course — keeping all plans patient-centered.

Take Action Now

- Continue to work on your draft business plan with the Business Plan Template from the previous chapter. (Didn't download it yet? Available below with the link or QR code!)

To support you incorporating the learnings from this chapter, access the Pharmovation Implementation Guide. Visit www.pharmovationguide.com or scan the QR code below for full access!

Chapter 6

Pharmovation TECHNOLOGY

"Technological innovation is indeed important to economic growth and the enhancement of human possibilities."
—Leon Kass, American Educator

In the 90's I was a student extern working at a hospital and the electronic health record was a brand new idea. A large chunk of my time in that position was spent working on a project that was twofold. First, we'd manually enter in all the patient medication history we already had documented. For new patients, we created a standardized form for patient history. This form included a section on medication history where we relied solely on the patient's memory to let us know what medications they were currently taking PLUS any medications they'd taken regularly in the past. Sometimes looking at what had been filled out later, it was clear the patient had misremembered their dosage, so we'd call pharmacies around town trying to verify what the proper dose was.

If that wasn't enough, once a patient filled out the form on paper, a pharmacist would review it and enter it into the system. These were the early days, and it was clunky to say the least. It wasn't easy to update, and it was incredibly difficult (if not at times impossible) to search for things within forms. Looking for trends was a nightmare.

I tell that story to orient us. Look how far we've come in a few decades!

But before we get too celebratory. Consider this: If I wake up in the middle of the night and think, "Oo, I need to get a haircut!" I can reach for my phone, get on my hairdresser's website, and book an appointment. It's that easy.

Technology has come a long way. Pharmacy care hasn't come as far as technology can go. There are a myriad of opportunities for pharmacy to take advantage of the wealth that's available in this golden age of technology.

Some people fear technology because they're afraid they'll lose their jobs as the robots take over. But research doesn't show this to be true. Technology makes us more efficient. It allows us to do the things we're meant to do and outsource the grunt work, the things we don't like. We are able to practice at the top of our licenses and capacity. Adopting technology and optimizing it to its maximum potential is part of this. Technology gives a wider capacity to serve more patients. Technology is nothing to fear. It is a resource we should be utilizing at every possible opportunity.

The goal of this chapter is to help you do just that: feel empowered to justify new technology to meet both your team's and your patient's needs. We'll start with some background and groundwork related to technology and innovation, discuss ways to apply new technologies in acute care, ambulatory care, personal applications, and patient technology. Then we'll wrap it all up with a case study.

Let's dive in.

Technology Innovation

SECTION PREVIEW | SECTION PREVIEW

In this section, we'll review...

- Background on Technology Innovation
- Pharmacy Strategy for Technology

Background on Technology Innovation

First off, don't panic when you hear the word disrupt again. We set it to the side a bit in the last chapter but it's time to bring it back into the conversation. There are quite a few technological predictions that will disrupt healthcare. When I say "disrupt," I mean in the sense of disruptive innovation, not that care will be interrupted or stalled. *Forbes Magazine* publishes a list each year that predicts which innovations will have the greatest impact on healthcare. While we won't go through the list exhaustively, it's enough to point out that these predictions are riddled with technology with artificial intelligence, digital health, data analytics, voice applications, interoperability, blockchain and precision medication being some of the key topics.[119,120]

We also need to consider the contributions of start-up initiatives[121] such as...

- **Mobile Health (mHealth)**: Mobile devices enable services like remote-monitoring, e-visits, and e-prescribing. This has resulted in a momentous change in patient behavior, improves outcomes and reduces costs.

- **3D Printing**: Prosthetics and dental implants and even personalized pills have already been printed successfully.
- **3D Imaging, Virtual Reality (VR)**: Increases the current state of physicians to view organs and tissue via scan. Leads to better precision as surgeons are able to see organs accurately. Reduces eye fatigues during operations.
- **Wearables**: Analyzes a patient's health status. Bio-sensing wearables monitor glucose levels, blood pressure and more.
- **Robotics**: More time available to medical professionals to replace the movements of manual work. Applications range from robotic arms for amputees to micro-robots repairing damage from the inside.
- **Artificial Intelligence (AI)**: Allows physicians to determine a patient's disease by analyzing their face, skin, etc. Transforms big data into actionable insights. Offers a range of applications from chatbots providing diagnostics to help physicians automate image-based diagnostics.
- **Big Data**: Enables the identification of risk factors, patient behavior and early signs of disease or illness.
- **Internet of Medical Things**: Plays a key role in facilitating the implementation of future health practices such as diagnostics and condition monitoring. Connected devices used for diagnostics, (remote) monitoring, and location systems.

We could go on for days. And it's clear that innovative technology covers a wide variety of areas in healthcare. To simplify, we'll further divide technological advancements in healthcare into four quadrants: infrastructure, payment models, care models, and disease management.[122]

- Technology Infrastructure
    - Population Health Solutions
    - Care Coordination
    - Readmission Management
    - Referral Management
    - Analytics
- Payment Models
    - Chronic Care Management/Transitional Care Management
    - ACO Enablement
    - Bundled Payments
    - Transparency
- Care Coordination
    - Telemedicine
    - Consumer Tools
    - Risk-Bearing Provers
    - On Demand Healthcare

    - Post Acute Care
    - Second Opinion
- Disease Management
    - Medication Adherence
    - Health Optimization/Wellness
    - Diabetes
    - Behavioral Health
    - Other Disease Management

All of these quadrants are key areas of investment. There's a lot of innovation and a lot of investment happening. It's an extremely exciting time.

I like to boil it down another way as well when I'm looking at a new technology opportunity. Is it **automation** or is it **analytics**? Is it automating practices we already have in place or is it analyzing data more quickly and in new ways? Ultimately, these are the two things we want to be doing with technology. These two factors allow us to have higher rates of safety and efficiency in the work we do in pharmacy. Again, we want to embrace this and not be fearful of it. True leadership doesn't fear technology. We know it will make us more efficient and allow both ourselves and our teams to practice at the top of our licenses and find more joy in our work.

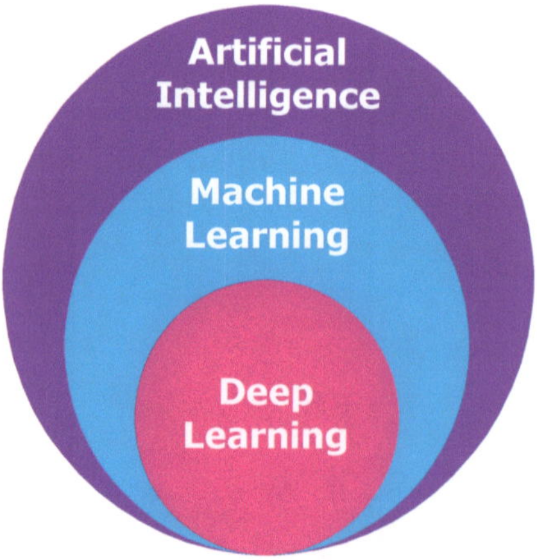

Artificial Intelligence Definitions

Let's talk a bit more about artificial intelligence. This is a really broad term that encompasses a lot of areas so we should define it a bit. Simply put, intelligence is the ability to learn and solve problems.[123] Then we have artificial intelligence (AI) which is defined as any technology which enables computers to mimic human behavior.[124] Within AI we have a subcategory called Machine Learning (ML). ML employs AI techniques which use statistical methods to enable machines to improve with their experiences.[125] With ML the computer is learning through information that's inputted so it can, over time, make better decisions. Even further down the AI rabbit hole we have Deep Learning (DL). DL is a subset of ML which makes computation of multi-layer neural networks feasible.[126] Basically DL gets into more complex tasks than ML has the capacity to do.

A few ways AI technologies are being implemented in the healthcare field are predictive analytics, translation, speech, expert systems, planning, scheduling and optimization, robotics, image recognition and machine vision.[127] There are also a myriad of healthcare startup companies with an AI focus that range from imaging, diagnostics, drug discovery, predictive analytics, risk scoring, genomics, hospital decision support, remote monitoring, clinical trials and even virtual assistants and compliance initiatives.[128] Many of the same ways you see AI showing up in your everyday life translate seamlessly into the healthcare field. It is easy to see how ubiquitous AI is becoming.

Pharmacy Strategy for Technology

But how do we see AI showing up in the pharmacy enterprise specifically?

We're seeing...

- More collaboration across many different entities serving the same patient
- Improved workflow efficiency and lower operating costs while promoting safety, accuracy, and efficiency
- Automated dispensing
- Health management centers instead of only medication fulfillment locations
- Personalized healthcare offerings including advice, guidance, and an expanded suite of services
- Growth in the availability of health-related data from personal and healthcare-related devices and records
- Development of pharmacogenomics and gene databases
- Drug discovery
- Clinical trials
- Specialty medication management

In short, we're seeing increases in efficiency gained throughout organizations. These are the catalysts which enable pharmacists (and other clinicians) to devote more time to providing personalized, detailed, high-touch care to their patients.[129]

The American Journal of Health-System Pharmacy has an article from 2019 that identifies ML as the most important subset of AI to pharmacy. It also discusses its future in the pharmacy field.[130]

They foresee ML supporting pharmacy in the following 5 ways[130]:

- Drug Product Decisions Using Pharmacy-Related Images
- Decisions to Treat

- Drug Selection Doses
- Dosing Decisions
- Inventory Management Decisions

They also recommend five things pharmacy leaders can do to prepare for machine learning and other AI occurring in health system pharmacy[130]:

- Engage
- Study
- Prioritize
- Collaborate
- Share

These aren't as simple as they appear at first glance. In order to **engage** with technology, we must have an appropriate balance of skepticism and open-mindedness. We'll have to learn about new topics and raise issues when we spot them, as well as point out opportunities that exist to the leadership of our organization. Plus, we have to **study** to know how it all works and get exposed to new tools to understand how to analyze key aspects of the new data we can obtain. After that we must make technology implementation a **priority** for our organization, which will require **collaboration** outside of just our pharmacy team. This will help us aggregate enough reliable data, analyze it, and understand it. We can do this through statewide, regional, and national networks. And through that collaboration we move seamlessly into the final recommendation: **share**. Share our successes and our challenges so that others who come after us can implement technology more easily and effectively.

But new technology doesn't just show up on your doorstep, although I wish it would! We've got to advocate and justify expenditures to those with the purse strings. You'll revisit situational analyses you've conducted previously, including the enterprise assessment and forecasts with an eye on technology. Please find the Technology Planning Worksheet, another useful template I've created for you, as a download through the link available at the end of this chapter. You'll find this is similar to the Service Planning Worksheet from Chapter 5.

You're going to include:

- What are your technology needs?
- What is the cost? (And note Capital or Operating Expense)
- Is it going to replace existing technology or allow you to retire existing technology?
- Is there a return on investment?
- Is it included in a business plan?

CATEGORY	TECHNOLOGY NEED	COST	TECHNOLOGY TO REPLACE/ RETIRE	ROI	BUSINESS PLAN RX OR IDN
Clinical Program Growth / Service Line Expansion					
Requested Pharmacy Technology					
PAI / Pharmacy Initiated					
TOTAL					
Technology to Replace / Retire		(-)			
		(-)			
NET TOTAL					

Technology Planning Worksheet

I want to highlight for you the sections that are both in the ASHP PAI 2030 and the ASHP forecast that focuses on the topic of technology. You can find that chart on the next page.

When you look further into this topic, you'll see that analytics and automation are the key topics where artificial intelligence is mentioned. Using health information technologies, advanced machine learning, emerging patients care technologies, wearable devices, health information technology, virtual pharmacy services, and more, should be a priority. We should keep these technologies in mind while creating business plans and deciding where to invest in the future of pharmacy. It's vital that we advocate for these technologies and, when doing so, we may need to add people to support the technology as well. We want to make sure we have access to an analytics resource either within our own department or through a partnership with a separate department or outside organization.

Training ourselves to advocate effectively for innovative technology within our organizations is an incredibly useful skill because we know how technology can be used in almost endless applications throughout healthcare. There are so many opportunities available, and this is especially true within pharmacy. We should always be exploring and learning about new ways for pharmacy to integrate technology into our practice.

In summary, we learned that technology innovation is vast and offers many possibilities, and that there are multiple areas for pharmacy to embrace technology innovation.

ASHP PAI 2030

C1. Pharmacists should **use health information technologies** to advance their role in patient care and population health.

C2. Pharmacy practice leaders should foster the development and application of **advanced analytics** (e.g., machine learning and artificial intelligence) in activities such as risk assessment, monitoring performance metrics, identifying patients in need of pharmacist care, optimizing medication use, and business management.

C3. Pharmacy practice leaders should be engaged in assessing **emerging patient care technologies** (e.g., mobile applications, monitoring devices, digital wearables or ingestables, blockchain technology) to support optimal medication use outcomes.

C4. The pharmacy workforce should be competent in **health information technology** (including but not limited to analytics, automation, and clinical applications of technology) with ongoing education and training embedded at all stages of career development.

C5. **Virtual pharmacy services** (e.g., telepharmacy) should be deployed to optimize operational and clinical services that extend patient care services and enhance continuity of care.

C6. The pharmacy enterprise must have **sufficient resources** to develop, implement, and maintain technology-related medication-use safety standards.

C7. Pharmacy departments should have **access to an analytics resource**, such as a data scientist, to collect, aggregate, measure, visualize, and disseminate data related to the financial and clinical performance of pharmacists.

C8. Pharmacy departments should use technology to ensure the **safe compounding of sterile products**.

C10. Pharmacy should advocate for information technology that is **interoperable and transparent** with respect to usability, security, and functionality across the continuum of care.

C11. Pharmacy should establish standards for the application of **artificial intelligence (AI)** in the various steps of the medication-use process, including prescribing, reviewing medication orders, and assessing medication-use patterns in populations.

ASHP Forecast

1. Invest in the collection of **PRO data** using validated questionnaires, and make the information readily retrievable in the EHR for frontline staff.

2. Develop and implement improved **documentation systems** that discretely capture pharmacy impact and enable analysis of the value of pharmacy services.

3. Lead your institution to proactively develop data systems that support the development of **validated AI applications**, providing the opportunity to redeploy human resources to other unmet patient care needs.

4. Assure the development of pharmacist expertise related to **genomic testing**, creating infrastructure and developing policies and practices that address the appropriate clinical and ethical use/interpretation of such testing.

5. Lead the management of **genetic modification therapies**, ensuring that required expertise is made available (in some cases in partnership with other departments) for cell-derived therapy.

6. Develop and implement **new technology in telemedicine** to improve access to the care of pharmacists in medically underserved communities.

5. Recognize the incentives and motivations that are encouraging **disruptive developments in healthcare**, particularly those driving entities not traditionally directly involved in delivering care. Develop and implement health system–based programs that respond to those same drivers.

Situational Analysis - Technology[55,85]

Acute Care Technology Innovation

In this section, we're given...
- Examples of Acute Care Technology
- Justifying & Supporting Technology

Now we'll look more specifically at opportunities available for innovative technology within the acute care setting. Here's a quote I like to use on this topic from Leon Kass, an American educator: "Technological innovation is indeed important to economic growth and the enhancement of human possibilities."[131]

Examples of Acute Care Technology

As we have before, we'll begin with our view zoomed out, taking in the scope of the pharmacy enterprise. In both operations and acute care clinical service, there are many aspects of the pharmacy enterprise that can be positively impacted by technology.

A few examples are:

- Operations
  - Dispensing and Workflow
  - IT and Robotics
  - Supply Chain and Procurement
  - Inventory Management
  - Centralized Compounding and Repackaging
  - Sterile Compounding
  - Provider Clinic and Urgent Care Med Fulfillment
  - Diversion Management
  - Infusion Centers
- Acute Care Clinical Service
  - Clinical Practice Model
  - Clinical Practice Standards and Stewardship
  - Formulary Management and Stewardship
  - Pharmacoeconomics
  - Medication Safety
  - Pharmacy Informatics and Clinical Decision Support
  - Quality and VBP Goals
  - Research

In short... almost every aspect of our jobs in both operations and acute care can be supported and improved through greater use of technology and automation. Every year the *Pharmacy Purchasing and Products Journal* publishes two key publications: their Resource Guide, and their State of Pharmacy Automation. In 2020 they found something interesting. Due to the scrambling nature and shifting priorities surrounding COVID in 2020 (and 2021), short-term projections for budget increases regarding automation are lower than expected, which is actually not surprising. But long-term, the overwhelming majority (59%) "of pharmacies are confident that their budgets will increase over the next 3-5 years."[132] Investment in automation is definitely on the horizon.

And I'll repeat, because it's worth repeating, that this is not something to fear. Our jobs are not in danger. Our expertise and training will still be valuable to the hospital enterprise. More than ever, in fact. Automation will help us perform our jobs better and more efficiently. It is not a threat!

Furthermore, the State of Pharmacy Automation reports the top key technologies in hospital pharmacy. Here are the top automated systems that are available to improve healthcare technology within hospital pharmacy in order of preference[132]:

- Automated dispensing cabinets (ADCs) (82%)
- Bar coded medication administration systems (76%)
- CPOE (Computerized Physician Order Entry) (74%)
- Smart pumps (69%)
- Bar coded unit dose packaging systems (46%)
- Temperature monitoring systems (40%)
- Automated anesthesia dispensing systems (27%)
- Automated drug storage and retrieval (22%)
- Automated remote systems to enable 24-hr pharmacy services (13%)
- Automated systems for medication reconciliation (10%)
- Physician order imaging systems 9%)
- Automated compounding devices for sterile compounding (9%)
- Computerized medication charts (6%)
- Intravenous (IV) Compounding robots (5%)
- Automated compounding devices for non-sterile compounding (3%)

These are the top options, and of course, many organizations are investing in more than one product. I want to make sure to point out that each director was choosing their top five and went on to rate their choices in terms of satisfaction. We'll look at satisfaction rates next. Remember that the top five technologies they're investing in might not be what they're most satisfied with. Additionally, satisfaction is rated based on user experience, not on the director's opinion.

Top products satisfaction ratings[132]:

1. Automated Dispensing Cabinets (ADC)
2. Medication Tray Management
3. Automated Drug Storage and Retrieval
4. Medication Distribution Systems
5. Automated Compounding Tools
6. Temperature Monitoring Systems
7. Smart Pumps

When it comes to technologies, hospitals are investing most heavily in those that increase efficiency and safety. As pharmacists, these should be our priorities as well. We must continue to invest in technologies that use our team's time as efficiently as possible so they can practice at the top of their license. Only through increased access to technology will we see improvements in patient safety and care.

Let's look at a few of these examples in a little more detail. We won't be able to go into every single example, so I do recommend that you find yourself a copy of this journal. Being familiar with these trending automations will be a great resource for your situational analysis.

Let's look first at **medication trays**, since these are really trending in hospital use. From 2016 onward, there has been a slow and steady growth in hospitals adopting the use of medication tray management. In 2016, only 15% of hospitals were using technology to support medication tray management but by 2020 nearly a quarter "of pharmacies have adopted an automated approach to increase the safety and efficiency of their medication tray systems."[132] The radio frequency ID tags on these products are a very helpful method to reduce manual time and increase patient safety. One thing I want to note in terms of justifying these types of resources is that there's usually a small upfront expense in terms of capital with procuring machines that activate these types of tools, then they potentially need to be updated every so often. So while there's some time involved in initially setting up the new product and may be ongoing operating expenses, most organizations find it to be worthwhile.

Next up are **automated dispensing cabinets (ADCs)**. As you know, this is another one of the most common technologies used in health systems. Note here that, "It is rare for pharmacies to rely on a single device to handle all medication distribution functions. Rather, most facilities utilize ADCs, which are then supplemented by a variety of other approaches."[132] Many organizations have pneumatic tubes where meds are shot through to a nursing unit as well as mobile computerized workstations. There can also be couriers where meds are delivered or med carts in rooms. Some organizations call these "nurse servers." There are also options for robotic delivery with machines delivering to separate floors. A lot of advances are happening with these tools that continue to show an improvement in safety and efficiency.

Automated drug storage and retrieval, also known as carousels, are another tool that is high on the investment list for many organizations. Carousels provide added efficiency and safety (you see this trend popping in again and again!), where meds are stored in an organized and compact way, this vertical storage cabinet allows for bar coding and better inventory management. Since 2012, Carousels have gained popularity and now have a 44% adoption rate.[132]

Barcode Medication Administration (BCMA) or **Computerized Physician Order Entry (CPOE)** is an interesting topic to explore. In many ways, it is a good example of the success of innovative technology as CPOE has reached nearly 100% utilization rates. The advent of CPOE was enhanced through the American Recovery and Reinvestment Act, which incentivized physicians to use it, but there are a couple of things to note. First, it took nearly a decade from when these devices and products were available to their utilization of 90% or more.[132] This is unfortunate since, the proof of this technology's success and added safety was available long before most physicians adopted it. This is related to the diffusion of innovation we've talked about before in previous chapters. Secondly, we're still not at 100% implementation, which is surprising to me. What would it take to get this to 100%?

Temperature monitoring is another area where automation is fast improving. 70% of pharmacies (and pharmacy departments) utilize a wireless approach to temperature monitoring. We have seen a downward trend as it pertains to monitoring temperatures manually, which is excellent. In fact, "the number of facilities without an automated solution for temperature monitoring continues to decline precipitously; projects indicate that the adoption rate for automated monitoring will reach 100% in the next few years."[132] One of the reasons this has been adopted so widely so quickly, is because it's incredibly cost effective. Pharmacies have strong satisfaction ratings with regards to automated temperature monitoring.

These five automations — medication trays, ADCs, automated drug storage and retrieval, BCMA and CPOE, and temperature monitoring — are being adapted most rapidly and regularly across the country, but I wanted to touch on one more before we move on.

Diversion software. This is an important topic as opioid stewardship is a growing need that pharmacists should be accountable for. Let's look at both identification of diversion and then tracking. With identification, we want to be able to better locate newer softwares that can help us to aggregate our electronic medical record data. This, with automated dispensing data, as well as automatic reviews, helps highlight potential situations that manually, would take a lot of time. This helps us identify potential issues more often and more quickly, so we can track and follow through. The annual survey does not mention these trends, but in my discussions with health system leaders I see that more and more emphasis is being placed on this diversion.

Another helpful resource in the *Pharmacy Purchasing and Products Journal* is a list of companies and manufacturers who are currently doing the work of advancing these technologies.[133] Of course, be aware that since the journal is free, many of these companies are also advertisers, but it's still a good starting point for further research. It includes companies working on automation systems, ambulatory automation, bar coding and unit dosing, capital equipment, compounding diversion returns, waste management, infusion products outsourcing and consulting, pharmacy supplies, pharmacy disposables, and software, to name a few.

Justifying & Supporting Technology

Let's focus back on your principal task of obtaining funding for technology innovations for your organization. You'll likely already know that you have two purchasing options when it comes to technology. This decision is really dependent on your financial assessment, what is available from the manufacturer, and some accounting principles, because there are some rules around how we do this.

One option is to purchase the product as an **operating expense**. In this case, you'll either be leasing the equipment or have some type of software contract where you're not actually buying the equipment outright — kind of like renting. Sometimes these requests can be easier than capital budgets which are often limited. This is often considered better when it comes to technology because there are aging and replacement needs. Technology can become outdated fairly quickly with all of the rapid advancement we're seeing, so this can be a good way to justify expenses and get budgets approved.

When it comes to **capital expenses**, there is usually a set threshold dollar amount. For some organizations this is between $3,000 and $5,000. In most cases, a single item can be considered capital. That purchase usually depreciates over multiple years. Just keep in mind that the capital request process is usually separate from your regular budgeting process. Plus, hospitals do have a limit in terms of how much capital they budget for each year.

It's important to understand what's available to you. Of course, your organization may not have an option, but keep this in mind when you're strategizing what and how to invest.

Also don't forget to include personnel resources to support technology (even dedicated FTEs) and training time in your requests to support implementation. For example, when I implemented a new IV workforce solution, it took weeks to train all of the staff to learn the new system, which is understandable. But if we hadn't budgeted for all that time in our planning, we may have been over budget or not had enough resources to cover the training. We know that automation can save us time in the long run, but in the short term it takes time to get things off the ground.

Another way to strategize and justify spending is to utilize the **ASHP Commission on Goals** as a resource guide. We should be thinking broadly about the fact that AI really is an opportunity. They outline these five goals related to the impact of artificial intelligence on healthcare and pharmacy practice[134]:

1. **Vision**: AI will create not only new products and processes but also new stakeholders; it is important to reaffirm from the start that the ultimate purpose of healthcare AI is the same as all healthcare: preserving the healthy, healing those who are ill, and comforting those who cannot be healed.
2. **Validity**: Sound epidemiology and evidence are the basis of medicine, and establish the trust that healthcare relies on; healthcare AI must be deployed only when its validity is proved.
3. **Viability**: Healthcare AI will find its highest use when it is clinically relevant and useful to the provider and the patient, which will require high utility in addition to high reliability.
4. **Vocation**: Healthcare AI must preserve the holistic nature of the caregiver's mission, not further fragment healthcare but further the quadruple aim.
5. **Value**: It is imperative to make healthcare more sustainable by improving outcomes while reducing costs; healthcare AI's impact must further these twin goals.

Another helpful resource may be the **Pharmacy Health Information Technology (HIT) Collaborative**.

Their goals are[135]:

1. **Interoperability**: Advance the adoption by pharmacists of systems capable of standards-driven health information exchange.
2. **Workflow and Usability for Systems/Providers**: Health IT supports the JCPP Pharmacists' Patient Care Process and provision of patient care services.
3. **Quality**: Facilitate the use of Health IT that supports effective quality measurement.

Keep an eye on the interoperability goal. Disparate systems in pharmacy, physicians' offices, long-term care facilities, hospitals, health systems, and laboratories all need to be able to provide communication and interoperability of patient centric data. A lack of interoperability can present challenges to practice advancement and safety. I know it has presented me challenges related to one of my passions — improving medication reconciliation. I'm happy that this organization exists and look forward to seeing additional outcomes of their work.

Before we move on to technology innovations in ambulatory care, I want to warn you (not for the last time) to beware of what I call "Shiny Object Distractions." Do not go after the newest, fanciest technology just because it is available.

WHAT TO WATCH FOR

Beware of Shiny Object Distractions.

Take your time when researching and strategizing to be sure that the hospital dollars you are requesting will be well spent. These advancements and innovation should be proven effective and save your team time while improving the safety and care of patients.

In summary, we learned that there are many examples of acute care technology innovation to advance pharmacy practice. Each example will add knowledge to your own practice advancement.

TAKE ACTION NOW

- Share in the Pharmovator Community what acute care technology innovation you are most interested in.

Ambulatory Technology Innovation

In this section, there are…
- Examples of Ambulatory Care Technology Innovation

Examples of Ambulatory Care Technology Innovation

Now let's explore what innovations are available in ambulatory care. The scope of the pharmacy enterprise as it pertains to ambulatory care, outpatient pharmacy and business and managed pharmacy solutions is quite vast.

It can include:

- Ambulatory Care
    - Clinic-Based Clinical Pharmacy Services
    - Clinic-Based Pharmacy Visits
    - Centralized Virtual Clinical Services
    - Telehealth
    - Population Health
    - Pharmacogenomics
- Outpatient Pharmacy
    - Outpatient/Retail
    - Mail Order/Home Delivery
    - Discharge Medication Delivery
    - Specialty Pharmacy
    - Medication Therapy Management (MTM)/Vaccines
    - Home Infusion
    - Bulk Compounding
    - Patient Advocacy/Medication Assistants
- Business & Managed Pharmacy Solutions
    - 340B Program
    - Payer Population Health

And that's just to name a few! Now from an outpatient pharmacy perspective, it is good to realize that many health systems are investing in adding their own outpatient pharmacies. And while this may be challenged by some, it has helped many health systems to improve continuity of care and reduce readmissions. When you look at the numbers you can see a steady increase in incorporation. Adoption rates of outpatient pharmacies are at 73% in larger health systems and at 80% in academic medical health systems, versus only at 35% in community hospitals.[132]

Now, let's explore some of the **automations** used in outpatient settings, just like we looked at in the acute care side.

- e-Prescribing (57%)
- Point-of-Sale Program (48%)
- Bar Code Verification (37%)
- Robotic Dispensing (34%)
- Automated Pill Counters (26%)
- Interactive Voice Response System (IVR) (22%)
- Automated Prescription Pick Up Kiosk (3%)

When we think about automation, we should understand that adoption percentages are much higher when it comes to the acute side of care, creating more opportunity for advancement. We also see bar code verification and robotic dispensing being utilized at a rising rate of 34-37%. Most shocking is the statistic that 13% of outpatient pharmacies currently have no automation in use.[132]

An aspect of ambulatory care which is growing at an extremely rapid rate is the use of **telehealth**. Let's take a minute to clarify the difference between telehealth and telepharmacy. I know there are different state laws out there which will facilitate some of this practice, but understanding what's included is really important. Here's a statement from the American Society of Health System Pharmacists (ASHP), which does support telepharmacy and telemedicine. They explain that telemedicine is defined by CMS or the Center for Medicare and Medicaid Services, which describes it as a means for improving patient health by permitting two-way, real-time, interactive communication between the patient and healthcare provider, when geographically separate. To meet the standards of telehealth, it can be conducted by interactive telephone communication equipment that includes both audio and video equipment. From a billing perspective, many times payors do require the video aspect, and while telehealth can occur without video, you may not be able to bill for the services. This is very much a changing environment right now, where laws are in flux because of COVID, which has been a driving force for public and organizational support for telehealth.[136]

The National Association of Boards of Pharmacy (NABP) defines the practice of telepharmacy as "the provision of pharmacist care by registered pharmacists and pharmacists located within US jurisdictions, through the use of their telecommunications or other technologies to patients or their agents, at distances located within the US. Some examples are remote pharmacy or remote dispensing.

Telepharmacy and **telemedicine** are not grouped together, because the activities are considered different. Telemedicine can include drug review and monitoring, but not necessarily some of the dispensing activities. I agree with the practice of thinking about these methods separately, because the activities are more in tune with what a provider does when you're talking about telemedicine or some of the clinical pharmacy services. This separation is important because there has been some confusion and unrest around telepharmacy rules, and I don't want it to negatively impact some of the great clinical ambulatory services we have integrated into these models. Again, the dispensing of medications is really more covered under the telepharmacy activities.

It's a great opportunity for advancement for us as health care providers. Getting patients the tools to be able to participate in telehealth is also an important initiative that could be supported under patient innovation advancement.

Another critical area for pharmacy leaders to step up to the plate is **Medication Access**. Especially in areas of **medication assistance** for patients, **real time prescription benefits (RTPB)**, and **electronic prior authorization (ePA)**. Many of the tools needed to facilitate this process are of little or no cost to the pharmacist of pharmacy, but it does take time to enforce new processes and train staff to use new methods.

I'm going to include a lot of detail in the chart below, and I'm not going to review all of it in depth, but I do want to share with you a little bit more about where we're seeing ambulatory pharmacy clinical services being supported with technology and the advent of the pharmacist **eCare Plan**. What is shown below is the history of the pharmacist eCare plan and how it has moved through a variety of venues. From its beginning in testing stages to being used to document the pharmacist plan, the Pharmacist eCare Plan is communicated between a pharmacy and an independent consultant pharmacist, as well as the payer or employer data.

Pharmacist Care Plan:

- **2013**: HL7 and NCPDP workgroups started drafting the HL7 version for the Pharmacist Care Plan.
- **2014**: NCPDP published "Recommendations for Use of the HL7 Consolidated CDA Templates for Pharmacy Version 1. Ø"
- **2015**: HL7 and NCPDP published first eCare Plan version "CDA® R2 Implementation Guide: Medication Therapy Management (MTM) Templates, Release 1 - US Realm"

- **2016**: Medication Management SNOMED CT codes were published (Pharmacy HIT Collaborative sponsored)
- **2016**: NCPDP published a summary document of Pharmacist Care Plan "Pharmacist eCare Plan Version 1.0: Guidance on the Use of the HL7 CDA Consolidated Templates for Clinical Notes R2.1 Care Plan" Pharmacist eCare Plan Version 1.0: Guidance on the Use of the HL7 CDA Consolidated Templates for Clinical Notes R2.1 Care Plan
- **September 2016**: Lantana Consulting Group was awarded ONC High Impact Pilot to complete Pharmacist Care Plan Implementation Guide
- **June 2017**: 1st electronic Pharmacist Care Plans were sent to Community Care of North Carolina as part of CMMI Pilot
- **September 2017**: Lantana Consulting Group published final report for ONC High Impact Grant
- **September 2017**: Pharmacist Care Plan C-CDA Implementation Guide and FHIR implementation Guide was submitted as a draft Standard in HL7 balloting process
- **2018**: NCPDP and HL7 Pharmacist Care Plan C-CDA Implementation Guide and FHIR implementation Guide reconciled ballot comments
- **2018**: ONC lists Pharmacist eCare Plan in Interoperability Standards Advisory tool
- **2019**: Current state - Lantana Consulting Group is incorporating Relevant Medication Management value sets to Pharmacist Care Plan C-CDA and FHIR Release 4 implementation guides and were prepared for Standard for Trial Use HL7 for May 2019 balloting process. Subsequently, the NCPDP/HL7 Pharmacist eCare Plan C-CDA template and Fast Healthcare Interoperability Resources (FHIR) Implementation Guides (IGs) completed balloting at HL7 and NCPDP in 2019. The HL7 FHIR Management Group requested some clarifications to the HL7 FHIR R4. These clarifications are related to the overall FHIR R4 standard not specifically to the Pharmacist eCare Plan.
- **2020**: When the HL7 FHIR Management Group completes their review, it will move to the HL7 Technical Steering Committee for approval. Once approved by HL7, NCPDP and HL7 will work jointly submit the IGs to the American National Standards Institute (ANSI) for accreditation and publication by HL7 and NCPDP

eCare Plan History[137]

There are quite a lot of companies getting involved in this aspect of medical technology, with multiple options supporting pharmacists who are doing independent MTM consulting arrangements or working in community pharmacies. In a health system where I've practiced, the pharmacists are documenting within the electronic health record itself, which is the same database as the physicians. This is a huge opportunity for interoperability to share pharmacy care plan information across the continuum of care. The broader topic in this ambulatory outpatient setting is **population health**. Coordinating health care and improving the overall health for populations is important. And as we have discussed, there is a move toward more payment models based on population health outcomes and our technology needs to be able to support and facilitate that information. There are several different companies out there that are working in this space, expanding our support from the topics of data aggregation and intelligence, risk management, clinical analytics, care coordination and patient outreach, as well as formation and advisory service.

As we wrap up our discussion on ambulatory technology, I want to quickly mention **blockchain**. I was confused to hear people speak about blockchain in the context of healthcare because I only understood blockchain as it relates to cryptocurrencies like Bitcoin. But as I've learned, blockchain itself is the supporting aspect that allows things like Bitcoin to be secure and has many applications in healthcare.

Blockchain by itself is a growing list of records that are called blocks, that are linked using technology called cryptography. It's resistant to modifications of data, which is really helpful. Another way to define it is as "an open, distributed ledger that can record transactions between two parties efficiently in a verifiable and permanent way."[138] Concerning interoperability, this type of data formation can definitely assist us in improving some of the challenges that arise.

With blockchain, you're able to see each piece of data through the history of that data's existence. Nothing is deleted, everything is timestamped with a name and is built upon, never erased. There are a lot of opportunities for blockchain in healthcare. Some of that work is being done at IBM. Technology like blockchain-stored records gives patients more control over their own information through verifiable consent. Blockchain's tools work in concert with electronic data to allow clinical data to be automatically aggregated. Blockchain's outcome-based contracts tie clinical outcomes to costs.[138] Some of the work being done by IBM Watson to utilize blockchain technology is fascinating. They are involved with patient consent, health data exchange, clinical trial management and outcome-based contracts. All of these topics have issues with ensuring the data is maintained, consistent, and communicated accurately between different systems. Blockchain is a tool that can improve some of the coordination and accuracy of data.[138]

In summary, there are a lot of opportunities for innovative technology within ambulatory care. However, both provider and patient acceptance is critical to the full integration of the available technology.

TAKE ACTION NOW

- Share in the Pharmovator Community what ambulatory care technology innovation you are most interested in.

•••

PERSONAL TECHNOLOGY INNOVATION

In this section, we'll discuss...
- Examples of Personal Technology Innovation

Examples of Personal Technology Innovation

In this section we'll look at examples of personal technological innovations that can allow you to be more effective in your work. Bill Gates has said that we are changing the world with technology, and I couldn't agree more. While we've touched upon ways technology can advance practice in different realms, it's important to remember that there are things you can use personally to experience efficiency and advancement in your own practice.

This includes tech like communication devices, voice activated notes, utilizing your computer, tablet or laptop in new ways, and incorporating medical information apps into your practice. We're not going to go into every single specific example of personal technology since that would be impossible. Apps are updating and changing all the time, and technology provides new tools almost daily. But when it comes to **communication devices**, there's definitely an opportunity for us to be able to communicate with our patients and providers with some of the newer technologies that have both video capabilities and secure text messaging. These allow you to send messages and images or other data in an encrypted and secure format. Having these types of communication channels available to us means they're also available to our patients.

When it comes to **voice activated notes**, we're seeing this become more and more popular in the home with Siri and Alexa. In the workplace this has been tested as well. I see more and more physicians using this type of technology so they don't have to write their notes during a clinic visit, but a system hears them and listens as a way to capture that information so a physician can focus on the patient. There is an opportunity here for pharmacy to incorporate this technology as well.

As for **computers and laptops**, I have been shocked to see many organizations don't provide laptops for all their leadership and staff. Functionality and flexibility is so much higher with laptops. We must ensure that team members have what they need to succeed. If you're tied to a desktop device and can't participate fully in rounds, this is certainly a detriment to the team and to your functionality as a pharmacy leader. We need to get people basic devices. And in many cases, we may need to increase the capacity of our devices in terms of memory. For example, some bigger data files may take up more space. Plus, all devices need to have video capability at this point. Working remotely needs to be an option with devices for all employees.

Finally, let's discuss **medical information apps**. This is a tough thing to simply mention, since there's a lot of resources out there, so we will only discuss it briefly. The fact is that you and your team need to have access to reliable medical information immediately. We need to justify access to drug information, books, and other references that might be more specific to infection, disease, pediatrics, or whatever other information your team needs. Dosing calculators and pharmacokinetic modeling are also important to justify. There are many reliable and respected online tools that require an investment. Your team should have access to these.

In summary, these are just a few examples for you to consider how you can be personally effective in your practice. When there's something you want to do and you have to do it manually, think about what technology you could use to replace that action to increase efficiency and allow you to practice at the top of your license.

Take Action Now

- Share in the Pharmovator Community what personal technology innovation you are most interested in.

Patient Technology Innovation

In this section, we'll discuss...
- Examples of Patient Technology Innovation

Before we look at our case study, we'll explore some innovations currently available in patient technology.

> ***"It can be argued that the largest yet most neglected healthcare resource, worldwide, is the patient..."***
> —Warner Slack

It's critical that we include the patient in their care decisions. There are many exciting innovations that patients can use for their individual healthcare, and we must assist in helping familiarize them with these innovations and how they can be utilized. This is an exciting area and opportunity for us to continue to be patient-centered while making sure patients have access to their health-related data and information technology that can improve our communication.

Examples of Patient Technology Innovation

When we discuss technology innovation in this section, there are a few key buckets to put these technologies in. The first is **mHealth** or health monitoring. This is the use of mobile devices to monitor or detect biological changes in the human bodies. Of course, it helps to record these changes and report back to your healthcare provider, and often the applications and devices used will keep a record of use, which is excellent. We also have **patient experience** topics such as journey mapping and other ways to ease entry into healthcare situations. Then there is **virtual reality**, which is a growing area for healthcare use. We see this technology being used to support things like rehab exercises or behavioral changes. And there are opportunities for pharmacy to potentially get involved or suggest that patients engage in these types of activities to improve overall outcomes. For example, smoking cessation could be amenable to this.

Here are a few more innovation examples with some additional detail[139]:

- Addam is a wearable technology for asthma that attaches to the body with a small adhesive patch. Sensors in Addam detect an asthma patient's symptoms and keep track of them. Symptoms include respiration patterns, cough rate, temperature, and heart rate. This device notifies patients when their symptoms are out of line with their norms. The device vibrates to alert patients and sends a text to a person chosen by the wearer.
- UCB is currently in trials for a wearable sensor that records symptoms of Parkinson's Disease. The company believes that the quality of the data collected will be more accurate than the data provided by patient logs or diaries during clinical trials.
- FreeStyle Libre, by Abbott is a two-piece system that measures the blood glucose levels of diabetic patients. The sensor is a small disc that attaches to the patient's body. The sensor sends information to a receiver or Android phone that is not attached to the patient. Each replacement disc has a lifespan of 14 days.
- The iTBra is a smart bra insert that fits into a woman's brassiere. There are two sensors, one for each breast that measures circadian temperature differences as a means of early detection of breast cancer.
- The Omnipod Insulin Management System is made by Insulet and holds as many as 200 insulin doses. This is one of the earlier proactive medical devices on the market. It was first approved and sold in 2005. The Omnipod is made up of a tubeless disposable insulin pump and a "Personal Diabetes Manager" that wirelessly signals the insulin pump when insulin is scheduled. It also helps the diabetic patient with calculating their insulin levels and measuring blood glucose levels.

With the advent of this technology, we have an opportunity to collect and aggregate the data from patients (with their written and verbal consent of course) and use it when formulating plans for their overall healthcare. These personal devices collect a lot of information, and we want to make sure it gets aggregated in a way that's meaningful and helps make better decisions.

When patients think about this topic, they define mHealth as an opportunity. These are outside devices like medicine dispensers, scales, pedometers, glucose meters, pulse oximeters, and blood pressure meters that connect to smart phones through Bluetooth. They're also internal devices like a device node accelerometer or smart patch ECG monitoring that connects to a phone as well. All of these devices, always with patient permission, upload data to a telemonitoring database or EHR and then share it with associated parties.[140]

And of course, we always want to know what patients think about integrating these technologies into their daily lives. Surveyed patients overwhelmingly state that they see this as an opportunity, and they want access and control. They want this data shared with their healthcare providers so they can make better decisions.[141] They also want more automation from providers on the whole, like reminders about appointments or when to take their medication. They want their specific conditions monitored and providers notified immediately if any problems arise. As pharmacists, we are healthcare providers too. And we want to ensure that we give individuals opportunities to access technology that could better their lives. We want to make sure that we're supporting these types of communication workflows with the pharmacist. The problem is that right now, there's very few examples of patients having this type of access to their pharmacies and not just with their provider.

The good news is that online access is both critical and growing. Surveys show that 90% of patients want online access to health information and education.[141] Regarding pharmacy, they'd like to refill Rxs and make appointments via digital channels (either via mobile phone or website.) While we've had automatic refill available for a while now, there are opportunities available to increase appointment availability. Think about it, we could have patients make appointments with their pharmacists, either at their pharmacy or an ambulatory clinic.

Another important topic around patient technology innovation is **medication adherence**. There is a useful diagram on the next page that summarizes all the different ways that we can monitor medication adherence, regardless of the different types of devices.

There are definitely opportunities here when we look across the top. Let me draw your attention to the second row from the bottom that states whether or not the data can be synced and integrated with the other information. We see things like sensors, smart pill bottles, pill dispensers and more. There can be sensors on the inhalers or insulin pens, or even the bottoms themselves. This allows for even greater technological innovation, such as digital medicine. Digital medicine is fully integrated with built-in sensors that help monitor patient adherence. There's a bio ingestible sensor, smart inhalers and smart insulin pens. Lots of opportunities when we look across the technology for helping patients with their adherence, which is of course, one of the most important ways that we can make medications effective.

Examples of the bio ingestibles include the etectRX (formerly EtectBio), which has received FDA clearance on their ID-cap system, and the Proteus digital health pill, which also encapsulates pills but tends to be used more with higher cost medications.

I want to mention again the importance of the patient experience. We know how important this is because we ourselves have navigated the healthcare environment and know it can be quite complex even when we are familiar with it.

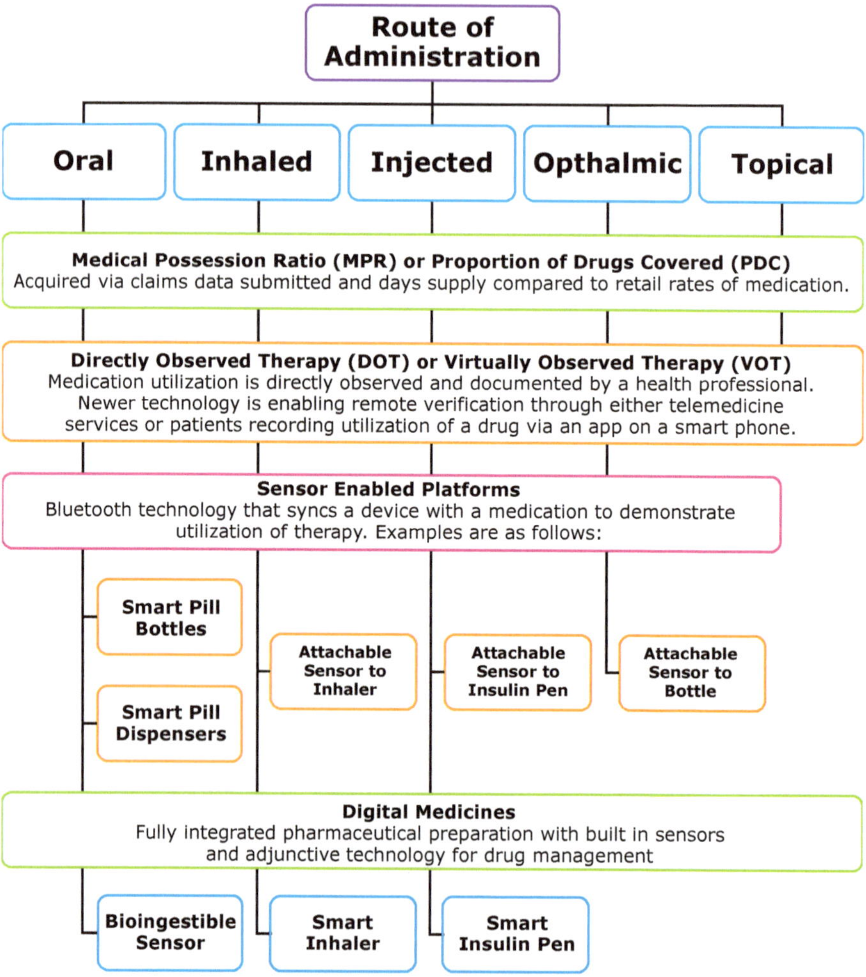

Medication Adherence[142]

There's an activity you can do called journey mapping. This is where you record (usually on a graph) every interaction that a person has with the healthcare system from the time they discover they have a disease or condition through all of the decisions that have to be made throughout the process. Also recorded is how easy or difficult it is to interact with the healthcare system. These types of examples can be helpful for us to look at and see what we could do from a safety perspective. Where are the gaps? Where are the opportunities to improve patient access to our health system? A key opportunity I see in journey mapping is for continuity touch points, such as when patients leave a clinic or are going home from the hospital. They are likely to go to their community pharmacy, infusion center, or a skilled nursing facility. They may interact with the healthcare system in other, unrecorded ways, that are often related to pharmacy. Medications may be changed at any of these touch points and what medications they should be taking and where to get their medications can be confusing. While I haven't created a specific journey map for pharmacy, I see a huge opportunity here to look into those decision points and activities.

I came to discover this opportunity through patient feedback. We hear from patients that they have huge amounts of stress and difficulty interacting with the healthcare system to optimize their medications throughout transitions of care. Another opportunity is to look at the actual, physical navigation maps in our health systems, which can often be extremely large and disorienting. Patients have to move throughout an overwhelming campus, navigate multiple buildings, get back in the car and drive across town, using GPS technology to find their new specialist's office. It can be mind-boggling and confusing to patients, who are already struggling with a new diagnosis. One technological solution to this is for each hospital to have a downloadable, GPS-navigable app that includes a map of facilities.

In summary, there are many examples of patient technology innovation to empower patients and providers.

Take Action Now

- Share in the Pharmovator Community what patient technology innovation you are most interested in.

•••

Case Study

In this section, we'll learn about...
- Technology Justification Case Study

Technology Justification Case Study

To round out this chapter, we'll explore a case study. This particular case study charts the course of the entire journey to justify resources, which we've discussed a bit in previous chapters.

Let me outline it more clearly now. When it comes to justifying resources, you're looking at a similar journey each time. It begins with your **strategic planning**, then your **FTE analysis** and **technology analysis**. Afterwards you'll research and put together whatever **business plans** you need, while assessing the **return on investment (ROI)**. Finally, once all of this is in place, you'll **seek approval** for your plan. Remember that this book can assist you throughout this journey with templates and other resources available in the Pharmovation Implementation Guide via the links at the end of each chapter. In fact, they're the same templates we'll be using in the case study.

For this project, we began with strategic planning and the technology planning worksheet that was filled out to assess where we had opportunities and needs.

Category	Technology Need	Cost	Technology to Replace/ Retire	ROI	Business Plan RX or IDN
Clinical Program Growth / Service Line Expansion	Renovations – Expand ADCs & Point of Care	$$	No	Partial	Capital +/- Operating
	Pharmacogenomic EHR Integration	$$	No	Partial	IDN Operating
	Anesthesia Bar Code Label System	$$	No	Partial	Operating
Requested Pharmacy Technology	Automated Drug Storage "Carousel"	$$$	Yes	Partial	Capital
PAI / Pharmacy Initiated	Automated Tray System	$$	No	No	Operating
	Diversion Software	$	Yes	Partial	Operating
	Drug Shortage Software	$	No	Partial	Operating
TOTAL					
Technology to Replace / Retire	Diversion Software	($)			
	Automated Drug Storage "Carousel"	($)			
		(-)			
NET TOTAL		$$			

Technology Planning Worksheet

For clinical program growth, the organization was experiencing nursing growth, and renovations were being done to nursing units. We were requested to collaborate with nursing which was a great opportunity. We found ways to expand automated dispensing cabinets (ADC) and actually convert them to point of care technology rather than something that was just being used for controlled substances. There was some ROI, when you look at some of the time-savings and medication waste. The majority of this expense was capital through renovations and equipment purchase.

There was also a growth of the pharmacogenomic program as discussed in the Chapter 5 Services Case Study. Integrating pharmacogenomics data into the EHR would allow clinical decision support much like we do with the identification of drug-to-drug interactions. There was partial ROI from some billable labs and patient encounters, the plan was part of the IDN business, and it was a software purchase.

The anesthesia department requested the barcode labeling system to support regulatory compliance and safety. This operating expense was partially offset by drug budget savings. It was great to have stakeholders advocate for this technology practice advancement.

Through PAI and department planning, several technology initiatives were identified, including automated drug storage 'carousels,' automated tray systems, diversion software, and drug shortage software. The largest investment in carousels allowed updating technology at one site and adding this technology at others to allow standardization of the pharmacy workflow across the system. This investment allowed the renovations planned for the pharmacies to occur in a smaller footprint and to comply with USP 797/800 standards. This supported the expense along with other savings from drug inventory management.

You can see below the status of the initiatives.

<table>
<tr><th>Category</th><th>Technology Needed</th><th>Notes</th><th>Status</th><th>Business Plan RX or IDN</th></tr>
<tr><td rowspan="2">Clinical Program Growth/Service Line Expansion</td><td>Renovations – Expand ADCs & Point of Care</td><td>Add with New Units & Phase in Full Transitions</td><td>In Progress</td><td>Annual Capital (Construction & Purchase)</td></tr>
<tr><td>Pharmacogenomic EHR Integration</td><td>Included in Precision Medicine Plan</td><td>Implemented</td><td>IDN – Operating</td></tr>
<tr><td>Requested Pharmacy Technology</td><td>Anesthesia Bar Code Label System</td><td>Added in Pharmacy Operating Budget Offset by Drug Budget Savings</td><td>Implemented</td><td>Operating</td></tr>
<tr><td rowspan="4">PAI/Pharmacy Initiated</td><td>Automated Drug Storage "Carousel"</td><td>Funded for Regulatory Compliance for Space in the Pharmacies</td><td>Implemented</td><td>797/800 Renovation Capital</td></tr>
<tr><td>Automated Tray System</td><td></td><td>Future</td><td>Operating</td></tr>
<tr><td>Diversion Software</td><td>Annual Budget</td><td>Planned</td><td>Operating</td></tr>
<tr><td>Drug Shortage Software</td><td></td><td>Future</td><td>Operating</td></tr>
</table>

Technology Planning Status

Of course, we had to make sacrifices and choices that would ensure the plan got approved. This meant we had to convert the purchase of some products for ongoing maintenance on current products, as well as set aside some goals that didn't have a clear ROI.

Cost Management	Savings
Medication Use Optimization	$XXX,XXX
Purchasing	$XXX,XXX
Inventory Management	$XXX,XXX
Waste Reduction	$XXX,XXX
Reimbursement	$XXX,XXX
Optimization	$4,500,000

Pharmacy Restructure & Business Plan Allocation	Cost
Technician Market Analysis	$XXX,XXX
Management Restructure	$XXX,XXX
Business Plan New Positions & Technology	$XXX,XXX
Total	$300,000
Net ROI	$1,500,000

Acute Care Business Plan ROI - Technology Included

Finally, we put together a business plan that included personal technology that had a clear ROI.

Some of this ROI was found by selling some of our older equipment to hospitals in need for a discounted cost. Additionally, some ROI was found through reduction in waste that happens naturally through better documentation and inventory management. Plus, because we had previously leased some of the equipment we were updating, it was a much smaller charge to lease upgraded equipment from the same manufacturer rather than starting from scratch with a new provider.

So, what happened? What was the final status of this journey to justify resources? The top item of the renovation was the expansion of the automated dispensing cabinets. We were able to add those new ones when the new units were being renovated and other areas were phased in for full transition, which would occur over the subsequent years. We weren't able to get them right away. A lot of that approval (or lack thereof) was related to the change from operating expense to capital expense. Remember, there's always a limited cap on capital expenses. So when we had to transition to a full purchase, rather than leasing, we weren't able to do it all at once. I also knew that we needed to invest in upgrading the smart pump technology because the organization didn't have fully integrated technology with their smart pumps. That took precedence, and was a big part of the capital expense for the coming year. In the end, there are compromises on every journey that we need to be prepared for, especially when we remember that healthcare still functions primarily as a business in the US.

I did want to emphasize that besides the specific software and hardware investments just discussed, there were additional technology supported PAI tactics. These are highlighted in the table below.

OBJECTIVES	Tactics
Clinical Practice Standardization	- EHR Workflow / Documentation Standardization - Acuity Scoring - Activity Prioritization - Scheduling/Shift Optimization
Service Line Support/Expansion	- Hospitalist Rounding - Oncology - Heart Failure/LVAD - Pulmonary/Adult ECMO - Emergency Departments - Primary Care & Specialty Clinics
Medication Reconciliation	- Admission - Discharge - Ambulatory
Residency Expansion	- PGY1 - PGY2
Students	- Intern Program - APPE Student Optimization including Pend Function
Precision Medicine	- Pharmacogenomic Testing w/ EHR Integration - Pharmacogenomic Clinic - Precision Oncology
Patient Experience	- Quiet at Night - Medication Education
Operations PAI	- Staffing Workflow & Tech Check Tech

Department PAI Objectives & Tactics
with Technology Highlights

In summary, the systematic journey to justify resources for technology-driven practice is worth the effort it takes to navigate the process. Our patients and employees deserve to spend less time on menial tasks, and more time getting the care they need and practicing at the top of their licenses. And it's our responsibility to advocate for them.

Take Action Now

- Share in the Pharmovator Community what technology you are going to advocate for in your practice.

To support you incorporating the learnings from this chapter, access the Pharmovation Implementation Guide. Visit www.pharmovationguide.com or scan the QR code below for full access!

Chapter 7

Pharmovation LEADERSHIP

"If you want to build a ship, don't drum up people together to collect wood and don't assign them tasks and work, but rather teach them to long for the endless immensity of the sea."
—Antoine de St. Exupery

Leadership can be summed up simply as accountability. Leaders are accountable for what happens in their department. Leaders hold themselves accountable. They hold others accountable. The proverbial buck stops with them. In pharmacy, this means that leaders must be responsible for integrating pharmacy within the rest of the organization. We are not a separate, siloed entity, but part of the whole.

Once upon a few years ago, I worked at Bayer Healthcare, on the "Big Pharma" side of the table. During our regular performance reviews, we had an additional component of responding to the values that Bayer ascribes to. Their values are: Leadership, Innovation, Flexibility and Excellence (L.I.F.E.). And Bayer takes adherence to these values extremely seriously. However, in the reviews, I began to notice that people who weren't managers were skipping over the leadership section. They even told others they didn't have to do either, because they weren't in leadership.

People often assume that leadership comes with a title. This isn't so. I like to think of leadership as having two sub-categories: Big Ls and Little Ls. The Big Ls are the leaders with official titles. They're on leadership teams and perhaps even attend leadership conferences. Little Ls are everywhere. They're encouraging their team members. They're showcasing excellence every time they arrive at work. They're inspiring to others on a daily basis.

You probably have a natural tendency to think from a leadership perspective. That's one of the reasons you're reading this book. **You already understand that it's important to have leadership at all levels, regardless of having "leader" as part of your title or department.** But your team members might not naturally think this way. They don't think they need a leadership mindset, because they're not natural leaders. These are the people that say, "Oh, don't worry about that. Nursing's responsible for that," or, "the techs take care of that. Just leave it," and so on and so forth.

This is an attitude that we, as leaders, must change both in ourselves and amongst our team. We are the medication experts. We must be accountable for the medications prescribed within our organizations. We must ensure the safety and positive outcomes of our patients from using these medications. Can we be everywhere at once? No. But we can make sure all the infusion pumps are running, the nurses have been properly trained on new equipment, and the pharmacy technicians have what they need to complete their job.

Leadership begins with adjusting your mindset, which we discussed in Chapter 1. It continues with action and accountability, which we'll explore now.

Our objective is to practice increased leadership and accountability regardless of your level in the organization. We'll explore five topics within leadership including the importance of:

- Leadership In Pharmovation
- Management & Leadership
- Big Ls & Little Ls
- Competency Identification & Assessment
- Key Knowledge, Skills, & Competencies

There are also a few tools available to accompany this chapter, so make sure to download those in the Pharmovation Implementation Guide with the QR code at the end.

Let's dive in.

•••

Importance of Leadership in Pharmovation

SECTION PREVIEW | SECTION PREVIEW

In this section, we'll learn about...
- What is Leadership?
- Why is Leadership Important to Pharmovation?

What is Leadership?

We'll begin with a definition of leadership and rooting ourselves in why this is an important topic for us to discuss related to Pharmovation.

Leadership is...

- The action of leading a group of people or an organization.[143]
- The set of characteristics that make a good leader.[143]
- The art of motivating a group of people to act toward achieving a common goal.[143]
- The process through which an individual attempts to intentionally influence another or a group in order to accomplish a goal.[144]

Leadership has a purpose. It is a process. It is intentional. Notice that the definitions above make it clear that it's not about the leader, but about the people.

Why is Leadership Important to Pharmovation?

But why do we need leadership in pharmacy? Shouldn't the hospital have leadership over pharmacy instead? Recent trends are showing us that leading change is a fundamental responsibility of being a pharmacist. When we think of the advancements we've had in our profession, we see that the status quo is no longer acceptable, and we identify the need to change and adapt to those advances. Change is happening. And we should be facilitating that change at as fast as possible, in the most responsible way possible, so that our patients receive the highest quality care possible.

So, we now understand that leadership is critical in pharmacy, so what about leadership and innovation? These two historically go hand in hand, but not always in a positive way. We will revisit some prior topics in Pharmovation from a leadership perspective, including the Innovation Do's and Dont's from Chapter 1. They have been included again on the next page for your convenience.

It's easy to see how well-intended leaders can fall into the traps of Innovation Dont's. As a leader, you'll be setting the stage, making innovation a process, and including it as part of your culture. Look for those big and small innovative ideas and ask questions. You can provide the resources to allow the investment of time, people, and money to support innovation.

Creating culture and systems isn't always as sexy sounding as "Let's try this crazy awesome new thing and let's do it in the next two months!" Leadership isn't about flash and excitement. It's about continuity, consistency, trust, and a solid base of communication. Because you will ask your team to do hard things. You will hold them to high

Innovation Do's	Innovation Dont's
Make innovation a process	Leaders just ask for ideas
Make innovation part of your culture	Accept the status quo
Build your persuasion skills	No buy-in from executives
Build change management skills	Same old thinking, same old results
Take customer input and build upon it as customers may not identify innovation	Avoid segmentalist organizations working in silos
Plan for integrative organization	Rely on customer feedback sessions
Accept big and small innovative ideas	Demand disruptive innovation
Consider a wide range of alternatives (resources, people, methods, business models)	Neglect alternatives
Know what you're trying to solve	Work on innovation only in a rush
Invest time, people, and money	Only have creative ideas and not implement innovation

Innovation Do's and Dont's

Systems	Structures	Strategic Direction	Policies & Procedures	People	Culture
Misdirected reward and evaluation systems Oppressive control systems Inflexible budgeting systems Arbitrary cost allocation systems Overly rigid, formal planning systems	Too many hierarchical levels Overly narrow span of control Responsibility without authority Top-down management Restricted communication channels Lack of accountability for innovation and change	Absence of innovation goals No formal strategy for entrepreneurship No vision from the top Lack of commitment from senior executives No entrepreneurial role models at the top	Long, complex approval cycles Extensive red-tape and documentation requirements Over-reliance on established rules of thumb Unrealistic performance criteria	Fear of failure Resistance to change Parochial bias "Turf" protection Complacency Short-term orientation Inappropriate skills and talents for managing entrepreneurial change	Ill-defined values Lack of consensus over value and norm priorities Lack of fit of values with current competitive context Values that conflict with innovativeness, risk-taking, and proactiveness

Barriers to Intrapreneurship[145]

standards. And you will expect results. You'll ask a lot from the people you work with. The only way they (and you) will be able to deliver will be on a foundation of trust, which can't be built overnight.

One effective way trust can be built is to allow your team to see how you deal with the Barriers to Intrapreneurship, which can be found on the previous page. These barriers are often common to intrapreneurship, which we discussed earlier on. Consider how a true leader might respond to the barriers.

Leaders must demonstrate and support the behaviors for intrapreneurship. Let's discuss some examples. People often have a fear of failure, how can you, as a leader, address that? Well, you can help make sure that they don't get scolded when they do fail. Allow for failures. You've probably heard the phrase "fail fast" so that we can move on and not get stuck on something that's not going to work. Responsibility without authority is a barrier in the structure of your organization. It allows leaders to push decision making on to lower levels and grant authority. Besides dealing with frustrating barriers to innovation, as a leader you'll also be responsible for managing change, which is another thing we've touched on before. During seasons of change in an organization, people typically become less effective and efficient. This isn't because they are lazy or stubborn, but simply adjusting to whatever change is taking place. A leader's role during this time is to reduce the negative consequences of change and accelerate the process so the period of change is shortened. Notice I said reduce, not eliminate. There will always be negative aspects of change. Humans are notoriously bad at changing or adapting quickly. A leader's job is to lessen these effects, not dismiss normal growing pains associated with change.

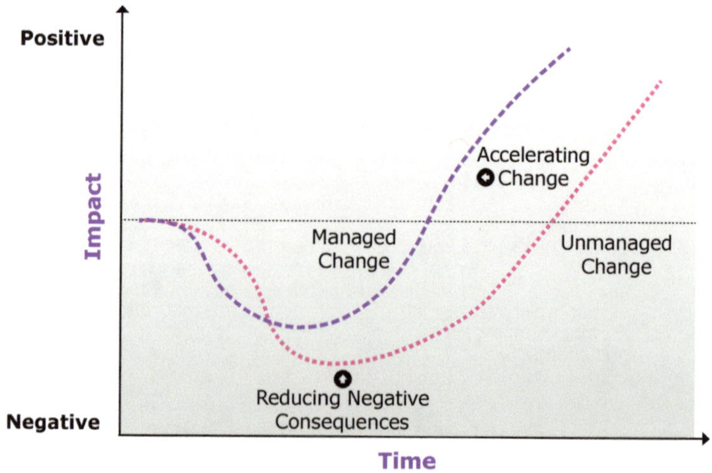

Using the Change Curve[20]

You may recall this change management curve where the managed change reduces the negative consequences of change to move towards accelerated change more quickly. We necessarily see a dip in productivity upon the initial impact of change. People become less effective and efficient during this time. As a leader, consider how you can support the knowledge around change management within your organization.

Here are three leadership practices that help drive innovation[146]:

1. **DEFINE a key innovation challenge**: This practice involves others and gives the team ownership of the coming project. They see this challenge as something that has persisted and may require changes within the organization to overcome and move past.
2. **UNDERSTAND the work of innovation by leader level**: You are not the only leader. Individual leaders are responsible for ideation and creation of innovation. They see novel solutions and approaches. Team managers lead the group innovation process and obtain necessary resources. Senior leaders set large-scale strategy and shape organizational culture. Leadership looks different on different people.
3. **DEVELOP what's needed for innovative thinking**: Your team needs the proper tool sets, skill sets, and mindsets to succeed in innovative thinking. This is worth investing time, money, and manpower into.

It's also imperative that pharmacy leaders are connected to leaders outside the pharmacy enterprise. This is one of the keys to full integration of the pharmacy into the rest of the organization. Pharmacy leaders, especially the CPO, must form relationships with other C-suite leaders, the administration council, medical executive committee, quality committee, and nursing leadership, as well as pharmacy-led committees.

What to Watch For

Don't just talk the talk,
you've got to walk the walk.

Watch out for leaders who talk the talk but aren't walking the walk. Don't just pay lip service to innovation. We need to support it and practice it.

In summary, remember that leadership is ultimately the art of motivating a group of people to achieve a common goal together. It's important to address innovations do's and dont's, remove barriers to intrapreneurship where you can, support change management, drive innovation and connect beyond pharmacy.

Take Action Now

- Identify a leadership barrier to Pharmovation you see in your organization.
- Consider a solution to this barrier and share in the Pharmovator Community.

•••

Management & Leadership

In this section, we'll learn…

- The Differences Between Management & Leadership

These two words are often used synonymously, but in reality, they are not the same thing. A manager is a person responsible for controlling or administrating all or part of a company or organization.[147] Management is the process of dealing with or controlling things or people.[148] A leader is the person who leads or commands a group, organization or country.[149] Leadership, as we've said, is the art of motivating a group of people to act toward achieving a common goal.[150]

The Differences Between Management & Leadership

It's the difference between the person and the overall process. Some key words here I want to point out are controlling, administrating, and dealing. A leader does not deal with people, they inspire people toward a common goal. A manager controls outputs and outcomes while a leader motivates others to be responsible for achieving an outcome together.

Put another way:

"Leadership is working with goals and vision; management is working with objectives."

—Russel Honore

There will be times when you are a leader, working with goals and vision and organizing around these things. There will also be a place for the manager, working with set objectives, managing resources, projects and programs. Leadership is concerned with doing the right thing while management concerns itself with doing things right. Leadership says, let's do it! And management says, go do it. A leader produces change and movement while a manager produces order and consistency. Can both exist within one person? Absolutely. Knowing when to act as leader and when to manage a project is a crucial skill in leadership.

It's also true that while leadership and management can mix well together, as you move up in an organization you will have less opportunities to manage and more opportunities to lead. Management functions lessen and are replaced by leadership functions as you move upward in your career. It will be necessary then, to replace some management function with leadership as you progress from position to position.

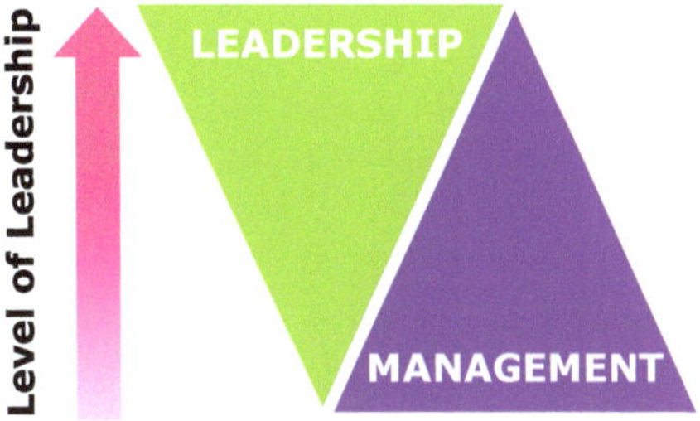

Mix of Leadership & Management Functions

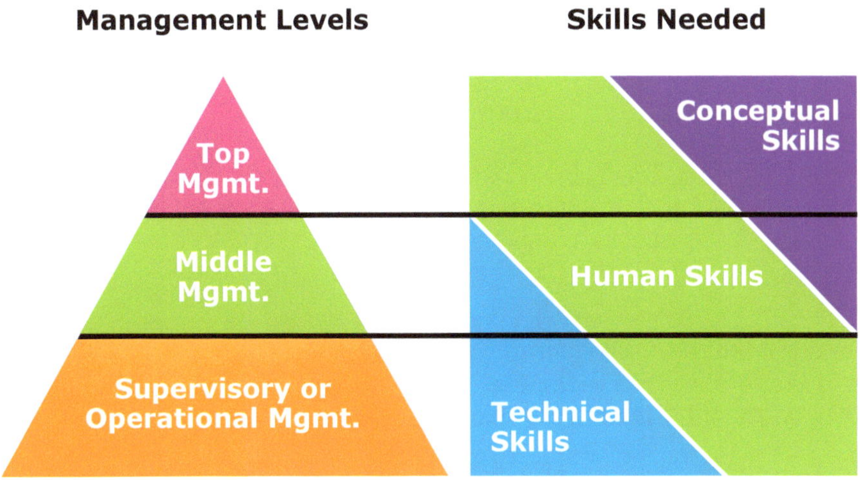

Management Skills Continuum[151]

This can also be explained by thinking of management in three parts: top management, middle management, and supervisory or operational management. The continuum of skills needed to be in management at any level are conceptual skills, human skills, and technical skills. But you'll need these skills in different doses at different levels.

Operational management needs high technical skills and human skills. Middle management needs a healthy dose of all three. While top management doesn't utilize their technical expertise very often, even though that's likely their background and training. Top management must be most proficient in human and conceptual skills.

I often think about an idea called **situational leadership**, which, in brief, states that different situations call for different types of leadership. You'll need a different mix of supportive behavior and directive behavior, depending on what kind of team member you're speaking to or what type of challenge arises. A good leader can flow easily between delegating, supporting, coaching, and directing throughout their day. Without thinking too much about it, they know, or have learned through their own coaching and experience, when to don a different hat. This goes hand in hand with the idea of a balanced manager. Remember how we said you can be both leader and manager? The concept of a balanced manager is like a venn diagram with three circles: management, coaching, and leadership.[152] These all must work together to create balance, progress, and innovation in the workplace.

There are entire books about this subject, and it would be impossible to cram all the theories into one section of one chapter, but understand that there are important differences between management and leadership, but almost every position will need to demonstrate both types of behaviors and skills at some point.

What to Watch for

Leadership is critical to getting your Pharmovation initiative approved, and management is critical to execute your initiative to completion.

To summarize, we explored the differences between management and leadership, but almost every position will need to demonstrate both types of behaviors and skills.

Take Action Now

- Reflect on a time when you demonstrated management when you should have demonstrated leadership.

•••

Big L & Little L

> In this section, we'll learn about...
> - What is the Difference Between a Big L and a Little L?
> - How Little Ls Can Contribute

What is the Difference Between a Big L and a Little L?

We touched on this topic at the beginning of the chapter, but I want to take a moment to really unpack the difference between big L, also known as capital L, "Leaders" and little L, lower case L, "leaders." We want to think of these two words — Leader and leader — as homonyms. Homonyms are two or more words having the same spelling or pronunciation but different meanings and origins.[153]

A Big L Leader is a person who has been given the formal title of leader. They manage other people in an organization. They may be good at their job. They may not be so hot at their job. Either way, they're considered a Leader.

A Little l leader, for the purposes of our conversation, is every pharmacist or technician on the front lines. Every person in the industry has the opportunity to be a leader in their current position. This pertains to managing their individual work, leading their practice, leading by example, and more.[154] Wayne Turmel puts it like this: "These people just lead, regardless of their job titles or positions. They are proactive, they lead by example and step up when things need to be done or tough decisions need to be made."[153]

How Little Ls Can Contribute

I'd like us to think of every person on our team as a Little L leader. They may not be conducting themselves in this manner at the moment, but every person has the potential to live their life this way. Our job, as Big L leaders, is to empower the rest of our team to lead as well. Because no one else leads us through life. Leaders make decisions, provide direction, develop plans, guide and nurture themselves and others, seek opportunities and make choices. Leaders make decisions that affect the way they think, live, interact, react, and learn. The reality is that each of us, and every member of our team is already a leader. What we do with the opportunities presented to us determines what kind of leader we are. Everyone on our team is leading themselves and leading those around them. However, this does not mean they are leading in a positive manner. And that's where the opportunity lies.

Turn the Ship Around: How to Create Leadership at Every Level is one of my favorite leadership books. As the Big L Leader, we have the chance to shift the culture of our team from a leader-follower approach, where people wait to be told what to do, to the leader-leader approach. One way to do this is the "think out loud" approach. In this method, you encourage everyone to say what they see, think, believe, fear, or hope. This facilitates open dialogue and opens the floor for new ideas and possibilities to come to light. It also begins to cement the idea that the team is in charge of their own destiny instead of the Leader being in charge of what happens next. Another way to encourage leader-to-leader behavior is to execute specific goals, not methods. Encourage team members to come up with different ways to get the job done. You should incorporate all of these new ideas with clarity so that the team members clearly and completely understand what the group is all about and trying to accomplish. Finally, you can train Little L "leaders" to use the phrase "I intend to", which allows people to verbalize what they want to do, thus allowing you to affirm their intentions or redirect as necessary. Incorporating these practices will create leadership at every level by having everyone recognize the inherent genius, energy and creativity in both themselves and others.[155] New talents will emerge, new practices will come into play, and your team will be full of newly empowered people.

What to Watch For

Avoid the urge to take control as a leader. Use the powerful leadership model and give control to your employees and create leaders.

But be aware: They say that power corrupts. This can be tempting as a leader, especially if you've been given the title of leader or position of power. Avoid the urge to take control and use a power-based leadership model. Instead, give control to your employees to build leadership skills in each of them.

In her Whitney Award address, Sara J. White shared the Seven Key Elements to Leadership[154]:

1. **Have a written work group vision and mission**: The power of this can be compared to a lighthouse or a foghorn. It is a department commitment that supports the overall organization, like your GPS to keep you on track.
2. **Work effectively to accomplish actual results**: We want to deliver, not just look as though we're working. It's important to measure our approach, manage our time, and ensure that results are achieved.
3. **Persevere and persist**: The one who has the strength of bamboo, that is the ability to bend and bounce back, is the one who will succeed. The bending is required to deal with different circumstances, adjust to changes, overcome adversity and meet every challenge with courage and compassion.
4. **Influence through attitude and approach**: Having a positive and enthusiastic attitude is crucial to supporting the mentality of your little l leaders in the team.
5. **Work well with others**: Successful leaders think of their staff as plants who need to bloom and thrive. To do so, your staff must be rooted in the rich soil of a nurturing work environment. Water them with care and attention, grown with the sunlight of appreciation.
6. **Lead yourself**: Lead yourself so people want to work with you. Having self knowledge and self awareness is critical to playing this part well.
7. **Invest in the future**: Successful leaders invest in the development of their staff, students and residents. They prepare them to lead others and take an active role in helping shape future leaders. We're not talking about innovation here, but investing in our people.

In summary, we learned that Big L Leaders may have an official leadership title while Little L leaders lead regardless of their title or position. Little l leaders have a tremendous impact on others and an opportunity to harness their inherent power. It is our responsibility to cultivate that in our staff and give them opportunities to harness their power and utilize their leadership skills.

Take Action Now

- Share in the Pharmovator community: Are you a Big L or a Little L and what opportunities do you see?

Competency Identification & Assessment

In this section, we'll learn about...
- Leadership Competency Assessment Methods

Now we're going to look at ways to improve leadership, self knowledge, and self study by identifying your key competencies and other assessment tools. A quote from Colin Powell that I think is appropriate here is, "Fit no stereotypes. Don't chase the latest management fads. The situation dictates which approach best accomplishes the team's mission."[156] Knowing yourself fully will help you remain confident in your own abilities and leadership, so you don't feel the need to chase new fads or readjust your style every time a new study is released. Remember how long it takes to implement change? Implementing new changes just for the sake of change is asking your team to go through a lot without much reward. Knowing yourself will help to avoid unnecessary stress for your team.

Leadership Competency Assessment Methods

Let's begin by looking more deeply into the idea of competencies. **Competency** is an observable and measurable knowledge, skill, ability (KSA) or other characteristic that contributes to successful job performance, workplace effectiveness, and career success. We'll look at competencies within two categories. Many people find themselves with a **cluster** of competencies. These are statistically supported groupings of related competencies within a broader scope of skills and behaviors. Clusters of competencies can be particularly helpful once you've discovered them and learn how to use these competencies effectively. The other category is career **stallers and stoppers**. You'll want to watch out for these as career stallers and stoppers are behaviors generally considered to be problematic or harmful to career success.[157]

Let's pause a moment for this brief digression. Knowing oneself can be difficult. This is why many people choose to avoid self knowledge and self discovery. Understanding your competencies means you will also need to identify your weaknesses and potentially problematic behaviors. It is a journey only for those willing to face challenges and potential difficult news. It is also an opportunity to discover your innate talents and how to turn your strengths into superpowers. A leader must approach this with humility above all else. Ok, are you ready?

Let's look at two tools that will help you assess and identify competencies.

First is the **Korn Ferry Leadership Architect Global Competency Framework**. Yes, it's a mouthful. But this tool provides a complete picture of the individual qualities that drive both performance and engagement. It's a unique holistic framework, anchored by comprehensive research on talent at all levels that addresses the foundations of human behavior such as traits, drivers, motivators, experiences and competencies. This framework comprises of four factors, twelve clusters and thirty-eight competencies with associated staged behaviors.

We'll look at this a bit later on as well and revisit it in the next chapter when focusing on your professional development plan. Here we're wanting to explore leadership skills and competencies that will help you be a successful Pharmovator.

The Framework is located on the next two pages. You'll notice there are four factors: thought, results, people and self. Scan through the clusters and competencies below those factors. Pay special attention to some of the career stallers and stoppers that can be troublesome in leadership since they don't inspire or build talent. Be honest with yourself and try to identify which ones pertain to you.

Now, I want to take a moment to preview the Competency Self Assessment Worksheet in the Pharmovation Implementation Guide that's available to you. (see link and QR code at the end of this chapter).

Factor	Cluster	Competency	Definition	Assessment Score (1-5)	Add to Development Plan	Year to Add	Comment
I: THOUGHT	A. Understanding the business	5. Business insight	Applying knowledge of business and the marketplace to advance the organization's goals				
		11. Customer focus	Building strong customer relationships and delivering customer-centric solutions				
		17. Financial acumen	Interpreting and applying understanding of key financial indicators to make better business decisions				
		35. Tech savvy	Anticipating and adopting innovations in business-building digital and technology applications				
	B. Making complex decisions	8. Manages complexity	Making sense of complex, high quantity, and sometimes contradictory information to effectively solve problems				
		12. Decision quality	Making good and timely decisions that keep the organization moving forward				
		32. Balances stakeholders	Anticipating and balancing the needs of multiple stakeholders				
	C. Creating the new and different	18. Global perspective	Taking a broad view when approaching issues, using a global lens				
		19. Cultivates innovation	Creating new and better ways for the organization to be successful				
		33. Strategic mindset	Seeing ahead to future possibilities and translating them into breakthrough strategies				
II: RESULTS	D. Taking initiative	2. Action oriented	Taking on new opportunities and tough challenges with a sense of urgency, high energy, and enthusiasm				
		27. Resourcefulness	Securing and deploying resources effectively and efficiently				
	E. Managing execution	15. Directs work	Providing direction, delegating, and removing obstacles to get work done				
		25. Plans and aligns	Planning and prioritizing work to meet commitments aligned with organizational goals				
		38. Optimizes work processes	Knowing the most effective and efficient processes to get things done, with a focus on continuous improvement				
	F. Focusing on performance	1. Ensures accountability	Holding self and others accountable to meet commitments				
		28. Drives results	Consistently achieving results, even under tough circumstances				

Competency Self Assessment Worksheet

Korn Ferry Leadership Architect: Global Competency Framework[158]

Factor I: Thought

A. UNDERSTANDING THE BUSINESS

5. **Business Insights**
Applying knowledge of the business and marketplace to advance the organization's goals.

11. **Customer Focus**
Building strong customer relationships and delivering customer-centric solutions.

17. **Financial Acumen**
Interpreting and applying understanding of key financial indicators to make better business decisions.

35. **Tech Savvy**
Anticipating and adopting innovations in business--building digital and technological applications.

B. MAKING COMPLEX DECISIONS

8. ***Manages* Complexity**
Making sense of complex, high quantity, and sometimes contradictory information to effectively solve problems.

12. **Decision Quality**
Making good and timely decisions that keep the organization moving forward.

32. ***Balances* Stakeholders**
Anticipating and balancing the needs of multiple stakeholders.

C. CREATING THE NEW AND DIFFERENT

18. **Global Perspective**
Taking a broad view when approaching issues, using a global lens.

19. ***Cultivates* Innovation**
Creating new and better ways for the organization to be successful.

33. **Strategic Mindset**
Seeing ahead to future possibilities and translating them into breakthrough strategies

Factor II: Results

D. TAKING INITIATIVE

2. **Action Oriented**
Taking on new opportunities and tough challenges with a sense of urgency, high energy, and enthusiasm.

27. **Resourcefulness**
Securing and deploying resources effectively and efficiently.

E. MANAGING EXECUTION

15. **Directs Work**
Providing direction, delegation, and removing obstacles to get work done.

25. **Plans and Aligns**
Planning and prioritizing work to meet commitments aligned with organizational goals.

38. ***Optimizes* Work Processes**
Knowing the most effective and efficient processes to get things done with a focus on continuous improvement.

F. FOCUSING ON PERFORMANCE

1. ***Ensures* Accountability**
Holding self and others accountable to meet commitments.

28. ***Drives* Results**
Consistently achieving results, even under tough circumstances.

Factor III: People

G. BUILDING COLLABORATIVE RELATIONSHIPS

6. **Collaborates**
Building partnerships and working collaboratively with others to meet shared objectives.

9. ***Manages* Conflict**
Handling conflict situations effectively, with a minimum of noise.

20. **Interpersonal Savvy**
Relating openly and comfortably with diverse groups of people.

21. ***Builds* Networks**
Effectively building formal and informal relationship networks inside and outside the organization.

H. OPTIMIZING DIVERSE TALENT

4. **Attracts Top Talent**
Attracting and selecting the best talent to meet current and future needs.

13. **Develops Talent**
Developing people to meet both their career goals and the organization's goals.

14. ***Values* Differences**
Recognizing the value that different perspectives and cultures bring to an organization.

*34. **Builds Effective** Teams*
Building strong-identity teams that apply their diverse skills and perspectives to achieve common goals.

I. INFLUENCING PEOPLE

7. **Communicates Effectively**
Developing and delivering multi-mode communications that convey a clear understanding of the unique needs of different audiences.

*16. **Drives*** **Engagement**
Creating a climate where people are motivated to do their best to help the organization achieve its objectives.

23. **Organizational Savvy**
Maneuvering comfortably through complex policy, process, and people-related organizational dynamics.

24. **Persuades**
Using compelling arguments to gain the support and commitment of others.

*37. **Drives*** **Vision and Purpose**
Painting a compelling picture of the vision and strategy that motivates others to action.

Factor IV: Self

J. BEING AUTHENTIC

10. **Courage**
Stepping up to address difficult issues, saying what needs to be said.

*36. **Instills*** **Trust**
Gaining the confidence and trust of others through honesty, integrity, and authenticity.

K. BEING OPEN

*29. **Demonstrates*** **Self-Awareness**
Using a combination of feedback and reflection to gain productive insight into personal strengths and weaknesses.

30. **Self-Development**
Actively seeking new ways to grow and be challenged using formal and informal development channels.

L. BEING FLEXIBLE AND ADAPTABLE

*3. **Manages*** **Ambiguity**
Operating effectively, even when things are not certain or the way forward is not clear.

22. **Nimble Learning**
Actively learning through experimentation when tackling new problems, using successes and failures as learning fodder.

*26. **Being*** **Resilient**
Rebounding from setbacks and adversity when facing difficult situations.

31. **Situational Adaptability**
Adapting approach and demeanor in real time to match the shifting demands of different situations.

Career Stallers and Stoppers

M. TROUBLE WITH PEOPLE
102. Blocked Personal Learner
103. Lack of Ethics and Values
110. Political Missteps

N. DOESN'T INSPIRE OR BUILD TALENT
101. Poor Administrator
104. Failure to Build a Team
105. Failure to Staff Effectively

O. TOO NARROW
106. Key Skill Deficiencies
107. Non-Strategic
108. Overdependence on an Advocate
109. Overdependence on a Single Skill.

Competencies *are observable and measurable skills and behaviors that contribute to workplace effectiveness and career success.*

Career Stallers and Stoppers *are behaviors generally considered to be problematic or harmful to career success.*

Clusters A-O *are statistically supported groupings of related Competencies or Career Stallers and Stoppers. They represent a higher order and broader scope of skills and behaviors that contribute to success or derailment.*

On your own time, you'll take this worksheet and begin to assess yourself to identify a career development plan. Again, this tool is only for those truly ready to embrace their leadership potential.

Briefly, what you'll do is begin with the factor on the left, the cluster, the competency, and then a brief definition of the competency. Then you'll give yourself an assessment score of one to five, one being on the lower end and five being very accomplished in this area. Then you're going to ask yourself, are you going to add it to your development plan? Yes or no. And then, what year would you want to add it? Finally add any other comments you would want to capture now in an ideal world. This competency self-assessment can also be done as a 360-assessment, where your peers would also evaluate you in these areas. I don't think that's necessary at this point in time, but you may wish to consider that when you're creating your continuous professional development plan. For now, I just want you to think about how comfortable you are in these areas across the 38 competencies.

Moving on. There's another tool I like to use that's a bit more focused on healthcare leadership. The American Council of Healthcare Executives (ACHE), of which I am a member, is a part of an overall leadership alliance in healthcare.

The Healthcare Leadership Alliance (HLA) is comprised of the following organizations[159]:

- American College of Healthcare Executives (ACHE)
- American Organization of Nurse Executives (AONE)
- Healthcare Financial Management Association (HFMA)
- Healthcare Information and Management Systems Society (HIMSS)
- Medical Group Management Association (MGMA)

This leadership alliance is a consortium of premier professional healthcare organizations and represents over 140,000 people. ACHE is comprised of not only healthcare professionals but individuals in healthcare leadership. The goal with this alliance is to pursue common interests and advance the healthcare management profession. To this end, they've created a competency directory that's available for healthcare leadership. It can be found on the next page.

The ACHE Competencies Assessment Tool is one of my go to development tools for myself, mentees, and coaching clients.[160] The competencies are grouped into five domains and shown here with a description.

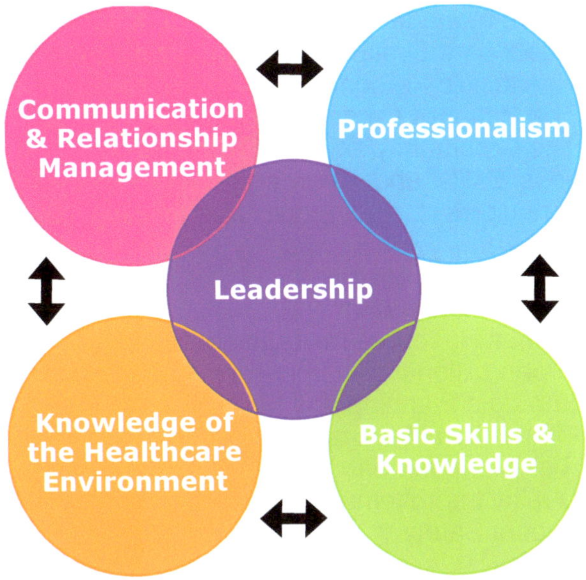

ACHE Healthcare Leadership Competencies[160]

1. Communication and Relationship Management. The ability to communicate clearly and concisely with internal and external customers, establish and maintain relationships and facilitate constructive interactions with individuals and groups.
    - Relationship Management
    - Communication Skills
    - Facilitation and Negotiation
2. Leadership. The ability to inspire individual and organizational excellence, create a shared vision and successfully manage change to attain the organization's strategic ends and successful performance. Leadership intersects with each of the other four domains.
    - Leadership Skills and Behavior
    - Organizational Climate and Culture
    - Communicating Vision
    - Managing Change
3. Professionalism. The ability to align personal and organizational conduct with ethical and professional standards that include a responsibility to the patient and community, a service orientation, and a commitment to lifelong learning and improvement.
    - Personal and Professional Accountability
    - Professional Development and Lifelong Learning
    - Contributions to the Community and Profession
4. Knowledge of the Healthcare Environment. The understanding of the healthcare system and the environment in which

healthcare managers and providers function.

- Healthcare Systems and Organizations
- Healthcare Personnel
- The Patient's Perspective
- The Community and the Environment

5. Business Skills and Knowledge. The ability to apply business principles, including systems thinking, to the healthcare environment.
    - General Management
    - Financial Management
    - Human Resource Management
    - Organizational Dynamics and Governance
    - Strategic Planning and Marketing
    - Information Management
    - Risk Management
    - Quality Improvement
    - Patient Safety

Self Assessment Scoring: You have access to the assessment to complete for yourself in the Pharmovation Implementation Guide's Competency Self Assessment Worksheet. ACHE recommends the following.

Novice (1) An individual's primary focus is understanding and gaining information in order to comprehend the skills needed. You have the level of experience gained in a classroom setting or on-the job training. You are expected to need help when performing this skill.

Competent (3) People with considerable experience develop competence in solving problems within the learned guidelines and rules. You are able to successfully complete the competency as requested. Help from experts may be required from time to time, but you can usually perform the skill independently.

Expert (5) Experts work intuitively analyzing, recognizing patterns, critiquing and solving problems with ideas and expertise. You are known as the expert in this area. You can provide guidance, troubleshoot and answer questions related to this competency.

Looking at this assessment, you'll see it includes many different areas from Korn Ferry's tool. As stated, it's much more geared toward the healthcare profession. Pay special attention to Knowledge of the Healthcare Environment as that is unique to this tool.

As a Pharmovator®, Leadership will be a key part of a continuous professional development plan — to be discussed in the next chapter.

These leadership self assessment tools will help you identify learning priorities. Keep in mind that your development will include enhancement of your strengths and developing areas for opportunity.

What to Watch for

Make note of career stoppers and stallers.

It's not necessary to address every weakness you may identify (that is why we have diverse teams), but make a special note to prevent any career stoppers or stallers. Only with introspection can you grow in self awareness and leadership.

In summary, we studied how to use Korn Ferry Leadership Architect Global Competency Framework as a tool to assess the foundations of human behavior. And in contrast the ACHE Leadership Competency Assessment Tool with more focus on healthcare related competencies.

Take Action Now

- Pick a leadership competency assessment tool to complete (use link at the end of the chapter to access). You will need it for your next steps in Chapter 8: Development.

•••

Key Knowledge, Skills, & Competencies

In this section, we'll learn about…

- Top 4 Leadership Competencies for Pharmovation
- New Leader Assimilation/ Onboarding

Top 4 Leadership Competencies for Pharmovation

Building on our knowledge of the thirty-eight leadership competencies, and more specifically the healthcare leadership competencies outlined in ACHE's assessment tool, now we'll focus in on four top leadership competencies that are crucial for Pharmovation. I'll also share a leadership tool that's not as well known, called New Leader Assimilation and Onboarding.

> **WHAT TO WATCH FOR**
>
> Leadership Pitfalls: Continue to get input and have confidants who will give you honest feedback.

I also want you to watch out for some typical leadership pitfalls. Leaders who refuse new input and don't have trusted people around them are doomed to fail. Make sure you are open to feedback, input on your decisions, and have confidants who will give you honest reactions.

Expanding upon this, here are six pitfalls of leadership[161]:

1. **Perceived knowledge**: Those who think they know, don't. We are all ignorant of what we don't know. Don't succumb to this as a leader.
2. **Isolation and disconnection**: There is a danger of disconnection when you get to higher levels of leadership. If you're not staying connected with others, you won't be in the loop or informed.
3. **Judging others through the lens of your strengths**: I resonate strongly with this one. It's easy to fall into the trap of believing that what's easy for us is easy for others. The truth is that what's easy for one is difficult for another. Difficulty is defined by individual abilities and the capacity to get things done. Arrogant leaders judge people through the lens of their own strengths.
4. **Failure to take responsibility**: When a team loses, it is oftentimes the fault of the coach. It's the same thing with a leader. If the team is failing, we have to look to the leader. And yes, it's a lot of pressure, but it's an important role.
5. **Double standards**: Treat people fairly. No one gets special perks or exemptions. Don't expect more from others than you expect from yourself.
6. **Self-importance**: What makes you a true leader is bolstering the importance of others, not yourself.

Now that we've covered the pitfalls, let's look into the four competencies I believe are critical for Pharmovation.

A Pharmovation leader…

- Cultivates innovation.
- Keeps a strategic mindset.
- Has high levels of financial acumen.
- Is skilled in persuasion.

We'll look at them through the Korn Ferry Framework, a tool which outlines competencies. It was documented in the book, *For Your Improvement* by Michael M. Lombardo and Robert W. Eichinger.[157] We will define which factor the competency falls under and which cluster it pertains to. Then we'll define what it looks like to be skilled, less skilled, or talented in a particular area. We'll also look at possible causes of lower skill and a few tips to develop the competency.

Let's unpack the identified Pharmovation competencies. First: **cultivates innovation**. This particular competency is within the thought factor and falls under the cluster of "creating the new and different."

- A leader skilled in this area...
  - Comes up with useful ideas that are new, better, or unique.
  - Introduces new ways of looking at problems.
  - Can take a creative idea and put it into practice.
  - Encourages diverse thinking to promote and nurture innovation.
- A leader less skilled in this area…
  - Stays within their comfort zone rather than experimenting with new ways of looking at things.
  - Presents ideas that are ordinary, conventional, and from the past.
  - Tends to be critical of others' original ideas.
  - Has a style that discourages the creative initiatives of others.
- A leader who is talented in this area…
  - Moves beyond traditional ways of doing things; pushes past the status quo.
  - Continually assesses the market potential of an innovative idea or solution.
  - Finds and champions the best creative ideas and actively moves them into implementation.
  - Tries multiple, varied approaches to innovative ideas.
  - Builds excitement in others to explore creative options.

Some possible causes of lower skill are…

- Caution or risk averse.
- Not open to new ideas.
- Has a narrow perspective.
- Lacks knowledge about process.
- Doesn't value innovation.

Here are a few tips to develop this competency:

1. Wonder what role you can play? Innovation takes a village.
2. Desire to enhance group creativity? Diversify.
3. Don't perceive yourself to be creative? Remove restraints.
4. Lack a climate conducive to innovation? Take the lead.

Next, we'll look at **strategic mindset**. This particular competency is within the thought factor and again, falls under the cluster of "creating the new and different."

- A leader skilled in this area...
    - Anticipates future trends and implications accurately.
    - Readily poses future scenarios.
    - Articulates credible pictures and visions of possibilities that will create sustainable value.
    - Creates competitive and breakthrough strategies that show a clear connection between vision and action.
- A leader less skilled in this area…
    - Is more comfortable in the tactical here and now.
    - Spends little time or effort thinking about or working on strategic issues.
    - Contributes little to strategic discussions.
    - Lacks the disciplined thought processes to pull together varying elements into a coherent view
- A leader who is talented in this area…
    - Sees the big picture, constantly imagines future scenarios, and creates strategies to sustain competitive advantage.
    - Is a visionary and able to articulately paint credible pictures and visions of possibilities and likelihoods.
    - Formulates a clear strategy and maps the aggressive steps that will clearly accelerate the organization toward its strategic goals.

Some possible causes of lower skill are…

- Doesn't like complexity.
- Prefers what is familiar.
- Has short-term focus.

- Lacks competitive drive.
- Is overly tactical.
- Has low curiosity.
- Is too busy with today's tasks.

Here are a few tips to develop this competency:

1. Can't anticipate what's to come? Become a trend-watcher.
2. Out of touch with customers? Make customer intimacy a priority.
3. Unclear about the competitive landscape? Get market smart.
4. Not standing out in the marketplace? Identify your distinctive advantage.

Third, we'll unpack **financial acumen**. This particular competency is within the thought factor (are you seeing a pattern here?) but falls under the cluster of "understanding the business."

- A leader skilled in this area...
    - Understands the meaning and implications of key financial indicators.
    - Uses financial analysis to generate, evaluate, and act on strategic options and opportunities.
    - Integrates quantitative and qualitative information to draw accurate conclusions
- A leader less skilled in this area…
    - Is unfamiliar with financial terms.
    - Is unclear about the cause-and-effect relationships among different business functions and overall financial performance.
    - Pays little attention to financial impact when drawing conclusions.
- A leader who is talented in this area…
    - Transforms financial information into business intelligence through analysis and integration of quantitative and qualitative information.
    - Identifies and monitors key financial indicators to gauge performance, identify trends, and suggest strategies that can impact results.

Some possible causes of lower skill are…

- Overwhelmed by data.
- Not curious.
- Ignores financial information.
- Not thinking strategically.
- Lacks basic financial skills.

Here are a few tips to develop this competency:

1. Don't know the basics? Get training.
2. Think finance is not your responsibility? Get involved.
3. Focus too narrow? Expand your perspective.
4. Emotional about decisions? Ground yourself in data.

Finally, let's look at the competency to **persuade**. This particular competency is within the people factor and falls under the cluster of "influencing people."

- A leader skilled in this area...
    - Positions views and arguments appropriately to win support.
    - Convinces others to take action.
    - Negotiates skillfully in tough situations.
    - Wins concessions without damaging relationships.
    - Responds effectively to the reactions and positions of others.
- A leader less skilled in this area…
    - Pushes own point of view too strongly.
    - Fails to win support or buy-in from others.
    - Is unable to negotiate solutions that are agreeable to all.
    - Responds negatively to the reactions and positions of others.
    - Has difficulty articulating a logical argument on their own position.
- A leader who is talented in this area…
    - Shares own ideas in a compelling manner that gains commitment from others.
    - Negotiates skillfully and creates minimal noise when working toward an agreed-upon solution.
    - Finds common ground and acceptable alternatives that satisfy the needs of multiple stakeholders.

Some possible causes of lower skill are…

- Has low personal confidence.
- Lacks allies or supporters.
- Is not confident in their own ideas.
- Comes on too strong.
- Does not listen or respond to objections.
- Has no plan of action or follow-up.

Here are a few tips to develop this competency:

1. Need to be heard? Speak up.
2. No allies? Build relationships first.
3. Need more help? Start with your boss.
4. Lack confidence? Address root causes.

Do not let the above information overwhelm you, but rather refer back to it when building your own competencies and considering where you may need to concentrate your efforts when developing areas you aren't as skilled in. A leader is not intimidated by their own lack of competency, but sees this as an opportunity to improve!

New Leader Assimilation/Onboarding

I also want to share a quick tool that you can use called New Leader Assimilation. This is available to download as well. I know that many people who pick up this book will be new to healthcare leadership and possibly struggling to thrive in this new role since leadership in healthcare often comes with limited leadership training. I know this can be frustrating.

What you'll do is conduct a new leader assimilation workshop for yourself. It can be done! You'll just need half a day where you get a group together of your direct reports or the entire team for which you're responsible. It just requires a few hours with the new leader (AKA you!), a simulation, and some leader feedback. We'll walk through it in just a bit.

The overall goal of why we would conduct an onboarding meeting or assimilation meeting (as GE who coined these events calls it) is that it's a technique to compress the period during which a new manager and the people who work for him or her sound each other out and become acquainted with the respective operating styles and expectations. Your team gets acquainted with the "new boss in town." Instead of a slow rippling effect throughout the office, it's a compact all-hands meeting where the new manager is able to hear more input and to express expectations and explain their operating style, so everyone is on the same page.

The process begins with questions from the team (you may collect these beforehand through an anonymous process if you wish) that are posted on a flip chart for all to see. You do not need to be in the room for this, but have someone else collect these questions. Then, while the team takes a quick break, you can review the questions and responses provided without them present. This way you can quickly get up to speed on issues that exist, lingering problems and questions the team has, and start to identify where you'd like to begin.

The overall objectives are to:

- Bring the new leader "up to speed" quickly.
- Reduce the level of preliminary apprehensions, which may exist for all parties.
- Provide a two-way flow of information on such points as style of operation, needs of the organization, and problem areas.

- Bring the organization together with the new leader as a unit at an early point in order to maintain momentum and commence the team building process.
- Provide a forum for the new leader to present ideas and philosophies.

It is recommended to do this within the first 90 days of a leader taking on their new role. I think the sweet spot is around 60 days because you've gotten to know the team a bit. You understand more of the challenges and are not completely fresh. You'll have had the opportunity to gain some of this information through initial one-on-one meetings, but this leader assimilation event is still very critical.

Some benefits for the new leader are…

- "Clears the air" from the beginning in manager-employee contact.
- Establishes the manager as a "real person" — puts name with face.
- Provides an opportunity for the manager to listen to the concerns of the organization.
- Provides input to the manager on key questions and issues.

Some benefits for the team are…

- Provides insight on manager's operating style, personal priorities, and expectations.
- Opportunity to ask questions on potentially sensitive matters.
- Team approach to getting acquainted with the new manager and demonstration of how they like to function as a group.

Plus this can be fun! It's a way to engage. It's also an opportunity for the team to agree on a code of conduct. For example:

- All Input is Accepted
- Everyone Participates
- Respect Confidentiality and Anonymity
- Avoid Acronyms (they can be alienating)

While you're free to use the rest of your time to cover any topics you feel are needed, here are nine key questions that have come to the surface since this process was developed:

1. What are your highest hopes for this team? (Team & leader respond)
2. What does the leader need to know about us as a group? What are the strengths and limitations, what do we do well, what is the team especially proud of? (Team responds)
3. In light of recent changes in leadership, what have you found to be the most challenging? What have you found to be positive?

(Team responds)

4. What do you want from your leader to help you do your jobs better? (Team responds)
5. What don't we know but would like to know about the leader? (Team responds)
6. What do you want to know about your leaders' management style? (Team & leader respond)
7. What would you like to see this leader do differently, less, more of, stop altogether, continue? (Team responds)
8. If you were in the new leader's shoes, what would you focus on over the next 6 months, a year? (Team & leader respond)
9. What does the leader need to know to be successful in their new role (Team responds)

Having this meeting with your team is extremely beneficial for everyone involved, as you can see. Additional questions that the leaders should answer include: How should we communicate with the Leader? Problem Solving/Decision Making Style? Other Preferences.

Make sure to take notes and incorporate what you learn from this meeting into your strategic plans for the future. You may also want to reference back to it when certain items are accomplished, even pointing to who had the original idea or made a comment that set the team in a new direction. Another great opportunity to empower your Little L leaders!

In summary, let's review the top four leadership competencies for Pharmovation: cultivates innovation, has a strategic mindset, possesses financial acumen, and is persuasive. Having a new leader assimilation meeting is the best way to engage with a new team and facilitate onboarding that benefits everyone. I hope you'll take advantage of all the resources available for you to download below before moving on to our next chapter: Development.

TAKE ACTION NOW

- What leadership competency do you want to develop further?
- Share your thoughts in the Pharmovator Community.

To support you incorporating the learnings from this chapter, access the Pharmovation Implementation Guide. Visit www.pharmovationguide.com or scan the QR code below for full access!

CHAPTER 8

Pharmovation DEVELOPMENT

"Continuous personal and professional development is your key to the future."
—Brian Tracy

Sitting outside your boss' office. Palms sweaty. Shallow breathing. Checking your watch for the tenth time. Why are they running so late? Let's just get this performance review over with. Phew. It's time. And it goes by fairly quickly. Not so bad. You've been doing good work. Whatever were you worried about in the first place? You even got a raise.

Then your boss abruptly switches gears. "Where do you see yourself in five years?" you hear them ask. What? You were just worried about getting through today. You haven't been giving much thought to the future in your current state of heightened anxiety.

And this, dear friends, is why I strongly advocate for separate professional development reviews, because it's a completely different state of mind for your employee. Development, coaching, and goal setting should be done on a separate day, at an appointed time.

These conversations can be difficult for many leaders. Nine times out of ten, that's because leaders have no experience with these types of meetings. No one has ever trained them. They've never been on the receiving end of this type of conversation. So, where to start?

Years ago, I was in a development meeting with a boss of mine, and I expressed an interest in learning more about IT. I was on the fence about whether or not I should go back to school and get a degree. She confidently asserted, "You don't need a degree. Let's get you some experience!" After that, I was placed on some new projects that allowed me to get on-the-ground training in an area that interested me. It was thrilling.

Now, as a leader myself, I try to bring this type of creativity to professional development meetings. Once, a technician in our department was considering leaving to pursue a career in nursing, or possibly IT, she wasn't sure. Through our conversation I was able to understand her strengths and what she wanted to do. Both pay and upward mobility were important to her. She had some great skill sets that weren't being fully utilized in her current position. With this information, the department was able to create a coordinator position for her, with a raise, and find some courses and on the job training for her with IT aspects. Everyone walked away happy.

But upward mobility isn't always the answer. Another pharmacist I had flagged for a leadership position didn't want to move into management. He liked being a direct patient care pharmacist. Through some coaching conversations we realized he wanted to dive deeper into nephrology so he could be a subject matter expert in the field. Plus, he was interested in ways to explore layered learning. For him, development wasn't "moving up", it was finding ways to gain mastery in current areas. His development, and expertise proved valuable to the department in the long run.

Development looks different for different people.

In this chapter, we will explore continuous professional development (CPD), find out how to do career planning, CPD self assessment, CPD action plan, and bring it full circle with developing others. The objective of this chapter is to take ownership of your career and encourage leadership growth by completing a 2-year development plan.

Investing in yourself through CPD provides you a personal ROI for your life and career. Through reading this book you will receive the tools to complete or update your CPD. I am so proud of you for investing in yourself.

•••

Continuous Professional Development (CPD)

In this section, we'll focus on...

- What is CPD?
- Steps
- Components
- Myths & Common Mistakes

What is CPD?

Let's first ground ourselves in the Connector Framework™ we've looked at before. This process guides your mission through to execution and excellence. We've reviewed before how your mission, vision, and values are important to developing your strategic plan, which ultimately helps you justify resources. The next steps are job recruiting and descriptions. We haven't spent a lot of time discussing these steps, but they are important to mention to connect the dots here. In this chapter, we'll differentiate between performance management and measures, and professional growth and development plans. Again, I'll reiterate that performance management and professional growth should be separated. Managing employee performance is not the same as coaching employees toward growth and development. They should not happen in the same meeting, in the same atmosphere, or under the same umbrella. Completely separate.

Within the category of professional development and growth plans, we have several components to assist us. These include competency assessments, an in depth look at strengths and opportunities, and the creation of an action plan for development activities. Professional development can also include movement on a career ladder or into a new position, but through the earlier example, we know that career development doesn't always include a position change.

Now, there are multiple terms used around development planning. In general, they are all very similar and used interchangeably. You might come across career development, personal development, professional development, and individual development. These are all terms that we can use. The only nuance is that personal development tends to focus on items that may not be directly related to your career.

When I think about a development plan, I like to think of it as a roadmap. The purpose of a personal development plan is to help someone reach their personal and career goals. The goals are the destination; the plan is the map. There isn't always only one way to reach a destination, perhaps multiple routes are available.

The official definition of **professional development** is learning to earn or maintain professional credentials such as academic degrees, formal coursework, attending conferences, and informal learning opportunities situated in practice.[162] It's been described as intensive and collaborative, and ideally incorporates an evaluative stage. I often add the term growth development to ensure a plan to achieve lifelong career goals is innovative and bold beyond current credentials.

Continuing pharmacy education differs a bit from continuing professional development. Our national organization Accreditation Council for Pharmacy Education (ACPE) helps differentiate between continuing pharmacy education (CPE) and continuing professional development (CPD). Continuing pharmacy education is "a structured educational activity designed or intended to support the continuing development of pharmacists and/or pharmacy technicians to maintain and enhance their competence. Continuing pharmacy education (CPE) should promote problem-solving and critical thinking and be applicable to the practice of pharmacy."[163] While continuing professional development (CPD) is "a self-directed, ongoing, systematic and outcomes-focused approach to lifelong learning that is applied into practice. It involves the process of active participation in formal and informal learning activities that assist in developing and maintaining competence, enhancing professional practice, and supporting achievement of career goals. The CPD approach is cyclical in nature where each stage of the process can be recorded in a professional learning portfolio."[163] And don't worry, of course I have you covered with a CPD template within the Pharmovation Implementation Guide.

Since the CPD approach is cyclical in nature, let's imagine that cycle. It's a "self-directed, ongoing, systematic and outcomes-focused approach to lifelong learning that is applied into practice.[163]

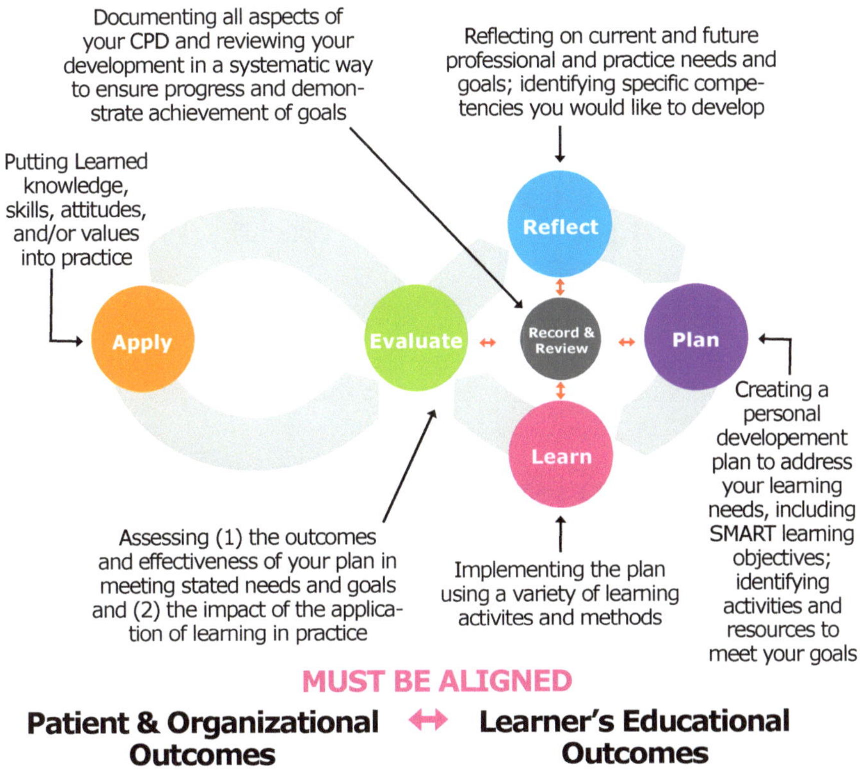

ACPE Continuing Professional Development[163]

As an ongoing cycle, there's no one place to start but we'll have to begin somewhere.

1. **Reflect**: Reflect on current and future professional and practice needs and goals. Identify specific competencies you would like to develop.
2. **Plan**: Create a personal development plan to address your needs, identifying activities and resources to meet your goals.
3. **Learn**: Implement the plan using a variety of learning activities and methods.
4. **Evaluate**: Assess the outcomes and effectiveness of your plan in meeting stated needs and goals and the impact of the application of learning in practice.

Throughout all four of these steps, it's imperative that the participant record and review throughout, documenting all aspects of CPD and reviewing development in a systematic way to measure progress and demonstrate achievement of goals.

Then, the knowledge can be **applied** into daily practice. After a certain amount of time (perhaps a set amount of time), you can then evaluate whether or not this application of knowledge has been successful or needs further development.

And... repeat as needed. To bridge this development to application within an organization, it's important to keep patient and organizational outcomes aligned with the learner's educational outcomes.

Steps

Let's outline the steps a bit more fully. I've used these steps many times in the past and aligned them with the CPD steps from a pharmacy perspective.

1. **Reflect**: During this step you'll conduct a self assessment to identify strengths, areas for improvement, and goals. The goals and objectives here will be to identify short, mid, and long-term career goals, plus, choose your top 3 development objectives to accomplish in the next 12 months. Sources for this step will be personal self reflection, tools like competencies lists and Discover Your Strengths, or 360 feedback from a manager, colleagues, employees or customers.
2. **Plan**: After the reflection step, it's time to enter planning mode. You'll take your top 3 development priorities and identify development actions in your development action plan. When planning, consider a mix of activities based on how people develop

(we'll explore this in more detail shortly). Then, communicate and discuss this plan by sharing and reviewing it with your manager, mentor, and/or HR colleague.

3. **Learn**: It's time to execute the plan. Schedule activities and complete by planned due date.
4. **Evaluate**: Revisit your plan quarterly at the least.
5. **Apply**: Confirm your ability to implement in practice or readjust as necessary.

Remember, that this is a journey, not a quick fix. I suggest that you do this for 12 months at a time. While you can plan forward into year two or three, make sure you're doing a minimum of 12 months.

Components

There's a template I've included in your Pharmovation Implementation Guide (available at the QR code or link at the end of the chapter). The worksheet has an **assessment** and **action plan** section. The template ties in with the previous leadership chapter where you've discovered your key competencies and strengths. There are places to include that information as well as a SWOT analysis of yourself, prior performance reviews, and then a 360 feedback or any other assessment you've completed in the past. Also included in the resources at the end of the chapter is a link to a CPD online tool from the National Association of Boards of Pharmacy (NABP) as an option when creating a personal development plan."[164]

This is a process that doesn't come into being overnight. But, as our quote at the beginning of the chapter reminds us: "Continuous personal and professional development is your key to the future." This is not something to overlook or brush to the side.

Myths & Common Mistakes

WHAT TO WATCH FOR

Don't believe the myths of professional development plans.

Something you want to watch out for is falling prey to some of the common myths of professional development plans. Some of these are believing that your manager is responsible for your professional development or that your company will provide you with everything you need. Perhaps you think you're done learning because you already have an advanced degree or you don't have the time since starting a new position. You may think that because you have an annual performance review that you don't need a professional development plan, or that you're too focused on your current job. Maybe you're worried you don't have time to devote to this or it costs too much. And finally, you may say "I already have one." But if you haven't looked at it every quarter or updated it at least once a year, then that plan is probably out of date. Beware of these excuses, they will hold you back. Only you are responsible for your professional development. While you can gain guidance from your manager or company, they are only there for support. You must shoulder the responsibility.

Here are a few rookie mistakes and tips for how to avoid them:

- **Waiting for manager or human resources**: Remember you are in the driver's seat. Take the initiative.
- **Not starting with an assessment or self-reflection**: Always take time to reflect. Consider a strengths finder or 360 feedback.
- **No long-term goal**: It's always helpful to identify short-term 1-5 year AND long-term 5+ year goals.
- **Too many goals or actions**: It's great to be bold in your goals, but consider focusing on 3-4 action items.
- **No clear action items and time frame**: Based on your goals choose how you will develop them and when.
- **Narrow methods for development**: Create diversity in your development methods. People typically learn 70% from experiences, 20% from coaching or mentoring, and 10% from courses.
- **Not using a tool or template**: Tools and templates can help you get all the pieces and track your progress.
- **Not updating regularly**: Consider updating twice per year at opposite times from job performance discussions.

To sum up, CPD is a self-directed, ongoing, systematic and outcome-focused approach to lifelong learning that is applied into practice. The basic steps are to reflect, plan, learn, evaluate, and apply. Components of these steps include a self assessment and an action plan. When embarking upon this journey for yourself or coaching employees along their professional development plans, take care to avoid myths and common mistakes.

•••

Career Planning

In this section, we'll learn about...
- Career Planning Questions
- Career Pathways Assessment & Options

Career planning can be daunting and overwhelming, which is why many professionals float along for decades with no real direction, staying in positions long after they've outgrown them. We need to be strategic about our careers just like our businesses. In this section, we'll outline helpful questions to consider when planning your career and introduce a Career Pathways Assessment and other options.

Career Planning Questions

For career planning, here are some **personal assessment** questions that are extremely useful. I've used them to coach individuals who are looking to advance their career but aren't sure which direction to go, as well as seasoned professionals who are looking for a change. These questions can be asked at any point in your career and utilized at any stage.

- What are you passionate about? (This can be personal and/or professional — finding an overlap can be the magic of work-life integration)
- What are your favorite competencies (knowledge, skills, abilities)?
- What are your favorite activities or tasks?
- What type of work do you like?
- When do you feel you are at your best (alone, in a group)?
- Ask 5 friends or family members to identify your greatest strengths.

You'll be able to download this as a resource at the end of the chapter, which will help guide you in creating your development plans from a self assessment career planning perspective. The next set of questions you will ask are to evaluate your **career options**. You may identify potential roles and jobs you could be doing. Consider writing down all the positions you're interested in, and possibly revisiting some nontraditional roles we've discussed in previous chapters. You can then use your personal assessment and highlight those positions that match more of your passions and values.

Once you've identified a few positions to consider, write down if there are any cons to these potential positions. Then, identify your top short- and long-term position targets. Which of the options is more in line with your short-term goals? What about long-term goals? Are there any overlaps that seem interesting to you?

Career Pathways Assessment & Options

Next is a tool I have used in the past that is relevant in terms of looking at the various roles available within pharmacy. You may not need to revisit this because you feel set already and have a direction, but it's worthwhile to at least do this critical factor assessment.

The APHA Career Pathways tool includes[165]:

- A Briefing Document
- Workshop Workbook
- Career Profiles
- Online Assessment Tool
- Career Resources
- Follow-up Materials and Exercises

The overall assessment tool they use is called the Vigilant Decision-Making Process. Through this process you'll appraise the challenge ahead, assess yourself, survey and evaluate alternatives, and finally commit to a next step.

The workshop workbook helps you dig into and rate some of your critical factors in a very systematic way. For example, you'll answer questions regarding how much time you want to spend doing specific factors, such as interaction with patients or conducting physical assessments. Questions are rated on a scale of 1 to 10 (one being none of my time and 10 being all of my time). Once all the questions are answered, it will be able to match you with career profiles that may be a good fit for you. As you know by this point, I appreciate a systematic approach to accomplish tasks. It helps us know that we're not inadvertently leaving things out or bypassing options we haven't thought of.

Career Critical Factors

- Interaction With Patients
- Conducting Physical Assessments
- Interpreting Laboratory Values
- Continuity of Relationships
- Helping People
- Collaboration With Other Professionals
- Educating Other Professionals
- Variety of Daily Activities
- Multiple Task Handling
- Problem Solving
- Focus of Expertise
- Innovative Thinking
- Applying Scientific/Medical Knowledge

- Creating New Knowledge via Research
- Management/Supervision
- Pressure/Stress
- Work Schedule
- Part-Time/Job-Share Opportunities
- Leisure/Family Time/Parental Leave
- Exit/Re-entry Opportunities
- Job Security
- Opportunities for Advancement/Leadership
- Professional Involvement
- Income /Benefits
- Geographic Location
- Autonomy
- Self-Worth
- Future Focus
- Professional/Community Prestige
- Unique Practice Environment
- Advanced Degree
- Entrepreneurial Opportunity
- Additional Training
- Interacting With Colleagues
- Travel
- Writing
- Working With Teams
- "On-Call"
- Work on Holidays/Weekends
- Presentations

Career Option Profiles

- Academia: Clinical Practice
- Academia: Economic, Social, and Administrative Sciences (ESAS)
- Academia: Pharmaceutical Sciences
- Ambulatory Care
- Association Management
- Chain Community Pharmacy: Management
- Clinical Specialists
- Community Health Center (CHC)
- Compounding Pharmacy
- Contract Research Organization
- Corporate Management
- Government/Federal Pharmacy
- Home Health Care
- Health System Pharmacy: Inpatient
- Health System Pharmacy: Outpatient
- Independent Community Pharmacy
- Long Term Care
- Mail Service
- Managed Care
- Medical Communications/ Drug Information
- Nuclear Pharmacy
- Office-based Medication Management
- Pharmaceutical Industry: Medical Liaison
- Pharmaceutical Industry: Research and Development (R&D)
- Pharmaceutical Industry Sale and Marketing
- Pharmacy Benefit Management (PBM)
- Pharmacy Law/Regulatory Affairs/Public Policy
- Specialty Pharmacy
- Entrepreneur
- Consultant

I really suggest this tool as a place to begin if you're stuck on your next career move. Even if you're not stuck, it's a wonderful tool to have in your back pocket for the next time a transition is on the table.

Find it in the References in the back of the book.[166]

What to Watch for

Career Planning does not need to be static. Revisit your assessment as part of your overall professional development process.

Keep in mind that career planning does not need to be static. You'll revisit assessments over the years as part of your overall professional development process. Career planning is a helpful step alongside professional development that can help you ensure that your career matches your passions and preferences. And the APHA Career Pathways Assessment is extremely helpful in uncovering your preferences and exploring new options.

In summary, we learned how career planning assessment can help you assure your career matches your passions and preferences. And that the career pathways assessment can help you uncover your preferences and explore new options.

Take Action Now

- Complete the career planning worksheet (available to download at the end of this chapter).
- Consider completing the APHA Career Pathways Critical Factors Assessment.

•••

CPD Self Assessment

In this section, we'll learn about...

- Self Assessment Sources & Methods
- Goals
- Prioritized Development Objectives

Now, we'll look at a few self assessment sources and methods, outline some goals, and explore prioritized development objectives. There's a downloadable worksheet available to help you through the process. I've mentioned this previously, but we'll go through it in more detail here.

"Unless you do something beyond what you have already mastered, you will never grow."
—Ralph Waldo Emerson

This is one of my all-time favorite quotes, and it has helped me at many transition points throughout my career. It's easy for us to get comfortable in our current roles, enjoying the ease that comes with mastery. But it's important for us to keep considering bold advancements and actions we can take to continue our growth. Remember we are striving to be both Big L's and Little L's — constant motion and experiencing new things is a part of this journey.

As we've discussed previously, self assessment is a critical step along the journey of Pharmovation. There are two different types of tools that can assist you when assessing yourself: solitary tools and those that you do with the feedback of others.

Self Assessment Sources & Methods

Some **self assessment** tools are:

- Competencies Assessment (discussed in Chapter 7)
- SWOT
- Strengths Finder
- Learning Activities (such as reading literature, engaging in teaching or precepting, involvement in research or writing, participating in a CE activity)
- Reading This Book or Taking the Pharmovation Course
- Center for the Advancement of Pharmacy Education (CAPE)

Some reflection sources **from others** are:

- Performance Reviews
- 360 Feedback from Manager, Peers, or Direct Reports

When you download the CPD in the Pharmovation Implementation Guide your assessment tab will look like the example on the next page.

There is space to record what types of self assessments you've completed and any short notes you wish to add. Then, you'll answer the following **reflection questions**:

Continuing Professional Development Plan (CPD)
REFLECT / ASSESSMENT

DATE CREATED: DATES REVIEWED/REVISED:

Assess / Reflect Sources

Y or N	Self- Assessment
	Competencies Assessment - ACHE
	Competencies Assessment - Korn Ferry
	SWOT
	Strengths Finder
	Learning Activities
	Center for the Advancement of Pharmacy Education (CAPE)

Y or N	From Others
	Performance Review
	360 Feedback

	Reflection Questions
1	List work-related situations in which you felt confident or competent:
2	What knowledge/skills contributed to the successes above?
3	List work-related situations that you need to feel more comfortable or satisfied with:
4	What knowledge/skills would you want to develop or improve to better manage similar situations in the future?

CPD Self Assessment

- List work-related situations in which you felt confident or competent.
- What knowledge or skills contributed to the successes above?
- List work-related situations that you need to feel more comfortable or satisfied with.
- What knowledge or skills would you want to develop or improve upon to better manage similar situations in the future?

After these reflection questions, you'll have an opportunity to document your competencies by listing your top strengths and areas for development. Let me tell you a bit more about the additional competency assessment tools you should consider.

I recommend a book written by Don Clifton called *Now, Discover Your Strengths.*[167] This book has been adopted by Gallup and used within their **Strengths Finder** assessment. Many times we focus too much time on our weaknesses or areas for improvement. And I like this book because it prompts you to focus on your strengths. It sorts your strength competencies into four domains: executing, influencing, relationship building and strategic thinking. A small fee does come with this assessment tool, but it can be a great guide. So go for it and turn your strengths into superpowers.

I also want to touch on something available from the **Center for the Advancement of Pharmacy Education (CAPE)**. In 2013, CAPE unveiled the fourth version of educational outcomes created to guide curricular discussions of faculty and preceptors within the academy and curriculum planning, delivery, and assessment within colleges and schools of pharmacy. While their assessment tool may be a bit too basic for some of the things you'll be planning and executing, the topics are worthwhile to look at and consider. Plus, you can use this scale with newer learners when you develop others, which we'll talk about shortly.

Here are the domains and sub categories that are included in the CAPE assessment[168]:

- Foundational Knowledge
    - **Learner**: A learner can develop, integrate, and apply knowledge from the foundational sciences to evaluate scientific literature, explain drug action, solve therapeutic problems, and advance population health and patient-centered care.
- Essentials for Practice and Care
    - **Patient-Centered Care (Caregiver)**: A caregiver provides patient-centered care as the medication expert who collects and interprets evidence, prioritizes patient care needs, formulates assessments and recommendations, implements care plan, monitors and adjusts plans, and documents activities.
    - **Medication Use Systems Management (Manager)**: At this level the professional manages patient healthcare using human, financial, technological, and physical resources to optimize the safety and efficacy of medication use systems.
    - **Health and Wellness (Promoter)**: A professional who designs prevention, intervention, and educational strategies for individuals and communities to manage chronic disease and improve

health and wellness.
    - **Population-Based Care (Provider)**: This individual describes how population-based care influences patient-centered care and the development of practice guidelines and evidence-based best practices.
- Approach to Practice and Care
    - **Problem Solver**: Identifies problems; explores and prioritizes potential strategies; designs, implements and evaluates viable solutions.
    - **Educator**: Educates all audiences by determining the most effective and enduring ways to impart information and assess understanding.
    - **Patient Advocate**: Assures that patients' best interests are represented.
    - **Collaborator**: Actively participates and engages as a healthcare team member by demonstrating mutual respect, understanding, and values to meet patient care needs.
    - **Cultural Sensitivity (Includer)**: Recognizes social determinants of health to diminish disparities and inequities in access to quality care.
    - **Communicator**: Effectively communicates both verbally and nonverbally when interacting with an individual, group, or organization.
- Personal and Professional Development
    - **Self-Aware**: Examines and reflects on personal knowledge, skills, abilities, beliefs, biases, motivation, and emotions that could enhance or limit personal and professional growth.
    - **Leader**: Demonstrates responsibility for creating and achieving shared goals, regardless of position.
    - **Innovator**: Engages in innovative activities by using creative thinking to envision better ways of accomplishing professional goals.
    - **Professional**: Exhibits behaviors and values that are consistent with the trust given to the profession by patients, other healthcare providers, and society.

If you've already completed your competencies assessment, slot your top strengths and areas for development in the chart on the next page. If not, this is another good time to do so. Knowing your competencies (and which of those are your favorite competencies, as we mentioned earlier) will be a key asset when creating the map you'll need for your professional development.

Goals

It's now time to capture your career goals. I have separated these out into short-term (1-2 years), mid-term (3-5 years) and long-term (5-15 years) goals to force you to think within each time horizon. And while we don't know exactly what's going to happen (our careers can be a jungle gym and not a ladder), I think it's important to put a stake in the ground for what you want to do in the future. Having long term career goals will help you to take the steps along the way. As they say: you can eat an elephant one bite at a time. Pharmovation is about thinking bolder so you can apply this innovation to your career.

Continuing Professional Development Plan (CPD)
REFLECT / ASSESSMENT

COMPETENCIES
(Knowledge/Skills/Abilities)

	Strengths
1	
2	
3	
4	
5	

	Areas For Development
1	
2	
3	
4	
5	

CAREER GOALS

	Short Term (1-2 years)
1	
2	
3	

	Mid Term (3-5 Years)
1	
2	
3	

	Long Term (5-15 Years)
1	
2	
3	

	Prioritized Development Objectives (SMART)
1	
2	
3	

CPD Competencies & Goals

If you are reading this book, you are likely interested in being a big L. Your career goals may be more clear as positions of advancement. If you are more interested in remaining a little L, it is important to note you will still have career goals. There is nothing wrong with assuming leadership in an informal capacity, we need leaders at all levels. You may want to develop deeper expertise within an area to become a subject matter expert. Spending time on this self assessment will help you to know yourself and allow you to own your career.

Prioritized Development Objectives

The last step in your CPD Self Assessment is to prioritize your development objectives. You want to take in all of the above information and filter down. These are your high-level priority development objectives. Keep in mind that you cannot develop everything at one time, so consider 2 - 3 to start.

Remember to make your objectives SMART.

S - Specific: State precisely what you'll be able to do.
M - Measurable: Include observable or quantifiable actions and behaviors.
A - Achievable: Be realistic about what you can accomplish.
R - Relevant: Align with your practice or organization's goals.
T - Timed: Include a target date to be completed.

Here's two examples using SMART formatting:

- By January 20XX, I will develop a medical education program for children and adolescents with ADHD who are receiving services at the community mental health clinic where I practice.
- By January 20XX, I will expand my knowledge and complete a certification program on revenue cycle management.

What to Watch For

Not thinking about the mid- to long-term. Start your development now for the big long term career goals.

In summary, remember to keep in mind your mid- and long-term goals as well. Start your development now to work toward the big long term career goals. You can use several assessment sources including self-assessments, reflection, and 360 feedback. Don't rely on one source to gain all the information you need. Once you've identified your SMART goals, prioritize them and set aside time so they'll be accomplished on schedule.

TAKE ACTION NOW

- Complete the self assessment tab on the CPD (available to download at the end of this chapter).

•••

CPD ACTION PLAN

In this section, we'll study...
- Learning Methods
- Action Plan Components

Your time spent in self assessment and competency discovery will lead you to develop wonderful and achievable short-, mid-, and long-term goals. But without a plan, those goals are just wishful thinking. You've got to have a strong plan to ensure you achieve your goals. And you know me, I love to connect the dots.

Learning Methods

Now we'll explore a number of different in-depth learning methods and the components needed to make your action plan sing — plan, learn, evaluate, and apply. Take a look at the Learning Methods chart on the next page.

We mentioned earlier the different percentages that are typically associated with different types of learning methods. This practice is known as the 70/20/10 rule, but let's go more into detail now.

There are three types of learning[169]:

1. **Structural Learning**: This is formal training or education that's completed away from your current place of employment. It's usually done before any other type of professional development

comprises about 10% of all learning. It can take place in the form of workshops, webinars, online learning portals, eLearning or mLearning.

2. **Learning from Others**: This is generally considered coaching and can take place near or on the job. This is exposure to different types of careers or new ideas. It takes place within communities of practice, subject matter networks, user generated-content, collaborative platforms, coaching, mentoring, or feedback. It's typically about 20% of your learning journey.
3. **Learning from Experience**: Here is where the bulk of learning occurs. Learning by doing. Learning on the job from your own experience. This is active learning and problem solving. It takes place within new placements, job rotations, job shadowing, self-directed and incidental learning, as well as through new projects or special assignments. This is where the majority of learning takes place.

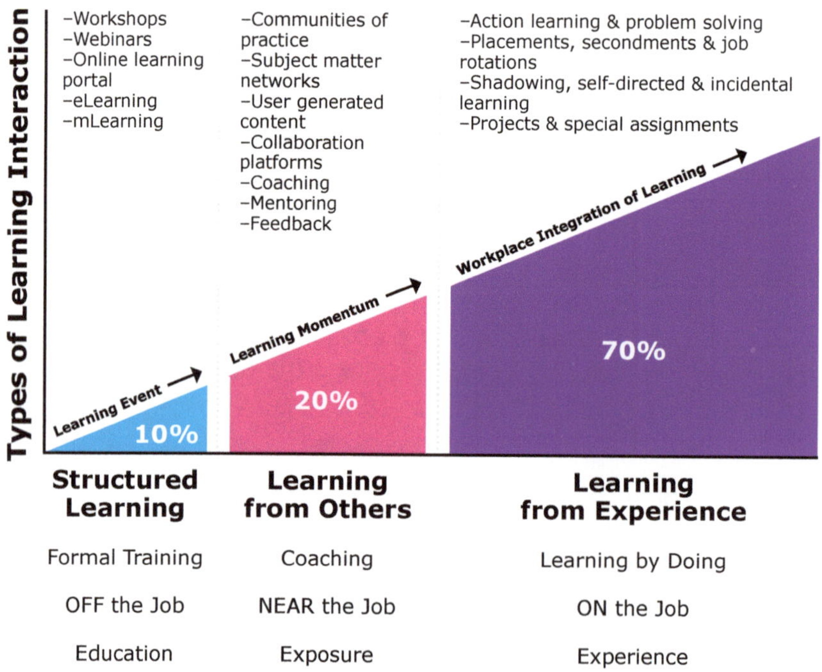

Learning Methods[169]

When creating a professional development action plan, it's imperative that you keep all three of these styles of learning in mind and in this balance. Going back to school may be exactly what you need, but in the end, that type of learning is only 10% of your professional development. You must create a balanced approach to your career. The 70/20/10 rule can help you keep it in perspective.

Another way to categorize professional development options is through ACPE's CPD Learning Categories. These are:

- **EDUCATION: A. Continuing Education**. Formal, structured continuing education activities (e.g. ACPE-accredited provider, Board of Pharmacy approved)
- **EDUCATION: B. Academic/Professional Study**. Structured non-CE education or unstructured autonomous learning activities
- **EXPERIENCE: C. Scholarly Activities**. Generation and dissemination of knowledge to advance practice or profession
- **EXPERIENCE: D. Teaching and Precepting**. Active involvement in the education and training of others
- **EXPERIENCE: E. Workplace Activities**. Workplace experiences that promote learning and professional development
- **EXPERIENCE: F. Professional/Community Service**. Contributions or leadership in professional or community activities that align with professional/career goals

Action Plan Components

Once you've identified your goals, you'll plan your next steps and document your action plan. These next steps typically involve some type of learning, which we've now outlined several ways to approach learning both inside and outside of the workplace.

I've made a downloadable action plan resource available for you to use. The worksheet tab is color coded so you can work on it in stages from plan, learn, evaluate, and apply. The top section allows you to document your development objectives, followed by the learning methods, and then your status updates. There is a preview of the lay out followed by the steps to fill out the action plan on the next page.

1. **Plan**: The development objectives will pre-populate from the self assessment tab. Then in the Plan Learning Activities section, you're going to identify learning activities (what) from a 70/20/10 perspective. This will help you identify ways to incorporate all three types of learning into your action plan.

   Then you'll list which objectives (by number) that specific learning activity covers and when you're going to complete it in terms of a due date. I like to do it this way because I find that certain learning activities do cover multiple learning objectives. For example, you may decide that you're going to get a master's in business administration and that's probably going to cover multiple of your learning objectives. Or if you work with a mentor, they will likely support several of your objectives.

Need help coming up with learning activities? Remember. you have resources in the competency tools from ACHE, Korn Ferry, and Strengths Finder that provide ideas for how you can grow the competencies you identify. There are two activities in the Exposure Method that I recommend for everyone (yes everyone). Find a mentor and create a networking plan.

PLAN		EVALUATE			APPLY
Prioritized Development Objectives (SMART) (Linked to Assessment Tab)		Achieved	Why or Why Not	Outcome of Learning	Implemented Into Practice
1	0				
2	0				
3	0				

PLAN		LEARN	EVALUATE		
Learning Method	Activity	Date Complete	Were my learning needs met?	What did I learn?	New learning needs identified
EDUCATION OFF the Job Formal Training					
EXPOSURE NEAR the Job Coaching/Mentoring					
EXPERIENCE ON The Job Learning by Doing					

EVALUATE - STATUS UPDATES			
Status Updates	Plan Status	In Progress Reason	Plan Changes
Q1			
Q2			
Q3			
Q4			

Action Plan Worksheet

2. **Learn & Evaluate - Learning Activities**: You'll then check in on your learning methods monthly or quarterly. Did you complete the activity and when? Were your learning needs met (fully, partially, or not at all)? Capture your insights about what you learned and if new learning needs were identified.
3. **Evaluate & Apply - Development Objectives**: We now want to connect back and reflect on our learning to evaluate our development objectives. Evaluate these on a regular basis to look at whether or not we achieved that objective either fully, partially or not at all, and why or why not. Identify the outcome of the learning. And you have three options there: what you have learned can reinforce your current knowledge, skills, or practice; you can plan to change your practice based on this learning; or you can plan to pursue additional learning or information. And then you'll be able to answer in the apply section, whether you implemented it into practice. Yes or no.
4. **Evaluate - Status Updates**: To support your own accountability to your CPD, you want to do quarterly status updates for the overall plan — or twice a year at a minimum. Document the plan status as in progress, complete, or unable to complete. If your goals are still in progress, what is the reason — more information or learning is needed, more time is needed. You may need to modify the development objectives if they don't fit anymore. Maybe you need additional reflection on your development needs. There is room to plan changes if needed.

What to Watch for

Don't try to develop too many areas at one time. It's a lifelong journey.

Remember that this is a lifelong journey. If you try to develop too many areas at once, you are likely to experience burnout and frustration.

In summary, in this section we studied learning methods with the 70/20/10 rule, and that the action plan components are: plan, learn, evaluate, apply.

Take Action Now

- Complete the plan section of the action plan tab on the CPD (available to download at the end of this chapter).

Developing Others

In this section, we'll focus on...

- Professional Development Plan vs Performance Review
- Myths for Managers
- Coaching Based on Performance/Potential

Before we close this chapter, let's bring it full circle to the discussion we began at the start: developing the members of our team. It's one thing (a very important thing!) to develop ourselves. This creates a culture of professional development where those we lead can see we are invested in our own advancement and are not simply sitting comfortably at the top. Invariably, this will lead us to encourage the development of those around us. We'll do this through the creation of a growth or development plan (instead of only performance reviews), busting some myths often perpetuated about managers, and coaching based on the performance and potential of our staff.

Jack Welch, the former CEO of GE has famously said, "Before you are a leader, success is all about growing yourself. When you become a leader, success is all about growing others." And that is an extremely important role a leader must inhabit. That of a coach, mentor, and guide.

Professional Development Plan vs Performance Review

Let's unpack the difference between a growth development plan and a performance review. We briefly mentioned this earlier, but it's well worth a deeper exploration.

	Professional Development Plan	Performance Review
Discussion Content	Discuss & adjust development objectives of the employee	Set and evaluate business goals & core success factors
Time Focus	Future	Current Year
Discussion Aim	Advancement of personal development	Align individual objectives to hospital/department goals
Role of the Mgr	Coach, Counselor	"Boss," Appraiser
In the"Driver's Seat"	Employee	Manager

Professional Development Plan vs Performance Review

When creating a growth development plan with an employee, you'll discuss and adjust development objectives with them. You'll focus on the future and discuss how to advance their personal development. Your role is that of a coach or counselor, and the employee drives the conversation. Alternatively, when in a performance review, the discussion focuses on setting and evaluating business goals and core success factors. You're focused on the current year, not the future, and aiming to align individual objectives to hospital or departmental goals. You're firmly in the role of boss or appraiser and the one driving the conversation. Because these meetings are so vastly different in content and purpose, they should never be conducted simultaneously. When you force your employee to juggle such starkly different situations, neither becomes productive. It becomes inevitable that one will overshadow the other, making both less effective.

Myths for Managers

What to Watch For

Don't spend all of your time developing your low performers.

Something that's not popular to say but is nonetheless true, is that not all of your employees will benefit the same amount from growth development meetings. And that's ok. Remember that they are the ones in the drivers' seat of their own professional development. Your role is to coach them, but they have to want to progress. Don't spend too much time trying to develop those who aren't fully committed to their own development.

However, it's a myth that the employee is solely responsible for their development. Your encouragement and coaching will be vital in their growth. You must also not succumb to the idea that there isn't enough time to conduct these meetings or invest in your employees' growth. Make time. You are a leader, not only a manager. So we have to look at the time we spend with our team as a good investment with a positive ROI of our time. Remember that there are things your employees wish for and aspire to beyond just a raise or promotion. Also, coaching them toward achieving their goals does not necessarily mean that they'll leave the company and desert the team. Sometimes it does mean that they'll grow into other positions outside the organization, but that is not a reason to lessen your investment in them. And again, make sure to support the range of performers in your department. Remember the high achievers may be the ones that are most vocal about their development desire, but middle achievers may just need encouragement.

Coaching Based on Performance/Potential

From this perspective, I want to turn to a small performance potential grid. You may also be familiar with a larger 9 block grid which adds an additional row and column. But we will keep it simple with these four boxes.

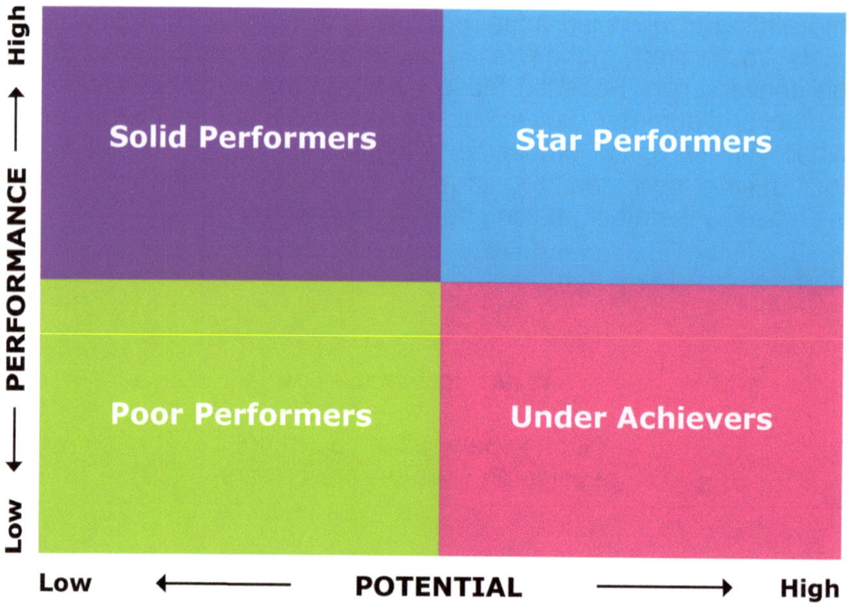

Performance Potential Grid

If it's helpful to have more defined categories and percentages, let's look at it this way. Think of your team in four different categories:

1. Star Performers: High potential with high performance.
2. Solid Performers: Lower potential but high performers.
3. Underachievers: Those with high potential but generally lower performance.
4. Poor Performers: Low potential and low performance.

By this breakdown, coaching time spent with underachievers garners you the most incremental increase in performance. This category has high potential but isn't sure how to maximize it, or finds themselves without encouragement or guidance. On average, an effective coach can help add another 10% in performance from their star achievers. These folks are already at the top of their game, and probably fully invested in their own growth. You can help them along, but they don't need as much encouragement as others.

To produce the most overall improvement in team performance, your time allocation should look like this:

- 20% to the poor and solid performers
- 50-60% to the underachievers
- 20-30% to the star performers

To summarize, conduct these development sessions separately from performance reviews. Steer clear of the myths and misconceptions outlined above and focus on coaching based on employee performance. This strategy will have the greatest impact on your entire team in the long run.

TAKE ACTION NOW

- Assess your team for performance/potential and reflect on your coaching time allocation.
- Share in the Pharmovator Community your insights on developing others and how you might change your approach.

To support you incorporating the learnings from this chapter, access the Pharmovation Implementation Guide. Visit www.pharmovationguide.com or scan the QR code below for full access!

Chapter 9

Pharmovation EXECUTION

"Vision without execution is hallucination."
—Thomas Edison

Pause. Close your eyes. Take a couple of deep breaths. Now imagine what your department would be like if you had every single resource you needed. Imagine overcoming the frustration of health system pharmacy chaos. Imagine enough technicians on your team, all practicing at the top of their licenses. Imagine aligned reimbursement for pharmacists' services with work that's being done instead of dispensing of product. Imagine you have no recruitment challenges and turnover rates are lower than other organizations because people love working on your team. Imagine the right technology, the right number of pharmacists at every level, being able to pay your team members what they deserve. Furthermore, you've got personal resources for each staff member and innovative technologies that drastically improve safety.

Because of all this, you feel comfortable knowing that safety has improved, you're not worried that things are being missed or overlooked because your staff is overworked. You walk into work each morning full of joy and greet team members who are also happy to be there. You're able to serve your organization and community fully and feel at peace in your choice of profession. You see high levels of patient engagement and collaborate effectively with other hospital staff.

Imagine all this, and more. This is the outcome of Pharmovation.

In this chapter, we will explore how to connect the dots, putting Pharmovation to practice, what best practices entail, and take those next steps into the future. The objective of this chapter is to be confident, able to realize the entire book promise by pulling it all together and implementing learnings into execution.

Connecting the Dots

In this section, we'll study...
- Pharmovation Framework™
- Connector Alignment™
- Execution

Pharmovation Framework™

I created Pharmovation to support the needs and vision for Pharmacy. By now you know that Pharmovation is the only implementation program of its kind that not only shows you exactly what to do to accelerate your career and advocate for resources, but ultimately how to advance pharmacy practice to bring joy to your work and improve patient outcomes. The above daydream can become reality with the rigorous application of what you've learned throughout this book.

We've journeyed together through the right mindset, explored the pharmacy enterprise, understood what strategies are necessary, what services are needed, what technology is available, what leadership potential you have, and how to develop all of the above to find the success you're longing for. With the tools in this book, you're finally ready to innovate both your practice and yourself.

Steve Jobs once said that "Creativity is just having enough dots to connect." What he means by his "dots" are the experiences that give you the knowledge to be able to make decisions. You have definitely expanded your knowledge through this book and you're learning how to connect the dots in many different ways.

Together we've explored the areas necessary to truly catapult you into the career you've always desired. Namely, we've looked into...

- **Pharmovation MINDSET**: You learned the importance of mindset to your success and how to incorporate it in your pharmovation journey.
- **Pharmovation OPPORTUNITY**: You know why staying aware of the bigger picture is vital and have realized that there's a huge need for pharmacists.
- **Pharmovation ENTERPRISE**: You've realized the potential reach of pharmacy and innovative growth. Capitalize on the value of the integration and reach of the pharmacy enterprise.
- **Pharmovation STRATEGY**: You know how to justify resources for both small and large needs.

- **Pharmovation SERVICES**: You're excited about the needs and opportunities for pharmacists and technicians to be accountable and innovative with their roles.
- **Pharmovation TECHNOLOGY**: You are empowered to justify new technology to meet your team and your patients' needs.
- **Pharmovation LEADERSHIP**: You're ready to practice increased leadership and accountability regardless of your current role in your organization.
- **Pharmovation DEVELOPMENT**: You feel a sense of ownership and increased motivation for your career. You are growing your interest in leadership and have created a development plan

And now we're concluding with…

- **Pharmovation EXECUTION**: You'll gain confidence and realize this entire book's promise by pulling all the skills you've gained into practice and implementing them into your career.

Connector Alignment™

All along we've followed the connector alignment framework, the steps connecting the dots from mission to execution.

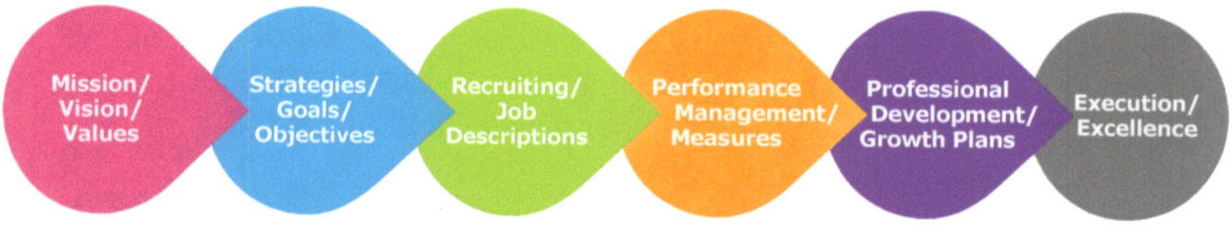

Connector Framework™

We started talking about the importance of building upon our mission, vision, and values to create our strategies, goals, and objectives. These middle dots of recruiting and job descriptions, and performance management were not covered in depth in this book, but they remain important in connecting the dots. They are covered in other programs of mine. We dove deep on professional growth development plans in chapter 8. And now we are ready to focus on the final dot — execution and excellence.

Execution

Finally, we've arrived. It's the moment to carry out and put into effect your plans and course of action. You're ready to accomplish, complete, and implement. It's great that we do all the strategy and planning to ensure we are innovative, but if we don't put it into effect, all of that planning is somewhat worthless. Your execution should be completed with excellence. When executing your well laid plans, focus on achieving excellence, not perfection.

Both during and after execution, it's important to check in with yourself occasionally along the way. I recommend that you build in reflection time to answer the following:

- Is what I'm doing "connecting the dots" and adding value?
- How do I spend my time?
- What should I prioritize?
- What can I do today to execute?
- What am I doing to support my team toward execution?

What to Watch for

"You can't connect the dots looking forward; you can only connect them looking backward. So you have to trust that the dots will somehow connect in your future. You have to trust in something — your gut, destiny, life, karma, whatever. This approach has never let me down, and it has made all the difference in my life."
—Steve Jobs

In summary, we've covered a lot of information throughout these pages together. The Connector Framework™ reminds us to connect the dots from our mission, vision and values all the way through to execution. Execution is the critical dot, the finish line, where you're able to accomplish, complete, and finally implement your plans.

•••

Pharmovation in Practice

In this section, we'll look at…

- Incorporate Into Your Practice
- Make Pharmovation Mindset a Habit
- Time Assessment & Prioritization

Incorporate Into Your Practice

Pharmovation is not a one-time action. You don't create one business plan, gain approval and pat yourself on the back. It's a mindset to incorporate into your practice moving forward. It's a habit you can create so that you're constantly innovating, leading creatively, and building your team.

Here are a few suggestions on how to incorporate elements of this book into your practice:

- **Mindset**: Use the innovation and intrapreneurship skills and behaviors regularly. Use change and transformation techniques throughout the strategy and execution process.
- **Opportunity**: Ongoing assessment of the need and opportunity for pharmacy and landscape surveillance for disruptive innovation.
- **Enterprise**: Ensure accountability and execution with your team for all aspects of the enterprise. Innovative assessment during strategic planning.
- **Strategy**: Use situational analysis, strategic planning, and business plans annually.
- **Services**: Innovative assessment during strategic planning.
- **Technology**: Innovative assessment during strategic planning.
- **Leadership**: Practice management and leadership daily as appropriate. Competency assessment annually.
- **Development**: Execute your development plan as scheduled and revisit quarterly. Innovatively plan annually. Develop others regularly.
- **Execution**: Use execution disciplines and best practices regularly.

Make Pharmovation Mindset a Habit

The foundation for all of Pharmovation is the proper mindset. So how do we make all of this part of our mindset? Remember that mindset is a habitual or characteristic mental state that determines how you interpret and respond to situations. We have the ability to control our mindset and change it when necessary. So much of Pharmovation is about creating a mindset of bold accountability within pharmacy. As we have discussed in the Mindset Performance Loop in Chapter 1, when you have the right mindset it affects your attitude, which in turn affects your behavior, changes your actions, drives better results, and increases performance. Everything begins with mindset. Never overlook this crucial step.

A quote I love on this topic is...

"Practice is the best of all instructors."
—Publilius Cyrus

As we talked about in the development chapter, putting things into practice is the best way to learn. You can't just shut this book and leave it on the shelf, you must take it and implement it into your day-to-day practice.

Time Assessment & Prioritization

Another thing to keep in mind is time. Time is our most valuable resource. So when you're asking yourself, "How do I incorporate all this into my practice?" The answer is, carve out the intentional time to do so. You need to complete a time study of yourself and engage in self reflection to ensure you're spending the right amount of time managing, leading and coaching. You need time for self development, developing others, planning strategy, and ensuring execution. You need daily, weekly, and quarterly prioritization of the most important tasks. To find this time, trim activities that do not add value.

To summarize, in this section you learned how to incorporate Pharmovation into your practice. And that you need to habitually assess your mindset and carve out time to prioritize what's important.

TAKE ACTION NOW

- Reflect on how you spend your time and answer the following:
  - Is what I'm doing "connecting the dots" and adding value?
  - How do I spend my time?
  - What should I prioritize?
  - What can I do today to execute?
  - What am I doing to support my team toward execution?

•••

BEST PRACTICES

In this section, we'll focus on...
- Execution Disciplines
- Failure To Execute
- Connector Foundation™

Execution Disciplines

So, what are the best practices surrounding execution? In this section we'll explore execution disciplines, what failure to executive looks like, and how this links back to our connector foundation.

As Thomas Edison's quote at the beginning of this chapter reminds us, "Vision without execution is hallucination." You've done so much work and invested a large amount of time to get to the execution step, now's not the time to blow it!

There are four disciplines to execution[170]:

1. **Focus on the wildly important**: You want to make sure you're prioritizing and focusing on what's most important. We've spoken about having big, hairy, audacious goals. Ensure that you and your team stay focused on these throughout execution.
2. **Act on the lead measures**: Don't bite off more than you can chew, but stay focused on acting on key measures. This is what you can control and track early on to ensure you're performing.
3. **Keep a compelling scoreboard**: Develop a way for employees and fellow leaders to track and engage with your progress. This will drive performance and ensure better communication with other stakeholders.
4. **Create a cadence of accountability**: This is where execution really takes place. The other three disciplines set the stage, but this final one is crucial. Focus on consistency and accountability. Make sure everyone has a purpose and is held accountable. Everyone should know their place and their responsibility within the overall plan.

Focusing on these four simple disciplines will conform and transform you from being a strategy-based leader to an execution-based leader. And this will showcase real results within your organization.

Another way to sum it up...

> ***"Execution is the ability to mesh strategy with reality, align people with goals, and achieve the promised results."***
> —Lawrence Bossidy

Here is a recommendation in terms of time breakdown. While I know that we've spent a majority of our time in this book focused on strategy and the justifying of resources, it's imperative that you don't lose sight of the fact that executing on that strategy is critical. What we find is that most people spend 95% of their time on strategy and the final 5% on execution. But this is the opposite of what is needed for success. What we should really plan for is about 5% of our time spent on strategy and 95% spent on execution. Sometimes strategic planning can stretch out though many months of the year, and it feels like we are in a constant state of designing and identifying new strategies. I am all for ongoing environmental scans, but we really need to focus on execution and avoid project creep.

Failure to Execute

Let's look now at why people and companies fail to execute. What holds them back?[171]

1. The 'dots' not aligned
2. 'Dots' not communicated
3. 'Dots' not memorable
4. Resources not provided
5. Quantity of strategies/projects
6. Inflexibility of plan
7. Lack of collaboration across units
8. Staff does not feel responsible for strategy
9. Confusion about activities that add value
10. Time management

These are all things we've discussed throughout planning and strategy phases, but it bears repeating that failure to do these will result in an ultimate failure of execution. You must align your purpose with that of your organization, communicate this connection in a memorable way, ensure that resources are provided, take on exactly what you can handle and no more, be flexible in your planning, collaborate across your organization with other units, hold your staff and yourself accountable, communicate the value you're adding and manage time effectively to execute properly.

Another best practice is communication, networking, and partnering. We've talked about where the Chief Pharmacy Officer (CPO) connects to a variety of organizational committees, as well as leaders within the health system. It's important that we are ensuring communication, involving them in our strategic planning, and networking to build personal relationships. We need to find ways that we can partner so that plans are not coming across as just the pharmacy initiative, but as true partnerships, because we all have the best goals in mind to achieve the triple aim and support our organizations.

Connector Foundation™

Another set of invaluable tools is the Connector Foundation. We've talked a lot about the connector alignment and that framework of connecting the dots from mission and vision to execution. These often underutilized tools will support your ability to have excellence and execute well.

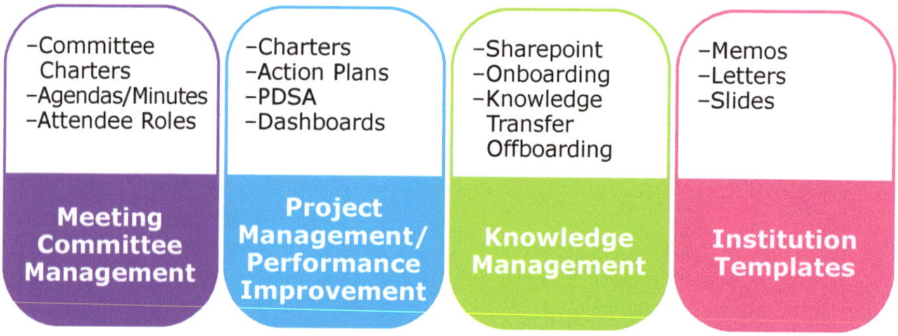

Connector Foundation™

- **Meeting/Committee Management**. Know what meetings are being held throughout your organization and what committees are formed. What do they do? Who's in attendance? What are their goals and agendas? What are the roles of attendees? How can they relate to pharmacy or benefit from pharmacy collaboration?
- **Project Management/Performance Improvement**. Each of the strategic plan goals we've identified in our strategic planning should receive a project charter and action plan created for it. There's a variety of templates and tools that can be used, but the key is to have it in writing. What's in the scope? What's out of the scope? What is the goal timeline? You must be tracking performance through dashboards, both for your projects and overall department performance.
- **Knowledge Management**. Once a project is approved, managing information that others receive on its progress is critical. I'm a big fan of using the program SharePoint from Microsoft, but there are other options. A centralized tool of some sort helps ensure collaboration and sharing. Onboarding and offboarding processes to support knowledge transfer between people during transitions is critical.
- **Institution Templates**. I'm a big fan of templates. Again, I'll point to a centralized location like SharePoint for everything to live and stay organized. Whether it's' memos, letters, slides, project plans, business plans or whatever, it's important to utilize templates whenever possible. We shouldn't be wasting time creating documents from scratch.

So, in summary, best practices include keeping in mind the four critical disciplines of execution, avoiding the 10 common reasons people and companies fail to execute, and using tools found in the Connector Foundation to support consistent execution.

Take Action Now

- Reflect on how much time you spend on execution.
- Assess which of the Connector Foundation tools you use regularly and what you may need to add to your practice.

• • •

Next Steps & Future

In this section, we'll focus on...

- The First Thing To Do
- Next Steps
- Future Growth & Development
- Celebrate

The grand finale is here. And yet, it's really just the beginning of your Pharmovation journey. As we conclude, we'll look at the first thing you should do after closing this book, address next steps, future growth and development, and pause to celebrate all you've already accomplished!

The First Thing To Do

After turning to the last few pages, I recommend you take a few moments to reflect on what you've learned and how you've grown from the moment you opened this book. Take this time to update your professional development plan with this learning activity and the insights you've gained. Begin with you. Where do you want to go next? Where do you want to develop? What areas have you been neglecting? Where are you now and where do you want to be in the future? What are you most passionate about? You may even want to revisit the development chapter to guide you through this step.

Next Steps

With your development plan in hand, remember all the resources that you received with this book in the Pharmovation Implementation Guide. Now's the time to take advantage of these goodies. Download everything provided at **www.pharmovationguide.com**. Open this book again and again to the appropriate chapters as you complete the materials available to you.

You may want to then schedule a session with myself. I love learning what Pharmovators are out there accomplishing, scheming, and dreaming of. Visit **www.kimberboothe.com/bookings** to schedule an exploration call to see how I can support you or your organization. If you're stuck, frustrated, or just need a little guidance, I'm here to cheer you on and help along the way.

Remember to reach out to the Pharmovator Community at **www.kimberboothe.com/community**. You're not alone! There are so many other pharmacy professionals on this journey of pharmovation with you. Make connections, garner support, and ask questions to others who are in the same boat as you.

And finally, identify and plan your next development activity. Don't stagnate, keep moving!

Future Growth & Development

If you discover that your next development steps align with my own, I'd love to find ways to work together. I serve our profession by providing coaching, consulting, courses, and memberships on strategic pharmacy leadership. As a strategic pharmacy consultant, I help organizations connect the dots from strategy to execution to advance pharmacy practice. Contact me if your organization needs help integrating the pharmacy enterprise, thinking strategically about innovation, business planning or project planning assistance.

In addition to the online courses and virtual membership, I also provide 1:1 career coaching and create personalized programs to help you get clear direction and gain confidence during every stage of your career. Let's collaborate to advance pharmacy practice.

Celebrate

The name Pharmovation comes from the concept of tying together our profession with the goal of innovation. Being a Pharmovator means being bold. It means striving to advocate for resources, advance pharmacy practice, and accelerate your career.

Pharmovation = Pharmacy + Innovation

"Pharmacy can do more with more!"
—Kimber Boothe

The first thing to do now is reflect on what you learned in this program and what new needs you identified. You can continue to implement what you learned. Please know that I am available to serve you in other ways. And last but not least. CELEBRATE!

Celebrate your success, move forward with confidence, and advocate for the resources you need to advance practice across the country. Let's go Pharmovators! So, what's next? Your pharmovation career. I wish you the best and look forward to staying in touch.

Thank you again and Happy Pharmovating!

TAKE ACTION NOW

- Please consider providing a review on Amazon or wherever you purchased this book.
- Email me your feedback to **kimber@kimberboothe.com**. I want to hear from you!

To support you incorporating the learnings from this chapter, access the Pharmovation Implementation Guide. Visit www.pharmovationguide.com or scan the QR code below for full access!

ACKNOWLEDGMENTS

As the saying goes, if you see a turtle on a fence post you know he did not get there alone. There were many people integral to my personal growth and my Pharmovation journey to advance pharmacy practice that has culminated in this book.

Family

- **Richard Boothe** - Thank you for being my best friend and partner in life, while being supportive of my career passions and sharing equally in managing our home and children. You make life fun.
- **Evan, Ethan, & Ella** - I love our family dinner games as I hear your innovative and thoughtful answers. While you are growing up too fast for me, I am excited to see how you will design the lives you want.
- **Francine Walter** - I am so blessed to have you as my mother. While our time was cut short, your love and modeling has shaped me. Thank you for encouraging me to dream big and be myself.
- **Edward Walter** - Your support at every stage of my life has been amazing. Thank you for identifying pharmacy as a career option in the US News & World Report which set me on this amazing path.
- **Leila Samuels** - You are the best mother-in-law a girl could ask for and have filled a void in my life. You're a great listener, raised an amazing son, and are a role model as a working mom who helped me balance everything.

Friends

- **Lisa Stanley** - You are my lifelong best friend and have been there for me despite my moves around the Eastern US. You ground me so that I can find the right balance in my life.
- **Patty Corrigan** - You are my best Pharmacy "Phriend" and have been my partner in crime since we started as freshman at UCONN.
- **Angela Cassano** - Thankful for building our friendship during our pharmacy school volunteer leadership work with APHA which grew during residency and continued during our career journeys. Your intrapreneurship and entrepreneurship have inspired me.

Career Leaders, Mentors, and Partners

- **Lori Lee** - You are a role model of supportive and assertive leadership. Thank you for believing in me and allowing for innovation as we created bold business plans to transform the department.
- **LeeAnn Miller** - You are a close friend and inspiring leader. Thank you for starting me on the journey of PAI by making it a priority for my role and for being a practical sounding board.
- **Marjorie Lazarre** - I have been moved by your leadership growth and style of accountability. My financial acumen and knowledge of the business of pharmacy has been greatly enhanced by your mentorship.
- **Lisa Stump** - You taught me bold leadership that extended beyond the pharmacy department and the value of technology in advancing care.
- **Marina Yazdi** - You have been a cheerleader for me from the time you were in my first precepted resident class. I am thrilled to see your career growth and appreciate your friendship and advice.
- **Eric Tichy** - While you admitted there were doubts about my returning to health systems after being in Pharma for a decade, you were first to recognize me for executing a bold strategy. Thank you for your early review and support of the Pharmovation program.
- **Amber Zaniewski** - Pharmovation was designed with you as my avatar to support aspiring leaders' bold strategic innovation. I am privileged to have been part of your growth and impressed by what you have achieved as a strategic pharmacy leader.
- **Brian Mansfield** - Thank you for hiring me as a student intern and creating opportunities for students to contribute to broad aspects of the department that set me up for success.
- **Carol Bright** - As my personal pharmacist you showed me the value of a pharmacist-patient relationship and opened my eyes to this career. You continued your support by taking me to my first pharmacy conference just after starting in Pharmacy School.
- **Jann Skelton** - From the time you were my preceptor during my APHA rotation you have inspired me toward advocacy. You have shown me the power that one person can have for a movement with the work you do for the Pancreatic Cancer Action Network.
- **Marrianne Ivey** - You are an inspirational leader who has been an advocate for the Pharmacy Enterprise and Chief Pharmacy Officer. I appreciate your mentorship and encouragement for my innovative intrapreneurship and entrepreneurship journey.
- **Doina Dumitru** - You have inspired me as a health system leader and with your passion for using information technology to advance patient care. I am thrilled to be partnering with you to support the

mindset and professional development of healthcare leaders.
- **Howard Cohen** - Thank you for bringing me under your wing for leadership mentorship and for your entrepreneurship guidance.
- **Jerry Siegel** - I have benefited by learning from you from many perspectives as a servant leadership role model, sharing the stage with you and being your client.

Medipreneurs

I have mentioned within the book that the Medipreneurs Summit was the inspiration for me to focus on advancing pharmacy as I connected my passion with the need to create Pharmovation. You each have individually touched me as well.

- **Anna Garrett** - You are the first pharmacist I followed who was sharing your knowledge in diverse platforms for a greater impact.
- **Michelle Fritsch** - You are a master of goals and I value your collaboration and appreciate your advocacy for patients.
- **Sue Paul** - Your passion for patient care and sharing that message is contagious. Thank you for partnering as we impact our profession through our accountability sessions and your development of teams that I have led.

Pharmfluencers

You are an amazing mastermind group that holds me accountable. I am in awe of what you are doing to advance pharmacy as entrepreneurs.

- **Kelley Carlstrom** - You have an amazing way of connecting with people and I appreciate your advocacy to support oncology practice.
- **Christina Madison** - I have learned so much from you on the opportunities for pharmacists in public health and how we can raise the voice of the profession through the media.
- **Blair Thielemier** - My teams and I have benefited from your programs to elevate pharmacy and have used the knowledge and inspiration to support ambulatory practice advancement.
- **Frank North** - Connecting the dots is one of my themes and I appreciate your passion to help people make connections for success.

Career Organization Teams

- **Yale New Haven Health** - I was born at YNHHS and my pharmacy path was nurtured there as I started as an intern and continued as I 'grew up' though to today. Thank you to my colleagues in the pharmacy department and beyond for your passion and engagement in the bold practice advancement accomplished.

- **St. Elizabeth Healthcare** - You are the most innovative community health system I have seen, and it was an honor to work with the family oriented leadership and team. Thank you for supporting the vision of pharmacy practice advancement.
- **Bayer Healthcare** - My decade spent with you helped me appreciate broader aspects of healthcare, strategy, and patient advocacy. I benefited from the large focus on professional development that accelerated my step into leadership.

Inspirational Pharmacy Leaders

You have touched me as a mentor or through your inspiring words and actions.

- Paul W. Abramowitz
- Nancy Alvarez
- Daniel Ashby
- Stuart Beatty
- Marialice Bennet
- Paul Bush
- Michael Cohen
- Harold Godwin
- Jean-Venable "Kelly" Goode
- Starlin Haydon-Greatting
- Douglas Hepler
- Mary Ann Kliethermes
- Scott Knoer
- Bonnie Levin
- Lucinda Maine
- Joseph Oddis
- Rita Shane
- Linda Strand
- Cedric Terrell
- Sara White
- William Zellmer
- David Zilz

Professional Organizations

- **American Pharmacists Association (APHA)** - My first flight ever was to an APHA national meeting. You have kept me flying through your advocacy for pharmacists and leadership experiences at student, regional, state, and national levels.
- **American Society of Health System Pharmacists (ASHP)** - You have been a huge part of my professional organization home. I owe much of my success to the education, inspiration, and networking relationships facilitated by you.
- **State Pharmacy Organizations in CT, FL, VA, KY, OH, NY** - Thank you all for your local work to advance the profession and for allowing me to be part of numerous committees and initiatives. It has been an honor.
- **American Council of Healthcare Executives (ACHE)** - I have gleaned so much value from the multidisciplinary content and networking relationships that ACHE has afforded me.

Pharmacy Schools

- **University of Connecticut (UCONN)** - Thank you to all the faculty and staff at UCONN who supported my pharmacy and leadership development during school and continued to support me in my career.
- **Medical University of South Carolina (MUSC)** - The two-year, post-baccalaureate PharmD exposed me to so many talented practice faculty in diverse patient service needs from emergency care, rural care, family medicine to the acutes of care.
- **Virginia Commonwealth University (VCU)** - My residency years were some of the most impactful and growth-inducing years of my life. Thank you to all who support me and the program.
- **University of Cincinnati (UC)** - Thank you for adopting me as a non-alumnus as I relocated to OH. I am honored to be a part of the Master of Science in Pharmacy Leadership to grow future leaders.

Residents & Students

One of my core values is to inspire and lifelong learning is one of my strengths. It is an honor to be able to be part of your development. You inspire me to do better and leave a legacy for future generations of pharmacists.

Clients

To my incredible clients, thank you for including me in your career and practice advancement journeys. I have learned much from you and you have supported the achievement of my goal to add new positions to pharmacy every year to advance practice.

Pharmovation Book Team

Thanks to everyone on the Holon Publishing team who helped me to bring this book to fruition. Catherine Valerio, Caroline Cole, Victoria Stingo, Leslie Cao, Mitchell Kennedy, Rebekah Spivey, Grace Beck Faile, Jeremy Gotwals.

Pharmacists and Technicians

I want to acknowledge what you do every day. I see your deep commitment to live your professional oath. But I also see the pain and burnout. You inspire me to show how 'Pharmacy Can Do More with More' so we can bring joy and impact to your career.

GLOSSARY & INDEX

Pharmovation = Pharmacy + Innovation

A

AAHC: Association of Academic Health Centers — 36

AAMC: Association of American Medical Colleges — 36

ACHE: American Council of Healthcare Executives — 43, 82, 196-200, 228

ACPE: Accreditation Council for Pharmacy Education — 115, 210-211

ACPE's CPD Learning Categories: A system for categorizing professional development options — 227

Acute Care Pharmacy: Including hospital stays and transitions of care — 41, 101-102, 122, 145

ADC: Automated dispensing cabinet — 85, 158-160, 176-177

ADC: Average Daily Census — 98

AI: Artificial Intelligence. Any technology which enables computers to mimic human behavior — 115, 151-154, 156, 162

AHA: American Hospital Association — 42, 47, 80, 82, 125

AHRQ: The Agency for Healthcare Research and Quality (In the United States) — 55

AMP: Average Manufacturuer's Price — 64

ANCC: American Nurses Credentialing Center — 109

AONE: American Organization of Nurse Executives — 196

APC: Ambulatory Payment Classification — 59

APHA: American Pharmacists Association — 120, 128, 216, 218

APM: Alternative Payment Models — 60-61

ASP: Average Sales Price — 64

ASHP: American Society of Health System Pharmacists — 65-67, 80, 82, 84, 94, 108-109, 111, 115, 120, 125-126, 139, 142, 143, 146, 155-156, 162, 165

B

BCMA: Barcode Medication Administration — 160

Blockchain Technology: A growing list of records that are called blocks, linked using technology called cryptography and resistant to modifications of data; an open, distributed ledger that can record transactions between two parties efficiently in a verifiable and permanent way — 114, 156, 168

Business: An organization or economic system where goods and services are exchanged for one another or for money; Every business requires some form of investment and enough customers to whom its output can be sold on a consistent basis in order to make a profit; Businesses can be privately owned, not-for-profit, or state-owned — 58-59

C

CHA: Catholic Health Association — 125

Change: To make or become different or to make things better as compared to the past — 20-25

CHIP: Children's Health Insurance Program — 60-61, 63

CHSP Initiative: Comparative Health System Performance Initiative: An AHRQ Initiative to study how healthcare systems promote evidence-based practices in delivering care — 55

CMS: Center for Medicare/Medicaid Services — 56, 60-61, 63, 82-83, 97, 99, 119, 165

CMS Measures Inventory Tool: A CMS tool which compiles various measures that are already in place within the organization that created them. This tool comes with the ability to prioritize which measures are applicable and most applicable to your organization — 83

Competency: Observable and measurable knowledge, skill, and ability (KSA) — 113, 181, 192-194, 196, 198-199, 201-205, 207, 210, 221, 225, 228, 238

CPD: Continuous Professional Development-learning to earn or maintain professional credentials such as academic degrees, formal coursework, attending conferences, and informal learning opportunities situated in practice — 209-214, 218-220, 223-225, 227, 229

CPE: Continued Pharmacy Education-to promote problem-solving and critical thinking and be applicable to the practice of pharmacy — 210-211

CPO: Chief Pharmacy Officer — 67, 185, 241

CPOE: Computerized Physician Order Entry — 106, 158, 160

D

Deep Learning (DL): A subcategory of Machine Learning and Artificial Intelligence which makes computation of multi-layer neural networks feasible — 152

Direct Cost: Costs related to the care of each patient — 96, 98

Disruptive Innovation: Innovation that creates a new market and value network and eventually disrupts an existing market and value network, displacing established market-leading firms, products, and alliances — 11-12, 34, 42-43, 46-47, 49, 52, 105, 119, 150, 183, 238

DRG: Diagnosis-related group payment — 59, 64, 97

E

F

G

H

common ownership or joint management; An accountable care organization is not, by itself, indicative of joint management — 55-58, 64, 105, 117, 128

HEDIS: National Committee for Quality Assurance's Healthcare Effectiveness Data and Information Set — 56

HFMA: Healthcare Financial Management Association — 196

HHS: Department of Health and Human Services — 47

HIMSS: Healthcare Information and Management Systems Society — 196

HIT: Pharmacy Health Information Technology Collaborative — 162, 167

HLA: Healthcare Leadership Alliance — 196

Homonyms: Two or more words having the same spelling or pronunciation but different meanings and origins — 189

I

IDN: Integrated Delivery Networks — 135-136, 140, 142-143, 155, 176-177

IHI: Institute for Healthcare Improvement — 30, 37-38, 125

Indirect Costs: Overhead costs unrelated to cost per patient — 96, 98

Innovation: A new idea, method or device; The application of better solutions that meet new requirements, unarticulated needs, or existing market need; Executing an idea which addresses a specific challenge and achieves value for both the company and the customer; Executing an idea which addresses a specific challenge and achieves value for both the company and customer — 2-12

Intrapreneur: A person within a large corporation who takes direct responsibility for turning an idea into a profitable finished product through assertive risk taking and innovation; Someone with a high degree of vision and high ability to act — 12-21

Intrapreneurship: Practicing entrepreneurship within a corporation — 12-21, 183-184, 186, 238

Invention: The creation of a product or introduction of a new process — 3

IVR: Interactive Voice Response — 165

J

JCPP: Joint Commission of Pharmacy Practitioners — 57, 117-118, 121, 163

K

KFF: Kaiser Family Foundation; A system which keeps track of average annual growth rates for select service types such as physicians, hospitals and prescriptions — 35

Korn Ferry Leadership Architect Global Competency Framework: A tool which provides a complete picture of the individual qualities that drive both performance and engagement. It's a unique whole person framework, anchored by comprehensive research on talent at all levels, that addresses the foundations of human behavior such as traits, drivers, motivators, experiences and competencies. This framework is comprised of four factors, twelve clusters and thirty-eight competencies with associated staged behaviors — 193-195, 199

Kotter's 8 Steps: A change management plan of action. These 8 steps are broken down into three phases: creating the climate for change, engaging and enabling the organization, and implementing and sustaining change — 23, 25

Kubler-Ross Change Curve: A model describing the four stages that most people go through as they adjust to change — 21-22

L

Leader (Big L): A person who has been given the formal title of leader. They manage other people in an organization — 180-181, 189-191, 219, 224

Leader (Little L): For the purposes of pharmacy, a little "l" leader is every pharmacist or technician on the front lines. Every person in the industry has the opportunity to be a leader in their current position. This pertains to managing their individual work, leading their practice, leading by example, and more — 180-181, 189-191, 219, 224

Leader: The person who leads or commands a group, organization or country — 186

Leadership: The art of motivating a group of people to act toward achieving a common goal — 182

Learning from Experience: This is where the bulk of learning occurs. Learning by doing. Learning on the job from your own experience. This is active learning and problem solving. It takes place within new placements, and job rotations, job shadowing or self-directed and incidental learning, as well as through new projects or special assignments. This is where the majority of learning takes place, or about 70% — 226

Learning from Others: This is generally considered coaching and can take place near or on the job. This is exposure to different types of careers or new ideas. It takes place within communities of practice, subject matter networks, user generated content, collaborative platforms, coaching, mentoring, or feedback. It's typically about 20% of your learning journey — 226

LTAC: Long Term Acute Care — 59

M

MACRA: Medicare Access and CHIP Reauthorization Act of 2015 — 60-61

Machine Learning: A subcategory of Artificial Intelligence-the employment of AI techniques using statistical methods to enable machines to improve with their experiences — 48, 114, 152, 154-156

Manager: A person responsible for controlling or administrating all or part of a company or organization — 187

Management: The process of dealing with or controlling things or people — 187

MGMA: Medical Group Management Association — 196

Mhealth: The use of mobile devices to monitor or detect biological changes in human bodies — 150, 171-172

MHT: Medication history technicians — 77, 95

Mindset: A habitual or characteristic mental state that determines how you will interpret and respond to situations; A fixed mental attitude or disposition that predetermines a person's responses to and interpretations of situations; A person's usual attitude or mental state is his or her mindset; A mental inclination, tendency, or habit; The established set of attitudes held by someone; A person's way of thinking and their opinions — 26-32

MIPS: Merit-Based Incentive Payment System — 60-61

MMS: Medication Management Services; medication management services are a spectrum of patient-centered, pharmacist provided, collaborative services that focus on medication appropriateness, effectiveness, safety, and adherence with the goal of improving health outcomes — 117-118

MTM: Medication Therapy Management — 70, 107, 127, 164, 166, 168

N

NGA: National Governors Association — 57

O

OECD: The Organization for Economic Cooperation and Development, a global organization of many countries who get together and assess different metrics impartially — 53-55

Organization Specific Method: There may be an organization specific method of conducting situational analysis that you should include in your formal business proposal. Be sure to keep this in mind when beginning any new journey to justify resources — 80

P

PAI: Practice Advancement Initiative-an elective organization that's dedicated to advancement of practice and excellence by fostering pharmacy leaders. It provides 59 recommendations regarding optimal, safe, and effective medication use, focuses on aspirational guidance to serve as a roadmap for pharmacy practice advancement, and a future-focused set of concepts looking beyond today's barriers to change — 80, 84, 94, 105, 108-111, 118-122, 126, 135, 137-141, 147-148, 155-156, 176-177, 179

PAI Self Assessment Tool: A tool to input the demographics and characteristics of your organization; It allows you to create an assessment summary regarding different sectors of your organization and helps create a prioritized action list — 84

PBM: Pharmacy Benefit Management — 48, 70, 99, 127, 132, 145, 217

PCOR: Patient-Centered Outcomes Research- helps people and their caregivers communicate and make informed health care decisions, allowing their voices to be heard in assessing the value of health care options — 55

PDI: Pharmacist Demand Indicator — 38

PDR: Pharmacy Demand Report — 38

Perspectives: Financial, customer, internal process, organizational capacity. Here you want to take different perspectives and analyze them. What's the financial situation? What are your customer's perspectives? What are the internal processes? How large is the organizational capacity? — 79

Pharmacy Enterprise: an integrated system of business units with accountability for clinical and financial outcomes related to medication use across the continuum of care in a health system — 1, 41, 43-45, 49, 51, 64-72, 80, 82, 87, 91, 108, 112, 114, 116, 118, 121, 123-124, 127, 129, 132-134, 144, 148, 153, 156-157, 164, 185, 235, 244

Pharmacists' Patient Care Process: A JCCP tool to clarify and outline the patient care process through collect, assess, plan, implement, and follow up; enhancing the collaboration, communication and documentation — 117-118, 163

PPS: Medicare Prospective Payment System — 59

Porter's Five Forces: Competitive rivalry, threat of new entrants, threat of substitution, power of customers, power of suppliers. Porter's five forces can be helpful when marketing new equipment or other types of merchandise. It's not used quite as often in healthcare, but when considering possible innovations, it's important to be aware of — 79

PROSCI-ADKAR: An acronym for the five outcomes an individual needs to achieve for a change to be successful: Awareness, Desire, Knowledge, Ability and Reinforcement — 23-25

PQA: Pharmacy Quality Alliance — 64

Q

QPP: Quality Payment Program. Through Center for Medicaid Services. This program began on January 1, 2017. Prior to QPP, payment increases for Medicare services were set by the Sustainable Growth Rate (SGR) law. This capped spending increases according to the growth in the Medicare population and had a modest allowance for inflation. However, as clinicians increased their utilization of services, the reimbursement for each unit of service had to be adjusted downward to hold costs constant. In practice, the SGR would have resulted in large decreases in the Physician Fee Schedule, which was not sustainable. To avoid these decreases in reimbursement, Congress had to pass a new law (every year) authorizing the current fee schedule and a small increase for inflation — 61

R

ROI: Return on Investment — 39, 74, 76, 78, 93-94, 96-103

RTPB: Real Time Prescription Benefits — 166

RUG: Resource Utilization Group — 59

S

SGR Law: The capping of spending increases according to the growth in the Medicare population with a modest allowance for inflation — 61

Situational Analysis: The starting point for developing an effective strategy and gaining insight into your situation starting with three basic steps: collect data, conduct a systematic assessment, compile your findings into a situational analysis framework. After this, you'll move onto your strategies, goals, and objectives — 42, 44, 74, 76, 79-88, 112, 121, 134-135, 139, 156, 159, 238

Situational Leadership: States that different situations call for different types of leadership — 188

SMART Objectives: An acronym for an accurate progress measurement with each letter representing respectively: specific, measurable, achievable, relevant and time-bound — 88, 90, 92

SNF: Skilled Nursing Facilities — 59-60

SHSMD: Society for Health Care & Strategy Market Development — 42

Strategic Plan Strategy: 10 steps including: Tactic Process; strategic pillar, goal brainstorming, objective brainstorming, prioritization and timeline, SMART objectives, metrics, actions/tactics, accountability RACI, resource needs, and plan summary — 92

Structural Learning: This is formal training or education that's completed away from your current place of employment. It's usually done before any other type of professional development and comprises about 10% of all learning. It can take place in the form of workshops, webinars, online learning portals, eLearning or mLearning — 225

SWOT: Strengths, weaknesses, opportunities, threats. This is a typical beginning analysis in many departments. Whatever situational analysis framework you complete, these factors should be considered either formally or informally — 79-80, 84-87, 213, 219

T

Telemedicine: A means for improving patient health by permitting two-way, real-time interactive communication between the patient and healthcare provider, when geographically separate. it can be conducted by interactive telephone communication equipment that includes both audio and video equipment — 128, 151, 156, 165-166, 174,

Telepharmacy: The provision of pharmacist care by registered pharmacists and pharmacists located within US jurisdictions through the use of telecommunications or other technologies to patients or their agents at distances located within the US. Some examples are remote pharmacy or remote dispensing — 44, 107, 114, 156, 165-166

Transformation: A thorough or dramatic change in form or appearance — 20-25

W

WHO: World Health Organization — 50, 52

REFERENCES

1. Innovation. Merriam Webster Dictionary. www.merriam-webster.com/dictionary/innovation. Accessed January 8, 2021.
2. Liozu S. What is innovation? Smart Business Online. https://www.sbnonline.com/article/what-is-innovation/. Published October 1, 2015. Accessed January 27, 2020.
3. Skillicorn N. 9 defining characteristics of successful INNOVATION (INFOGRAPHIC). Inc.com. https://www.inc.com/nick-skillicorn/9-defining-characteristics-of-successful-innovation.html. Published April 19, 2016. Accessed March 17, 2020.
4. Rogers EM. *Diffusion of Innovation.* New York: The Free Press; 2003.
5. Adair J. *Effective Innovation: The Essential Guide to Staying Ahead of the Competition.* London: Pan; 2009.
6. Drucker P.F., Maciariello J.A. *Innovation and Entrepreneurship: Practice and Principles.* Abingdon, Oxon: Routledge; 2009.
7. Gallo C. The *Innovation Secrets of Steve Jobs: Insanely Different Principles for Breakthrough Success.* New York, NY: McGraw-Hill; 2017.
8. Daskal L. 7 Smart Habits of Great Innovators. Inc. https://www.inc.com/lolly-daskal/the-seven-habits-of-successful-innovators.html. Published September 8, 2014. Accessed February 21, 2020.
9. Entrepreneur. Merriam-Webster. https://www.merriam-webster.com/dictionary/entrepreneur. Accessed April 6, 2020.
10. American Heritage® Dictionary of the English Language, Fifth Edition. Copyright © 2016.
11. Pinchot III G. *Intrapreneuring: Why You Don't Have to Leave the Corporation to Become an Entrepreneur.* 1985.
12. Foley S. 5 reasons why Intrapreneurship is important. Corporate Entrepreneurs. https://corporate-entrepreneurs.com/2013/11/08/5-reasons-why-intrapreneurship-is-important/. Published February 26, 2016. Accessed January 16, 2021.
13. Chamorro-Premuzic, T. How bad leadership spurs entrepreneurship. Harvard Business Review. https://hbr.org/2012/09/how-bad-leadership-spurs-entrepreneurship. Published August 7, 2014. Accessed May 1, 2020.
14. Pinchot G. Evaluating intrapreneurs. Pinchot.com, https://www.pinchot.com/perspective/intrapreneuring/. Published May 27, 2020. Accessed January 13, 2021
15. Haller HE. *Intrapreneurship – Ignite Innovation.* Silver Eagle Press; 2014.
16. Covin JG, Kuratko DF, Morris MH. Corporate Entrepreneurship & Innovation. Mason, OH: South-Western; 2011.

17. Change. Merriam Webster Dictionary. https://www.merriam-webster.com/dictionary/change. Accessed March 9, 2020.
18. What is change management? ASQ. https://asq.org/quality-resources/change-management. Published 2021. Accessed September 9, 2021.
19. Transformation definition & meaning. Dictionary.com. https://www.dictionary.com/browse/transformation. Accessed March 9, 2020.
20. The Mind Tools Content Team By the Mind Tools Content Team, Team the MTC, wrote M, wrote E. The change curve: Accelerating change, and improving its likelihood of success. Change Management Training from MindTools.com. https://www.mindtools.com/pages/article/newPPM_96.htm. Accessed March 10, 2020.
21. Inc. P. The prosci adkar® model. Prosci. https://www.prosci.com/adkar/adkar-model. Accessed January 14, 2021.
22. Kotter JP. *Leading Change.* Boston (Massachusetts): Harvard Business Review Press; 2012.
23. Company HMHP. The American Heritage dictionary entry: Mindset. American Heritage Dictionary Entry: mindset. https://www.ahdictionary.com/word/search.html?q=mindset. Accessed February 27, 2020.
24. Mindset - dictionary definition. Vocabulary.com. https://www.vocabulary.com/dictionary/mindset. Accessed February 27, 2020.
25. Mind-set medical definition. Merriam-Webster. https://www.merriam-webster.com/medical/mind-set. Accessed February 27, 2020.
26. Mindset english definition and meaning. Lexico Dictionaries I English. https://www.lexico.com/en/definition/mindset. Accessed February 27, 2020.
27. Mindset. Cambridge Dictionary. https://dictionary.cambridge.org/dictionary/english/mindset. Accessed February 20, 2020.
28. Clinician resilience and well-being. National Academy of Medicine. https://nam.edu/initiatives/clinician-resilience-and-well-being/. Published July 15, 2021. Accessed August 17, 2021.
29. Durham ME, Bush PW, Ball AM. Evidence of burnout in health-system pharmacists. *American Journal of Health-System Pharmacy*, Volume 75, Issue 23_Supplement_4. Published December 1, 2018. Accessed May 3, 2020.
30. Western D. 15 different types of mindsets people have. Wealthy Gorilla. https://wealthygorilla.com/15-different-types-mindsets-people/. Published June 3, 2021. Accessed August 22, 2021.
31. Dweck CS. *Mindset: The New Psychology of Success.* New York: Random House; 2016.
32. *IHI framework for improving joy in work*: IHI. Institute for Healthcare Improvement. http://www.ihi.org/resources/Pages/IHIWhitePapers/Framework-Improving-Joy-in-Work.aspx. Accessed April 6, 2020.
33. 5+ ways to develop a growth mindset using grit and resilience. PositivePsychology.com. https://positivepsychology.com/5-ways-develop-grit-resilience/. Published August 26, 2021. Accessed September 15, 2021.
34. 2018 health care cost and Utilization Report. HCCI. https://healthcostinstitute.org/annual-reports/2020-02-13-18-20-19. Accessed January 11, 2021.
35. Kamal R. How has U.S. spending on healthcare changed over time? Peterson-KFF Health System Tracker. https://www.

healthsystemtracker.org/chart-collection/u-s-spending-health-care-changed-time/#item-usspendingovertime_7. Published December 23, 2020. Accessed January 12, 2021.

36. Kamal R. What are the recent and forecasted trends in prescription drug spending? Peterson-KFF Health System Tracker. https://www.healthsystemtracker.org/chart-collection/recent-forecasted-trends-prescription-drug-spending/. Published April 12, 2019. Accessed May 1, 2020.
37. Knickman JR, Snell EK. The 2030 problem: Caring for aging baby boomers. Health services research. https://www.ncbi.nlm.nih.gov/pmc/articles/PMC1464018/. Published August 2002. Accessed January 22, 2020.
38. Long, G.The Biopharmaceutical Pipeline: Innovative Therapies in Clinical Development. Analysis Group Inc. http://phrma-docs.phrma.org/files/dmfile/Biopharmaceutical-Pipeline-Full-Report.pdf. Boston, MA: July 2017. Accessed March 20, 2020.
39. Let there be change. Accenture. https://www.accenture.com/_acnmedia/PDF-95/Accenture-Aamc-2018-Workforce-Rrojections-Update-April-11-2018.pdf%E2%80%8B. Accessed March 14, 2020.
40. Out Of Order Out Of time: The State of the Nation's Health Workforce. A Report by the Association of Academic Health Centers. Published 2008. https://www.aacp.org/sites/default/files/aahc_outoforder_outoftime.pdf. Accessed March 3, 2020.
41. Triple aim for populations: Ihi. Institute for Healthcare Improvement. http://www.ihi.org/Topics/TripleAim/Pages/default.aspx. Accessed January 20, 2020.
42. Knapp, DA. Professionally Determined Need for Pharmacy Services in 2020. American Journal of Pharmaceutical Education. 2002, Vol. 66. https://www.aacp.org/sites/default/files/2020needforservices.pdf. Published Winter of 2002. Accessed February 1, 2020.
43. Pharmacists: Occupational outlook handbook. U.S. Bureau of Labor Statistics. https://www.bls.gov/ooh/healthcare/pharmacists.htm. Published September 13, 2021. Accessed September 16, 2021.
44. Home: Occupational outlook handbook. U.S. Bureau of Labor Statistics. https://www.bls.gov/ooh/healthcare/pharmacy-technicians.htmand. Published September 15, 2021. Accessed September 23, 2021.
45. https://pharmacymanpower.com/about.php. Accessed March 23, 2020.
46. Pharmacist demand indicator. AACP. https://www.aacp.org/article/pharmacist-demand-indicator. Accessed February 3, 2020.
47. Pharmacy demand Report (PDR). AACP. https://www.aacp.org/article/pharmacy-demand-report-pdr. Accessed April 8, 2020.
48. Pedersen CA, Schneider PJ, Ganio MC, and Scheckelhoff DJ. ASHP national survey of pharmacy practice in hospital settings: Prescribing and transcribing-2019. *American Journal of Health-System Pharmacy*, Volume 77, Issue 13, 1 July 2020, Pages 1026–1050, https://doi.org/10.1093/ajhp/zxaa104. Accessed March 14, 2020.
49. Crighton M, Toscani M, Barone J, Colaizzi J. Are pharmacy schools growing too fast? Pharmacy Times. https://www.pharmacytimes.com/view/are-pharmacy-schools-growing-too-fast. Published February 16,

2016. Accessed January 12, 2020.
50. Cain J, Campbell T, Congdon HB, et al. Pharmacy student debt and return on investment of a pharmacy education. American Journal of Pharmaceutical Education. https://www.ajpe.org/content/78/1/5.full. Published February 12, 2014. Accessed March 15, 2020.
51. 2019 Environment Scan. American Hospital Association. https://www.aha.org/system/files/media/file/2020/11/2021_Environmental_Scan.pdf. Accessed May 4, 2020.
52. Futurescan 2020-2025: Health Care trends and implications. SHSMD. https://www.shsmd.org/resources/display/futurescan-20202025-health-care-trends-and-implications. Accessed January 21, 2020.
53. Top issues Confronting hospitals in 2019. American College of Healthcare Executives. https://www.ache.org/learning-center/research/about-the-field/top-issues-confronting-hospitals/top-issues-confronting-hospitals-in-2019. Accessed February 9, 2020.
54. Vermeulen LC, Swarthout MD, Alexander GC, et al. ASHP foundation pharmacy forecast 2020: Strategic planning advice for pharmacy departments in hospitals and health systems. OUP Academic. https://academic.oup.com/ajhp/article/77/2/84/5653009. Published December 5, 2019. Accessed March 7, 2020.
55. DiPiro JT, Fox ER, Kesselheim AS, et al. ASHP Foundation Pharmacy Forecast 2021: Strategic Planning Advice for Pharmacy Departments in Hospitals and Health Systems. OUP Academic. https://academic.oup.com/ajhp/article/78/6/472/6128834. Published February 4, 2021. Accessed April 20, 2021.
56. Disruptive innovation. Wikipedia. https://en.wikipedia.org/wiki/Disruptive_innovation. Published August 28, 2021. Accessed September 20, 2021.
57. Christensen CM, Grossman JH, Hwang J. *The Innovator's Prescription: A Disruptive Solution for Health Care*. New York: Mcgraw-Hill Education; 2017.
58. American Patients First: The Trump Administration Blueprint to Lower Drug Prices and Reduce Out-of-Pocket Costs. Department of Health and Human Services. https://www.hhs.gov/sites/default/files/AmericanPatientsFirst.pdf. Published May, 2018. Accessed May 1, 2020.
59. Market insights: Disruptive innovation. Aha. https://www.aha.org/center/emerging-issues/market-insights/disruptive-innovation. Accessed February 21, 2020.
60. Fein AJ. Insurers + PBMs + Specialty Pharmacies + Providers: Will Vertical Consolidation Disrupt Drug Channels in 2020? Drug Channels. https://www.drugchannels.net/2019/12/insurers-pbms-specialty-pharmacies.html. Published December 12, 2019. Accessed May 2, 2020.
61. Vermeulen LC, Eddington ND, Gourdine MA et al. Pharmacy forecast 2019: strategic planning advice for pharmacy departments in hospitals and health systems. OUP Academic. https://academic.oup.com/ajhp/article/76/2/71/5289845. Published January 16, 2019. Accessed January 11, 2020.
62. Healthcare English definition and meaning. Lexico Dictionaries I English. https://www.lexico.com/en/definition/healthcare. Accessed

February 26, 2020.
63. Healthcare definition & Meaning. Dictionary.com. https://www.dictionary.com/browse/healthcare. Accessed February 26, 2020.
64. Healthcare. The Free Dictionary. https://www.thefreedictionary.com/Healthcare. Accessed February 26, 2020.
65. Vellanki M. Who are the key players in the healthcare industry? Mahesh VC. http://mahesh-vc.squarespace.com/blog/understanding-whos-paying-for-what-in-the-healthcare-industry. Published April 5, 2016. Accessed April 15, 2020.
66. Health at a glance 2019. OECD iLibrary. https://www.oecd-ilibrary.org/social-issues-migration-health/health-at-a-glance-2019_4dd50c09-en. Accessed January 7, 2020.
67. Furukawa MF, Kimmey L, Jones DJ, Machta RM, Guo J, Rich EC. Consolidation Of Providers Into Health Systems Increased Substantially, 2016-18. Health Aff (Millwood). 2020 Aug;39(8):1321-1325. doi: 10.1377/hlthaff.2020.00017. PMID: 32744941. Accessed April 5, 2020.
68. Defining health systems. AHRQ. https://www.ahrq.gov/chsp/chsp-reports/resources-for-understanding-health-systems/defining-health-systems.html. Published September, 2016. Reviewed September, 2017. Accessed April 22, 2020.
69. Patient centered agenda. Patient Centered Agenda. https://www.phrma.org/advocacy. Accessed January 18, 2020.
70. The Patient-Centered Medical Home: Integrating Comprehensive Medication Management to Optimize Patient Outcomes. Patient-Centered Primary Care Collaborative; Second Edition. https://jcpp.net/wp-content/uploads/2015/09/PCPCCmedmanagement.pdf. Published June 2012. Accessed February 17, 2020.
71. Giberson S, Yoder S, Lee MP. Improving Patient and Health System Outcomes through Advanced Pharmacy Practice; A Report to the U.S. Surgeon General, Office of the Chief Pharmacist. U.S. Public Health Service. https://jcpp.net/wp-content/uploads/2015/09/Improving-Patient-and-Health-System-Outcomes-through-Advanced-Pharmacy-Practice.pdf. Published December 2011. Accessed February 19, 2020.
72. Isasi F, and Krofah E. The Expanding Role of Pharmacists in a Transformed Health Care System. National Governors Association Center for Best Practices. Washington, D.C. https://jcpp.net/wp-content/uploads/2015/09/NGA-TheExpandingRoleOfPharmacists.pdf. Published January 13, 2015. Accessed April 18, 2020.
73. Business.Business Dictionary. http://www.businessdictionary.com/definition/business.html. Accessed May 2, 2020.
74. CMS' value-based PROGRAMS. CMS. https://www.cms.gov/Medicare/Quality-Initiatives-Patient-Assessment-Instruments/Value-Based-Programs/Value-Based-Programs. Accessed January 24, 2020.
75. The quality payment program. The Quality Payment Program. https://qpp.cms.gov/. Accessed January 26, 2020.
76. Miller HD. Why Value-Based Payment Isn't Working and How to Fix it: Creating a Patient-Centered Payment System to Support Higher-Quality, More Affordable Health Care. CHQPR. 2017; First

Edition. https://www.chqpr.org/downloads/WhyVBPIsNotWorking.pdf. Published October, 2017. Accessed March 11, 2020.
77. Innovation models: CMS Innovation Center. Innovation Center. https://innovation.cms.gov/innovation-models#views=models&stg=accepting%20letters%20of%20intent,accepting%20applications,ongoing. Accessed February 18, 2020.
78. S. Knoer. Stewardship of the Pharmacy enterprise, American Journal of Health-System Pharmacy. DeepDyve. https://www.deepdyve.com/lp/ou-press/stewardship-of-the-pharmacy-enterprise-5JD3ODAKm0?key=OUP. Published July 15, 2014. Accessed May 3, 2020.
79. Zellmer WA. Inventing our future. Am J Health-Syst Pharm. 2007; 64:(12). 1262. Accessed January 16, 2020.
80. Draft: long-range vision for the pharmacy workforce in hospitals and health systems. American Society of Health-System Pharmacists Council on Education and Workforce Development. ASHP. 2006; 63:661–5. Accessed March 17, 2020.
81. Powell MF, Knoer S, Couldry R. What is the pharmacy enterprise? A framework for success and the future of the profession. Presented at ASHP Midyear Meeting. Las Vegas, NV; December 3, 2012. Accessed February 21, 2020.
82. Ivey FM. Rationale for having a chief pharmacy officer in a healthcare organization, *American Journal of Health-System Pharmacy*, Volume 62, Issue 9, 1 May 2005, Pages 975–978, https://doi.org/10.1093/ajhp/62.9.975. Accessed March 12, 2020.
83. Berra A. Realizing pharmacy's full value. Advisory Board. https://www.advisory.com/topics/pharmacy/2019/02/realizing-pharmacy-full-value. Published February 28, 2019. Accessed February 7, 2020.
84. Lohr R. Elevating pharmacy leadership to meet System goals. Advisory Board. https://www.advisory.com/topics/pharmacy-and-lab/2017/06/elevating-pharmacy-leadership-to-meet-system-goals. Published June 7, 2017. Accessed February 24, 2020.
85. About PAI 2030. ASHP. https://www.ashp.org/Pharmacy-Practice/PAI/About-PAI-2030. Accessed January 8, 2020.
86. PAI self-assessment tools. ASHP. https://www.ashp.org/pharmacy-practice/pai/pai-self-assessment-tools. Accessed February 9, 2020.
87. Solving the healthcare value equation. Healthcare IT News. https://www.healthcareitnews.com/sponsored-content/solving-healthcare-value-equation-0. Published June 30, 2016. Accessed April 18, 2020.
88. ASHP Guidelines on Medication Cost Management Strategies for Hospitals and Health Systems, *American Journal of Health-System Pharmacy*, Volume 65, Issue 14, 15 July 2008, Pages 1368–1384, https://doi.org/10.2146/ajhp080021. Accessed April 1, 2020.
89. Pedersen CA, Schneider PJ, Scheckelhoff DJ. ASHP national survey of pharmacy practice in hospital settings: Dispensing and administration—2011, *American Journal of Health-System Pharmacy*. 2012, Volume 69, (Issue 9): Pages 768–785, https://doi.org/10.2146/ajhp110735. Published May 1, 2012. Accessed April 16, 2020.
90. Kaboli PJ. Clinical pharmacists and inpatient medical care. Archives of Internal Medicine. https://jamanetwork.com/journals/jamainternalmedicine/fullarticle/410298. Published May 8, 2006. Accessed January 18, 2020.

91. De Rijdt T, Willems L, Simoens S. Economic effects of clinical pharmacy interventions: A literature review. OUP Academic. https://academic.oup.com/ajhp/article-abstract/65/12/1161/5127894?redirectedFrom=PDF. Published June 15, 2008. Accessed February 17, 2020.
92. Touchette DR, Doloresco FD, Suda KJ, et al. Review of Therapeutics: Economic Evaluations of Clinical Pharmacy Services: 2006–2010. PHARMACOTHERAPY. 2014; Volume 34 (Number 8). https://www.accp.com/docs/positions/whitepapers/EconEvalClinPhcySvces_Pharmaco_8-14.pdf. Accessed January 17, 2020.
93. The Patient-Centered Medical Home: Integrating Comprehensive Medication Management to Optimize Patient Outcomes. PCPCC. 2012. Second Edition. https://jcpp.net/wp-content/uploads/2015/09/PCPCCmedmanagement.pdf. Published June 2012. Accessed March 2, 2020.
94. Isasi F, and Krofah E. The Expanding Role of Pharmacists in a Transformed Health Care System. National Governors Association Center for Best Practices. Washington, D.C. https://jcpp.net/wp-content/uploads/2015/09/NGA-TheExpandingRoleOfPharmacists.pdf. Published January 13, 2015. Accessed May 4, 2020.
95. Magnet recognition program®: Ancc. ANA. https://www.nursingworld.org/organizational-programs/magnet/. Accessed February 27, 2020.
96. Progress Measures: ASHP Hospital and Ambulatory Care Self-Assessment Data, Collected 2011-2017 Care Team Integration. Ashpmedia. http://www.ashpmedia.org/pai/docs/PAI-Progress-Measures.pdf. Accessed January 14, 2020.
97. ASHP Practice Advancement Initiative 2030: New recommendations for advancing pharmacy practice in health systems, *American Journal of Health-System Pharmacy*, Volume 77, Issue 2, 15 January 2020, Pages 113–121, https://doi.org/10.1093/ajhp/zxz271. Accessed February 19, 2020.
98. Consensus of the Pharmacy practice Model summit. OUP Academic. https://academic.oup.com/ajhp/article-abstract/68/12/1148/5129369?redirectedFrom=fulltext. Published June 15, 2011. Accessed April 28, 2020.
99. Home. JCPP. https://jcpp.net/. Published October 5, 2015. Accessed January 14, 2020.
100. Pharmacists' Patient Care Process. JCCP. 2014. https://jcpp.net/wp-content/uploads/2016/03/PatientCareProcess-with-supporting-organizations.pdf. Published May 29, 2014. Accessed February 5, 2020.
101. Center for Innovative Pharmacy Solutions. https://www.pharmacy.umaryland.edu/centers/cips/. Accessed May 3, 2020.
102. Innovations in pharmacy. https://pubs.lib.umn.edu/index.php/innovations. Accessed February 20, 2020.
103. Department of Pharmacy. School of Pharmacy. https://sop.washington.edu/department-of-pharmacy/research/institute-for-innovative-pharmacy-practice-i2p2/. Accessed March 3, 2020.
104. Center for Pharmacy Innovation. Cedarville University. https://www.cedarville.edu/center-for-pharmacy-innovation. Accessed March 11, 2020.
105. Center for Pharmacy Practice innovation. Center for Pharmacy

Practice Innovation I Center for Pharmacy Practice Innovation I VCU School of Pharmacy. https://cppi.pharmacy.vcu.edu/. Accessed April 6, 2020.
106. Practice innovation. APhA Foundation. https://www.aphafoundation.org/practice-innovation. Published July 21, 2021. Accessed August 1, 2021.
107. Innovation. ASHP. https://www.ashp.org/Innovation. Accessed May 4, 2020.
108. ASHP launches Innovation center at Midyear Clinical Meeting. ASHP. https://www.ashp.org/News/2019/12/07/ASHP-Launches-Innovation-Center-at-Midyear-Clinical-Meeting. Accessed January 22, 2020.
109. Age-Friendly health Systems: Center: AHA. American Hospital Association. https://www.aha.org/center/new-payment-and-delivery-models/age-friendly-health-systems. Accessed March 4, 2020.
110. Thurston MM, Liao T-chun V, Lim T, Pounds T, Moye-Dickerson PM. Utilization of a multidisciplinary team to reduce the rate of hospital readmissions in high-risk heart failure patients at a community teaching hospital: The pharmacist's role in transitions of care. American College of Clinical Pharmacy. https://accpjournals.onlinelibrary.wiley.com/doi/abs/10.1002/jac5.1072. Published January 11, 2019. Accessed April 8, 2020.
111. Innovations in Pharmacy. Iip. 2021; Volume 12 (No. 3). https://pubs.lib.umn.edu/index.php/innovations. Published June 23, 2021. Accessed August 16, 2021.
112. Practice innovation. APhA Foundation. https://www.aphafoundation.org/practice-innovation. Published July 21, 2021. Accessed August 3, 2021.
113. Perdew C, Erickson K, Litke J. Innovative models for providing clinical pharmacy services to remote locations using clinical video telehealth. OUP Academic. https://academic.oup.com/ajhp/article-abstract/74/14/1093/5102598?redirectedFrom=fulltext. Published July 15, 2017. Accessed February 1, 2020.
114. Shapiro SD. Promise of precision medicine for health systems. OUP Academic. https://academic.oup.com/ajhp/article-abstract/73/23/1907/5102123?redirectedFrom=fulltext. Published December 1, 2016. Accessed April 8, 2020.
115. Kathleen Vest PD, Brooke Griffin PD. Finding your passion in a nontraditional pharmacy career path. Pharmacy Times. https://www.pharmacytimes.com/publications/career/2019/CareersFall2019/finding-your-passion-in-a-nontraditional-pharmacy-career-path. Published March 8, 2021. Accessed March 10, 2021.
116. Pedersen CA, Schneider PJ, Scheckelhoff DJ. ASHP national survey of pharmacy practice in hospital settings: Dispensing and administration—2014. Am J Health Syst Pharm. 2015;72(13):1119-1137. doi: 10.2146/ajhp150032. Accessed January 11, 2020.
117. Schneider PJ, Pedersen CA, Scheckelhoff DJ. ASHP national survey of pharmacy practice in hospital settings: Dispensing and administration—2017. Am J Health Syst Pharm. 2018;75(16):1203-1226. doi: 10.2146/ajhp180151. Accessed February 21, 2020.
118. Castle M, Boothe K, Sinclair P. Practice advancement initiative (PAI) supported by medication cost management strategies in a community

health-system. 2018 ASHP Conference for Pharmacy Leaders. Dallas, TX (Poster Abstract). Accessed March 23, 2020.
119. Das R. Top 8 Healthcare predictions for 2019. Forbes. https://www.forbes.com/sites/reenitadas/2018/11/13/top-8-healthcare-predictions-for-2019/?sh=a58f4a8700eb. Published November 13, 2018. Accessed April 28, 2020.
120. Das R. Top 8 predictions that will Disrupt healthcare in 2020. Forbes. https://www.forbes.com/sites/reenitadas/2019/12/04/top-8-predictions-that-will-disrupt-healthcare-in-2020/. Published December 5, 2019. Accessed April 28, 2020.
121. Healthcare innovation map reveals emerging technologies & startups. StartUs Insights. https://www.startus-insights.com/innovators-guide/healthcare-innovation-map-reveals-emerging-technologies-startups/. Published March 20, 2020. Accessed May 2, 2020.
122. 15 amazing healthcare technology innovations in 2016. ReferralMD. https://getreferralmd.com/2016/01/healthcare-technology-2016/. Published March 18, 2021. Accessed March 21, 2021.
123. Intelligence. Merriam-Webster. https://www.merriam-webster.com/dictionary/intelligence. Accessed January 15, 2020.
124. Artificial intelligence. Merriam-Webster. https://www.merriam-webster.com/dictionary/artificial%20intelligence. Accessed January 15, 2020.
125. Machine learning. Merriam-Webster. https://www.merriam-webster.com/dictionary/machine%20learning. Accessed January 17, 2021.
126. By: IBM Cloud Education. What is deep learning? IBM. https://www.ibm.com/cloud/learn/deep-learning. Accessed January 15, 2020.
127. Artificial intelligence: An introduction. GeeksforGeeks. https://www.geeksforgeeks.org/artificial-intelligence-an-introduction/. Accessed January 3, 2020.
128. CB Insights. AI in healthcare: 90 startups making noise in the industry: CB Insights. CB Insights Research. https://www.cbinsights.com/research/artificial-intelligence-startups-healthcare/. Published August 14, 2020. Accessed April 7, 2021.
129. Soffar H. Artificial intelligence in pharmacy, and will pharmacists be replaced by robots? Science online. https://www.online-sciences.com/robotics/artificial-intelligence-in-pharmacy-and-will-pharmacists-be-replaced-by-robots/. Published August 29, 2019. Accessed March 5, 2020.
130. Flynn A. Using artificial intelligence in health-system pharmacy practice: Finding new patterns that matter. OUP Academic. https://academic.oup.com/ajhp/article-abstract/76/9/622/5466525?redirectedFrom=fulltext. Published April 17, 2019. Accessed March 16, 2020.
131. Leon Kass QUOTES. BrainyQuote. https://www.brainyquote.com/quotes/leon_kass_295641. Accessed March 17, 2020.
132. Halvorsen RM. The 15th Annual State of Pharmacy Automation: Results from PP&P's 2020 national Survey. Pharmacy Purchasing & Products. 2020; 17(6). https://www.pppmag.com/digitalmag/Main.php?MagNo=277&PageNo=1. Published August 2020. Accessed May 1, 2021.
133. Halvorsen RM. Resource Guide. Pharmacy Purchasing & Products. 2020. https://www.pppmag.com/digitalmag/Main.php?MagNo=254&PageNo=1#page/2. Published January 2020. Accessed

January 14, 2021.
134. Executive summary of the 2019 ASHP Commission ON Goals: Impact of artificial intelligence on healthcare and Pharmacy practice. OUP Academic. https://academic.oup.com/ajhp/article-abstract/76/24/2087/5580763?redirectedFrom=fulltext. Published October 4, 2019. Accessed February 17, 2020.
135. The Roadmap for Pharmacy Health Information Technology Integration in U.S. Health Care: 2018 to 2021 Update. Pharmacy HIT Collaborative. http://www.pharmacyhit.org/pdfs/workshop-documents/PHIT_Roadmap_2018-2021_Final.pdf. Accessed May 5, 2021.
136. SOPIT BP Telepharmacy statement - Ashp. https://www.ashp.org/-/media/assets/pharmacy-informaticist/docs/sopit-bp-telepharmacy-statement.ashx?la=en&hash=FEA67B8E2CD6AEEE6F73DA5DB72D71536ACB59D2. Accessed May 5, 2021.
137. Software solutions. eCarePlan. https://www.ecareplaninitiative.com/software-solutions. Accessed February 8, 2020.
138. What is blockchain technology? IBM. https://www.ibm.com/blockchain/what-is-blockchain. Accessed January 15, 2021.
139. Wearable technologies in the pharmaceutical industry. Pitstop. https://www.pitstophealth.com/blog/wearable-technologies-in-the-pharmaceutical-industry. Accessed January 14, 2020.
140. Van Terheyden N. Personal Health – Navigating Healthcare – Patient Safety and Personal Healthcare Management. https://navigating-healthcare.wordpress.com/category/personal-health/. Published November 7, 2014. Accessed May 4, 2020.
141. Methananda N. Mobile Health – A ubiquitous approach to healthcare. Digital Pulse. https://www.digitalpulse.pwc.com.au/mobile-health-ubiquitous-healthcare/. Published August 24, 2012. Accessed April 19, 2020.
142. Aungst T. How to track medication adherence with digital health technologies. The Digital Apothecary. https://www.thedigitalapothecary.com/pharmacy-innovation-news/2019/1/5/yx173nd9rhez4eh4235jg7wpe1l3jy. Published January 21, 2019. Accessed April 6, 2020.
143. Ward S. What is leadership? The Balance Small Business. https://www.thebalancesmb.com/leadership-definition-2948275. Accessed January 26, 2020.
144. Holdford DA. *Leadership for Pharmacists: Facilitating Change in Pharmacy Practice*. Washington, D.C.: American Pharmacists Association; 2018. Accessed March 5, 2020.
145. Covin JG, Kuratko DF, Morris MH. *Corporate Entrepreneurship & Innovation*. Mason, OH: South-Western; 2011.
146. 3 practices that will help drive innovation in your organization. CCL. https://www.ccl.org/articles/leading-effectively-articles/hr-pipeline-3-ways-to-get-more-innovation/. Published August 31, 2021. Accessed September 6, 2021.
147. Manager. Dictionary.com. https://www.dictionary.com/browse/manager. Accessed February 6, 2020.
148. Management. Dictionary.com. https://www.dictionary.com/browse/management. Accessed February 6, 2020.
149. Leader. Dictionary.com. https://www.dictionary.com/browse/leader.

Accessed February 7, 2020.
150. Leadership. Dictionary.com. https://www.dictionary.com/browse/leadership. Accessed February 7, 2020.
151. Remya Menon Follow Research Assistant. Managerial skills. SlideShare. https://www.slideshare.net/RemyaRavindran/managerial-skills-32845051. Published March 28, 2014. Accessed March 4, 2020.
152. Situational leadership theory. Wikipedia. https://en.wikipedia.org/wiki/Situational_leadership_theory. Published August 24, 2021. Accessed September 5, 2021.
153. Turmel W. Leadership: Big "L"s and Little "l"s. Management.Issues. https://www.management-issues.com/opinion/4302/leadership-big-ls-and-little-ls/. Published June 25, 2007. Accessed February 18, 2020.
154. Harvey A.K. Whitney Award Lectures. Harvey A.K. Whitney Award Lectures: Sara J. White. https://www.harveywhitney.org/lectures/sara-j-white/. Accessed March 17, 2020.
155. Marquet LD. *Turn the Ship Around!: A True Story of Turning Followers into Leaders.* New York: Portfolio; 2019.
156. Colin Powell quotes. BrainyQuote. https://www.brainyquote.com/quotes/colin_powell_393609. Accessed January 12, 2020.
157. Lombardo M, Eichinger R. *FYI: For Your Improvement : A Guide for Development and Coaching : For Learners, Managers, Mentors, and Feedback Givers.* 5th ed. 2014.
158. Korn Ferry Leadership Architect™ Global Competency Framework: Frequently Asked Questions. Korn Ferry. https://www.kornferry.com/content/dam/kornferry/docs/article-migration/KFLA_FAQs.pdf. Accessed February 11, 2020.
159. Healthcare leadership Alliance - home. Healthcare Leadership Alliance - Home. http://www.healthcareleadershipalliance.org/. Accessed March 4, 2020.
160. Ache Healthcare Executive 2020 Competencies Tool. American College of Healthcare Executives. https://www.ache.org/-/media/ache/career-resource-center/competencies_booklet.pdf. Published 2020. Accessed April 8, 2021.
161. The six pitfalls of leadership. Leadership Freak. https://leadershipfreak.blog/2018/03/23/the-six-pitfalls-of-leadership/. Published March 23, 2018. Accessed January 10, 2020.
162. Professional development. Wikipedia. https://en.wikipedia.org/wiki/Professional_development. Published July 21, 2021. Accessed August 24, 2021.
163. Accreditation Council for Pharmacy Education Guidance on Continuing Professional Development (CPD) for the Profession of Pharmacy. acpe-accredit.https://www.acpe-accredit.org/pdf/CPDGuidance%20ProfessionPharmacyJan2015.pdf. Published January, 2015. Accessed April 8, 2020.
164. CPE monitor. National Association of Boards of Pharmacy. https://nabp.pharmacy/cpe-monitor-service/. Published September 28, 2021. Accessed October 2, 2021.
165. APHA career pathway evaluation program for pharmacy professionals. American Pharmacists Association. https://portal.pharmacist.com/apha-career-pathway-evaluation-program-pharmacy-professionals.

Published August 23, 2016. Accessed January 6, 2020.
166. Career Option Profiles. American Pharmacists Association. https://www.pharmacist.com/career-option-profiles. Accessed March 3, 2020.
167. Clifton D. *Now, Discover Your Strengths: The Revolutionary Gallup Program That Shows You How to Develop Your Unique Talents and Strengths.* New York: NY. Gallup Press; 2020. https://www.gallup.com/cliftonstrengths/en/253922/popular-cliftonstrengths-books.aspx. Accessed January 18, 2020.
168. Cape educational outcomes. AACP. https://www.aacp.org/resource/cape-educational-outcomes. Accessed February 1, 2020.
169. The 70, 20, 10 rule for developing your employees. The Manager's Resource Handbook I Tools, Resources and Guides for Managers and Business Leaders. Real Advice from Real Bosses. https://www.managersresourcehandbook.com/the-70-20-10-rule-for-employee-development/. Published March 23, 2019. Accessed February 23, 2020.
170. The 4 disciplines of execution. FranklinCovey. https://www.franklincovey.com/the-4-disciplines/. Published June 29, 2021. Accessed July 6, 2021.
171. Kraaijenbrink J. 20 reasons why Strategy execution fails. Forbes. https://www.forbes.com/sites/jeroenkraaijenbrink/2019/09/10/20-reasons-why-strategy-execution-fails/. Published September 10, 2019. Accessed March 27, 2020.